PLANT
COMBINATIONS
for Your
LANDSCAPE

CRE▲TIVE
HOMEOWNER®

PLANT COMBINATIONS
for Your
LANDSCAPE

by TONY LORD PHOTOGRAPHY by ANDREW LAWSON

CREATIVE HOMEOWNER®, Upper Saddle River, New Jersey

First published in North America in 2010 by

CRE**A**TIVE
HOMEOWNER®

Creative Homeowner® is a registered trademark of Federal Marketing Corporation

Plant Combinations for Your Landscape, First Edition
Library of Congress Control Number: 2010923023
ISBN-13: 978-1-58011-509-4   ISBN-10: 1-58011-509-8

Current Printing (last digit): 10 9 8 7 6 5 4 3 2 1

First published in Great Britain as *Summer Plant Combinations* by Mitchell Beazley, an imprint of Octopus Publishing Group Ltd, Endeavour House, 189 Shaftesbury Avenue, London, WC2H 8JG
An Hachette UK Company   www.hachette.co.uk   ISBN: 978-1-84533-445-1

RHS Publisher Susannah Charlton
RHS Commissioning Editor Rae Spencer-Jones
Commissioning Editor Helen Griffin
Art Directors Tim Foster and Pene Parker
Senior Editor Leanne Bryan
Editor Helen Ridge
Executive Art Editor Victoria Easton
Designer Murdo Culver/Airedale Publishing
Picture Researcher Janet Johnson
Proofreader Ruth Baldwin
Indexer Helen Snaith
Production Manager Peter Hunt

Printed in China

CREATIVE HOMEOWNER, A Division of Federal Marketing Corporation
24 Park Way, Upper Saddle River, NJ 07458

www.creativehomeowner.com

How to use this book

This book is not meant to be a series of recipes for perfect planting but rather a menu of suggestions from which readers can choose, revise, or augment combinations to suit their own tastes and conditions. Some combinations are bright to the point of garishness; others delicate to the point of blandness, depending on one's view. As the book does not discuss the culture, propagation, or a wide range of varieties in the detail found in a plant encyclopedia, such a work would be invaluable used with this book, both to supply such detail, and to show similar but different varieties that could be used to refine combinations suggested here, or to rework them in different colors.

Key to symbols

These indicate the main characteristics of the plant and its cultural requirements.

H & S (Height & Spread)	These are given at reasonable maturity. For tender perennials used for summer bedding or containers, they represent the dimensions reached by a plant overwintered from cuttings taken the previous year.
✿	The flower symbol indicates the typical flowering season. Accurate matching of flowering season is essential for successful combined floral effect, and can be judged from plants that flower together in your locality.
▬▬	The colored bar represents the range of light levels from full, day-long sun on the left to dense shade on the right. The bar beneath represents the plant's preferred part of this range (black) and the part it will tolerate (white).
△△△	The raindrop symbols show the plant's preferred soil water content. One raindrop indicates dry conditions; two raindrops, soil that is always moist, never waterlogged, or dry; three indicate plenty of moisture year-round.
▦■■■	The colored squares show the plant's preferred soil conditions. From left to right: light, well-drained, e.g. chalky or sandy; medium with adequate drainage, e.g. silty loam; heavy soil; humus-rich, e.g. peaty soils.
Z3 pH	The hardiness zone on the left is explained on pp.358–9. The pH range shows the soil acidity or alkalinity that the plant will tolerate, pH7 being neutral, lower values acidic, and higher ones alkaline.

Plant portraits
These are chosen to show the featured plant in an effective combination, whether a harmony or a contrast, with one or more other plants.

Plant entry headings
The full botanical name is given for each featured plant. The genus, written in italics, is followed by the species, also in italics, and, where appropriate, the cultivar, which is written in roman. A multiplication sign indicates that the plant is a hybrid.

Gentiana asclepiadea
WILLOW GENTIAN

How it works: *Gentiana asclepiadea* is one of the easiest gentians to grow. Here, its intense, deep pure blue flowers stand out dramatically against the yellow-green foliage of *Rubus cockburnianus* 'Goldenvale'. Grown in light shade, the rubus leaves remain bright and avoid being scorched by the sun.

Recommended partners: *Anemone* × *hybrida* 'Honorine Jobert', *Geranium* 'Johnson's Blue', *Hedera helix* 'Buttercup', *Hosta* 'Sum and Substance', *Lilium lancifolium* var. *splendens*

H: 36in (90cm) **S: 24in** (60cm)
✿ **Mid-summer to early autumn**
◊◊ ☐-■ Z6 pH5–7.5

How it works
This gives detailed information on the color and form of the plants shown in combination, with prominence given to the featured plant.

Cultural information
These symbols indicate the main characteristics of the plant and its cultural requirements. See Key to symbols (left) for a full explanation.

Common name
The plant's common name, if it has one, follows the botanical name and is given in small capitals.

Recommended partners
At the end of each plant entry are further suggestions for effective planting partners.

Introduction

Summer is the apogee of the gardener's year. There are flowers and foliage of almost every hue and the potential for endless combinations. But there are limitations: after the gorgeousness of late spring, summer starts with something of a lull, the "June gap." Then come the glories of high summer – but by late July it can be hard to keep the display going unless gardeners use all their wile.

Tricks of the light

The consecutive seasons, spring and summer, present some strikingly different considerations for the gardener. The quality of light changes markedly, from the rather soft, sometimes watery spring sunshine illuminating from a relatively low angle, to the hard and braying light of summer, almost directly overhead, increasing contrast so that the garden seems zebra'd black and white; some colors, especially purple, will scarcely show in sunny weather. Pity the poor garden photographer who at this time of year becomes crepuscular, emerging only at dawn and dusk. As always, gardeners who make most use of the quality and direction of the light get more out of

their gardens, especially if they align their planting to be seen against the rising or setting sun. Red or orange foliage and flowers and thin-textured plants like grasses especially lend themselves to such *contre-jour* effects, provided the gardeners are around to see them. The far haze of balmy late summer days has been recognized by gardeners as a chance to add color as a means of emphasizing distance, an example of which would be using a cloud of pale blue flowers at the farthest point from the viewer to make it look as though the planting is even farther away than it actually is.

There is also a seasonal change in the prevalent range of colors: from the blues and yellows that predominate in spring with foliage that is usually a bright, sometimes yellowish, green to the cool colors of summer – pinks, mauves, lavenders, purples, and crimsons with rather duller green foliage – though there are plenty of white flowers at both seasons. Scarlet is becoming more popular in early summer, supplied by plants such as poppies and tender perennials, such as salvias, cannas, begonias, verbenas, and penstemons that come into their own in late summer and continue

into the autumn, combining agreeably with the prevailing fall colors. Yellows become numerous through July, with the advent of many herbaceous composites, most of them from local plants.. Among the late flowers such as daisies, hardy salvias, and grasses are lots that lend themselves to the New

This border contains a complete spectrum of colors. Such a feast is not planned to be consumed all at once: the hot-colored section of the border is the main course for late summer and autumn, when color is provided by *Rudbeckia fulgida* var. *deamii* and *Monarda* 'Mrs Perry', with bold vertical accents from *Kniphofia uvaria* 'Nobilis'.

Perennial style, with its preponderance of flowers that like prairie conditions with relatively nutrient-poor soil and good drainage in full sun.

Bedding and borders

One of the earliest summer jobs is the replacement of spring bedding annuals – wallflowers, violas, primroses, forget-me-nots, and the like – with summer annuals. It may well be worthwhile using later-flowering biennials such as Siberian wallflowers, stocks, sweet Williams, rocket, honesty, *Smyrnium perfoliatum*, and foxgloves for bedding that bridges the gap between spring and summer, continuing into the "June gap": thus the chore of bedding out for later in the year is staggered until late June or early July, when annuals for late summer or autumn such as

Far left: In this garden, the paving gives structure and emphasis to the rounded forms of *Berberis thunbergii* 'Atropurpurea Nana' and *Lavandula angustifolia* 'Hidcote', which by themselves could seem amorphous and dull.

Left: Repeated vertical stems of *Digitalis grandiflora*, *Phlomis russeliana*, and salvias provide unity in this scheme by the renowned designer Tom Stuart-Smith.

salvias or chrysanthemums can take their place.

Planting annuals remains an exceptionally popular form of summer gardening, whether for complete beds or for areas around the garden where a focus of bright color is needed. There is a popular misconception that it is an outdated style, unsubtle, unbearably vulgar and that, of course, no modern gardener with good taste would touch it. We gardeners might think we are using the plants for something other than bedding, yet almost every garden has sections of beds or borders that are bedded out each year to provide a display that permanent planting would not supply so well, nor for so many months. Annuals can be subtle enough not to disturb the most sensitive soul, though there are times when it must have impact, for instance in townscapes where it is seen fleetingly *en passant*. A very large proportion of the display at many public gardens depends on patches of annuals. In many places, annuals are used to extend the season beyond mid-summer in most areas. It is principally bedding plants that create the display, whether used in traditional beds or in hanging baskets, window boxes, and other containers, themselves also forms of bedding albeit on a smaller scale.

Bedding annuals have much the same requirements as other sorts of plant combinations: it should have good use of texture and structure, so that it succeeds seen at close range as well as from a distance. Where a whole bed is concerned, the front rank is usually an edging that neatly defines the plants behind. Then comes a "ground" of a taller plant. This generally should not be too short, especially not for civic planting seen at a shallow angle from a distance, where short plants would subtend an infinitesimal angle to the eye and would scarcely be visible. Either the ground or the edging and preferably both should have definite texture or form; it would not be effective if both were amorphous.

More-complex schemes could have a ground made up of several bands or of two or three plants intermixed, as in the "shot silk" effect beloved of the Victorians in which *Verbena rigida* is interplanted with a geranium. Plants used as focal points, generally having architectural form – for instance spiky cordylines or bold-leaved castor oil plants – stand out from the ground plants and rise above

them. Whether for the ground or the edging, mixtures are of limited use, their jumbled colors often cancelling each other out, giving a messy and muddled effect and diminishing impact. ("Designer mixes," in which a few harmonious or effectively contrasting colors are combined, are more useful.) Suitable edgings include shorter *Tagetes* or *Begonia*

Semperflorens Cultorum Group, while there are some perennials that can be used in the same way, such as heucheras or the neater grasses, though these generally have the tidiest and most attractive foliage if replanted each year. There are many possible plants to use as grounds, including pelargoniums, larger petunias and tagetes, *Salvia*

Annual bedding schemes can make a significant floral contribution to a garden, as can be seen here. The effect of color, repetition, and balance is clear for all to appreciate.

splendens, and calceolarias as well as foliage plants like coleus and amaranthus.

Unlike Victorian gardeners, we do not demand that annuals always be contrasting in color: there are situations where something more tranquil is needed, for instance wherever in the garden one wants to sit and rest. For our own gardens we can please ourselves whether

Dahlia 'Bednall Beauty' and *Crocosmia* 'Lucifer', here planted with *Cordyline australis* Purpurea Group, have both achieved numerous awards.

bedding should be bold and exhilarating or subtle and restful, but for public spaces it needs to appeal to most people who see it: if it is so garish that 30 percent hate it or so subtle that 30 percent don't notice it, it is failing to satisfy its viewers and can scarcely be cost effective. However, this must not be allowed to become a recipe for middle-of-the-road mediocrity.

Summer containers

Containers, including window boxes and hanging baskets, are often essentially bedding schemes in miniature, having similar elements: a trailing plant often replaces the usual edging, softening the edges of the container and extending the display downwards; the ground is often primarily of two flowering plants, perhaps most effectively one with small and one with relatively large flowers, while the focal point, as for conventional bedding, is usually a foliage plant of striking form, perhaps with strappy or spiky leaves. All but the biggest and grandest hanging baskets can dispense with the central focal point plant, which might not be clearly seen from below and might look like a faintly ridiculous topknot, like plumes on the hat of a courtier. In hanging baskets, trailing plants add grace and help prevent the outline being too unnaturally spherical. One of the most common sorts of hanging basket is the gigantic football of vegetatively propagated

petunias. (The Surfinia Series is the most famous.) Most are stunningly floriferous and easy to grow. But this is not enough for me – I want hanging baskets that have a pleasing balance of good foliage as well as flowers. It must be owned that foliage plants for hanging baskets are relatively scarce and that the trailers are the most useful: among the silvers and grays, one of the best is *Helichrysum petiolare*, a plant with poise and character, though it can be a thug, becoming enormous within a couple of months and demanding gallons of water every day unless judiciously pruned in mid-season. Its habit of arranging its sprays of foliage facing upwards makes it less effective for baskets or window boxes that are set very high. *Helichrysum microphyllum* is almost as commonly used but less successful, smaller, and scruffier and without the ability to arrange itself gracefully. Some relative newcomers seem promising – for example, *Dichondra argentea*, while among variegated plants, *Plectranthus madagascariensis* 'Variegated Mintleaf' is among the most versatile, modestly pleasing without being flashy and useful for breaking up vast expanses of flower into more digestible pieces. Flowers that face resolutely upwards, away from the eyes of the viewer, are less useful for window boxes or hanging baskets, especially if high up.

Conversely, those that face down are especially effective: I am very fond of Pendula begonias, especially the Illumination Series; these have a near perfect balance of good foliage and flowers, are tolerant of both shade and the sun, and are almost good enough to be used on their own, though the *Plectranthus* makes a good companion. Their colorings are more subtly varied and shaded than some newer sorts, such as the Panorama Series.

It is perfectly possible, though uncommon, to plant containers entirely with foliage plants. However, containers with solely flowering plants and indifferent foliage or leaves hidden entirely by flowers seldom have enough structure or texture to succeed. My preference (perhaps not yours) is for a simple treatment for smaller containers, such as hanging baskets and window boxes, with a handful of plant components each playing a defined role. What we most often see seems to me to be a jumble and an opportunity missed, with too many components, sometimes jarring, sometimes too similar to

each other, diminishing the impact. On a bigger scale, a more complex treatment is possible, in which the plants do not just play the roles of the elements of a bedding scheme: the very largest displays can be almost symphonic in their sustained development, almost like a section of a well-designed border.

Containers are usually seen at fairly close range but in the urban environment should be effective from some distance away: in such situations, a bold and simple color scheme is preferable to a very complex one. Dark colors, such as violet, purple, crimson, and even scarlet, can become almost invisible from a hundred or more yards away, especially in shade; something brighter, such as yellow, orange, or vivid pink, might work over a greater range. In such an environment, a simple, repeated planting using the same colors can help unify, say, the facade of a single building or emphasize the architectural cohesion of a terrace, while a series of baskets or window boxes in different color schemes would be visually disruptive.

In containers, when so few plants are involved, the brassiest yellows can be difficult combined with other colors and can entirely ruin the effect: *Calceolaria integrifolia*, *Lysimachia congestiflora*, and *Bidens ferulifolia* (and its close relatives) do not flatter most other hues in the way that sulphur yellow or soft lemon would. Though they contrast well with strong blue or purple and can be used with scarlet and orange, perhaps with bronze foliage, they can utterly overpower rose or salmon or mauve in the most unpleasant way. However, no yellow petunias or calibrachoas are fierce enough to argue with their neighbors and they often have a pleasantly leavening effect.

Hanging gardens

Containers and especially hanging baskets usually support a large expanse of foliage and flower with a small volume of compost: adequate watering is essential, especially for those subjects that do not recover adequately if allowed to wilt.

Verbenas usually cease flowering for two or three weeks if they get too dry, and lobelias rarely fully recover. A solution is to incorporate water-retentive polymer granules: the

Violas and sunflowers (*Helianthus* 'Choc Chip') are traditional cottage garden plants, although they have not been used in this pot in a cottage garden way.

plants will still use the same amount of water, but the soil will retain more moisture and there will be less chance of the plants suffering. The small volume of soil is also likely to run out of nutrients unless six-month slow-release fertilizer granules have been incorporated. Alternatively, a weekly feed with high-potash liquid fertilizer (such as tomato feed) will provide adequate nutrients and can help in cool weather, when slow-release fertilizers do not work. With such provisos, containers and hanging baskets should perform until after the first ground frosts, which, being raised, they will not suffer. Conversely, many container plants, especially near-hardy perennials, will tolerate being planted before the traditional local first frost-free planting day for annuals (for example, March 21 for Atlanta and April 19 for Chicago both probably now earlier as a result of climate change). However, there are a few plants, such as *Ipomoea* and *Colocasia* species, that need warmer nights before they will start to grow: these should not be planted until later.

If the point of suspension of a basket is only a little more than its radius away from the wall, the plants are likely to form a blister-shaped mass against the wall. If the basket is hung significantly farther than its radius away, the mass of plants will remain more or less round and separate from the wall, a significantly different and more dramatic effect. The weight of a hanging basket, especially after watering and if it contains a large volume of fleshy plants, such as pendula begonias, can be very considerable: the support needs to be strong and adequately fixed, especially for baskets over public streets and particularly if hung well out from the wall, exerting extra leverage.

It has to be owned that not all of the most popular annuals will flower reliably throughout the season. Seed-raised pelargoniums tend to flower well when first planted (as they are bred to be colorful when sold) but are seldom floriferous after mid-summer and can be marred by seedheads unless deadheaded, not usually an option if they are out of reach in baskets; cutting-raised pelargoniums tend to flower more reliably, though the longer-lasting flowers of the doubles can be balled by botrytis in wet weather. Petunias do not perform well in prolonged wet weather, not even the Multiflora sorts that are supposed to be more resistant, and by September the

In this hanging basket of impressive size, *Petunia* Surfinia Blue Vein 'Sunsolos' is prevented from forming a solid and indigestible mass of flower by being mixed with *Calibrachoa* Million Bells Orange Glow 'Sunbelore', *Nemesia*, and *Verbena*, which are lightened by the silver-gray foliage of *Helichrysum petiolare*.

blooms start to get marred by dew. However, they perform better off the ground in containers or hanging baskets. One species that is usually both tolerant and easy to grow in sun or shade in warm climates is *Impatiens alleriana*, the busy Lizzy. But it is not indestructible. In the dismally wet summer of 2008, the *Impatiens* downy mildew devastated most plants in the United Kingdom. This most useful species might now be hard to grow, even in an average summer there. Though isolated plants of common tobaccos (*Nicotiana sanderae*) may survive, plantings of more than a handful usually succumb to tobacco blue mold by mid-July in warmer, moister climates, but they can survive longer in the drier climates. Other species of *Nicotiana*, such as *N. langsdorffii* and *N. sylvestris*, usually survive unless grown near to *N. sanderae*, though their foliage is generally disfigured by the mold.

Meadow planting

Annuals and biennials are also useful for summer effect in flowery meadows. There are numerous ways of managing these, but most depend on reducing the fertility of the soil before sowing or planting by constant removal of grass clippings so that the flowers can compete with more vigorous grasses. After flowering, the flowers should be left to set seed. The site can then be mown, scattering the seed, and cultivated to produce a fine tilth, suitable for another year's meadow flowers to germinate and thrive.

The June gap

Perennials that are especially useful for bridging the June gap include columbines, not only the old-fashioned granny's bonnets and other selections of *Aquilegia vulgaris*, but species such as *A. canadensis* and *A. fragrantissima* plus the long-spurred hybrids. Bearded irises are also immensely useful, though only the Tall Bearded sorts will continue into summer: generally the shorter they are, the earlier they bloom. The myriad hardy perennials that follow include many that will last in bloom much longer if frequently deadheaded, increasing the number of their possible combinations.

The majority of garden shrubs flower as spring turns to summer, with the likes of philadelphus, deutzia, weigela, and roses following in quick succession. Most have foliage of depressing dullness and benefit from being draped by some attractive climber, either an annual such as morning glory or a perennial such as clematis or everlasting pea, both to break up the monotonous expanse and to give later interest. Some, such as many modern shrub roses, can be encouraged to rebloom by deadheading, as can many herbaceous perennials, encouraging lateral stems for later flowers.

The late spring chop

Staking is not a matter for a book on plant combinations, except to say that most gardeners want to avoid plants that need it. However, there are some techniques that reduce the need for staking and allow relatively floppy subjects to be used without making extra work. One is the "late spring chop," cutting back perennials such as asters, *Eupatorium*, *Helianthus*, *Monarda*, *Phlox*, and *Sedum* by about one-third around the third or fourth week of May. This encourages bushy growth but also has the effect of making flowering a little later, often about two weeks, which may affect the choice of suitable companions. For subjects that open a terminal spike, which then gets deadheaded and is followed by a succession of lateral flowerheads, the chop tends to produce more flowerheads lasting a slightly shorter time over a shorter period: one might choose not to use it for the stateliest spikes, such as delphiniums, or for the broadest-headed achilleas. Replanting will also make for sturdier growth and slightly later flowering: using a single rooted piece of rhizome to replace each clump of monarda or Michaelmas daisy every year can produce healthy, vigorous, and relatively mildew-free new clumps.

Late summer color

Whether for shrubs, perennials, or annuals, the use of colored foliage in combinations helps meet the criteria of the "one-third rule," i.e., that at least one-third, and preferably one-half, of the plants in a grouping should be in display at any one time for the scheme to "read" and to provide color from spring right through to autumn.

Among hardy perennials, there are a few stalwarts that continue to bloom profusely into the lean months of late summer, such as *Aster amellus* and *A.* × *frikartii*, as well as the Japanese anemones. Generally, it helps to incorporate some tender perennials (effectively bedding plants), such as penstemons, argyranthemums, salvias, or osteospermums, to keep the display going through late summer and into autumn.

In the woodland garden, the canopy of deciduous tree foliage will have often cast much of the area into shade, limiting the possibility for plant associations to lighter glades, especially because many woodlanders can become besmirched by sooty mold dripping from above in such situations.

Where there is more light, there are still some shrubs, such as some of the later rhododendrons (for instance 'Aladdin' or 'Azor'; there are hundreds more), that will serve well into summer, while there are also many hydrangeas, not only cultivars of *H. macrophylla* and *H. serrata* but species such as *H.*

Above: Flowers of bold shape can be effectively set against a cloud of much smaller flowers in a contrasting color, as here with *Osteospermum* 'Pink Whirls' and *Veronica austriaca* subsp. *teucrium* 'Crater Lake Blue'.

Left: Whether bedded out annually or, in favored climates, overwintered *in situ*, penstemons such as 'Alice Hindley' are valuable for extending the season of display into late summer and beyond.

quercifolia, both hybrids and species, that can be used in the display.

Bulbs and climbers

It is the lilies that are the most useful of all summer-flowering bulbs, for their fragrance, their wide range of colors, and the bold shape of their blooms, their "line quality." They add a note of luxury that can be supplied by few other flowers, with thousands of cultivars for sun or shade, all of them best planted forward of other plants of their own height. Crinums have similarly classy blooms and, once established, are easy and may be left to their own devices, though they are rather marred by their foliage, which tends to kink and arrange itself in an ungraceful and messy way. After lilies, gladioli constitute perhaps the next most numerous genus, but I have to admit that I find them difficult: though clumps or looser groupings of the smaller Nanus or Primulinus sorts can be charming and often persist nowadays from year to year without being lost to winter cold, the largest sorts can look very stiff and can seem unappealing as the lowest florets shrivel and die unless they are deadheaded almost daily. And yet, I have this sneaking feeling that they could be used in a way that would make them seem thrilling and exotic, and might even unfetter them from their association with Dame Edna Everage. Their colors are so varied, from green through orange to violet, and their form so bold and striking that some exciting associations should be possible – it's just that I haven't seen them yet.

Growing summer bulbs through grass is difficult: it is hard to avoid having to cut the grass during July and August. Those bulbs that just get into either end of summer – camassias in June or colchicums in August – are primarily for spring and autumn. But there are some other useful bulb genera, from *Allium* and *Eremurus* at the start of summer to *Galtonia* and *Eucomis* at its end, that play an important role in summer beds and borders.

Among climbers for summer combinations, it is the roses, both Climbing and Ramblers, and the clematis that are the most versatile and useful. However, we should not forget a wide range of others, including herbaceous *Lathyrus* and slightly tender seed-raised genera like *Maurandya*, *Rhodochiton*, and *Lophospermum*. Their usefulness for breaking up dull shrub foliage has already been mentioned, but they can also help to carry a planting scheme upwards, perhaps where a wall backs a border.

Summer is not a time for gardeners to rest on their laurels: the autumn can be as glorious as any other season if gardeners spend a little time on planning and preparation. And we can always reflect on this summer's successes and failures and plan how to make next year's garden better.

Climbers such as roses and clematis (here 'Albertine' and 'Etoile Violette') make a classic combination. Trained to pillars, perhaps with connecting swags or arches, they can add height and define separate areas of the garden.

Shrubs and Small Trees

The essential building blocks of a garden, shrubs and small trees should be chosen with care to ensure interesting shapes and attractive foliage and flowers all year, as well as to provide shelter, vistas, and focal points. Every garden needs trees and shrubs to create a basic structure.

Introducing shrubs and small trees

In most garden plantings, a proportion of shrubs and a small selection of trees are essential to provide height, bulk, structure, and, with the inclusion of some evergreens, year-round interest. The boundary between shrubs and small trees is a blurred one. Pittosporums, lilacs, philadelphus, and many others, start their life as shrubs but develop tree-like proportions and, with help from the gardener, eventually make picturesque small trees. Trees display all the attributes of shrubs, but higher above ground level, often on trunks that have their own merits of elegant outline or attractive bark.

Making a selection

Trees and shrubs contribute to both the structure and the decoration of the garden, and it is important to bear these two aspects in mind when selecting and arranging them. In most situations, it is best to avoid thinking in terms of the "shrub border" and to plan instead to use trees and shrubs to enhance the whole garden. Selecting only those species that will grow well in the particular soil and situation will ensure that they thrive with minimum effort and will create a strong sense of unity in the garden.

Small trees and the taller shrubs can be used as focal points and to create height. Birches with their pale trunks or the very elegant paperbark maple, in groups or as single specimens, will draw the eye, frame views, and create a canopy to capture views of the sky. In large enough groups – even a well-placed trio in a small garden – the atmosphere of a wood or wild garden can be created: viewed from the rest of the garden, the trees form attractive masses, while under their canopy is a scene of vertical trunks and cool green shade with a rich woodland ground flora.

Once the high points have been decided on, the major shrubs can be distributed to form bold accents at a lower level. Mahonias and many of the conifers are good for texture and greenery all year round, playing an especially important role in maintaining structure and interest through the winter.

When the star cast of trees and specimen shrubs has been assembled, attention can be turned to the chorus, the less dramatic but no less important plants that will enclose and shelter the garden, guide people through it, sub-divide larger plots into smaller and more comfortable spaces, and conceal any undesirable views. For these purposes there are many well-behaved but less-exciting (and usually much less expensive) shrubs.

Finally, having established the structure of the garden with shrubs growing from waist height (where they will obstruct physical movement) to eye level and above (as visual barriers), attention can be turned to the ground plane. Here low plants can be woven together: lavenders, cistus, and rosemaries do well on dry soils, while the heathers, leucothoes, smaller rhododendrons, and many others are ideal for moist, acid situations. Knee-high shrubs will cover the ground to reduce the necessity for weeding; they will also soften the transition between lawns and paving and fences, walls, and trees, and will create their own tapestry of foliage, flowers, and form.

Shrubs and small trees can be used to extend a planting scheme upwards. In a small garden where space is restricted, they can allow the border to be steeply banked, hiding the garden's boundaries with a wall of foliage and flowers.

Designing a shrub border

- What is needed in shrub planting is great variation in grouping, from individual specimen plants to substantial masses of 10, 20, or more lower ground covers.
- The outlines of the larger groups should be irregular, like pieces in a jigsaw, so that they are linked together more firmly.
- The spacing between specimens in a group should also be varied, unless formality is intended.

- Lessons can be learned from natural groupings of trees, rocks, or even animals in a field, and it is worth spending time playing with circles on paper to achieve the right effect.

This planting, which includes *Lavandula* 'Aphrodite' and *L. dentata*, *Salvia officinalis*, and white-flowered *Thymus*, produces a wonderful aroma and provides useful culinary herbs.

Finishing touches and care

Woody plants usually start off much too small for their situation but then grow inexorably, often becoming too large. Thinness in the early stages can be compensated for by interplanting the permanent selection with short-lived and quick-growing shrubs, herbaceous perennials, or annuals.

In fact, useful though trees and shrubs are in a garden, it is neither necessary nor desirable to grow them to the exclusion of other plants. Lilies will push through the lower shrubs to flower in late summer. Herbaceous plants extend the flowering season and break the monotony of an over-reliance on shrubs. Stout clumps of peonies and arching sheaves of daylilies will create a greater sense of seasonal change and welcome lightness among the woody permanence of the shrubs.

Once the permanent shrubs and trees have reached the desired size, it may be necessary to restrict their growth to prevent the garden from deteriorating into a tangle of the more thuggish species. If time is available, rule-book pruning can be adopted. This is an art in itself and very satisfying.

Blending a range of plant groups, such as dark green columnar yew, white-flowering yucca, and pink-flowering *Armeria maritima*, is a different approach to gardening with plants that need little water.

Abutilon vitifolium var. *album*

How it works: Crowded spikes of white foxgloves (*Digitalis purpurea* f. *albiflora*) lift themselves high enough to offer a contrast of floral form with *Abutilon vitifolium* var. *album*, while providing a quiet harmony of color.

Recommended partners: *Buddleja alternifolia* 'Argentea', *Clematis* 'Bees' Jubilee', *Delphinium* Galahad Group, *Eremurus robustus*, *Onopordum nervosum*, *Rosa* 'Fantin-Latour'

H: 16ft (5m) S: 8ft (2.5m)
✿ **Late spring to mid-summer**

 ◊◊ □-■ Z8 pH5.5–7

Acer griseum
PAPERBARK MAPLE

How it works: The rich brown bark of the paperbark maple (*Acer griseum*) glows orange where lit from behind by the sun, allowing it to harmonize with *Crocosmia* 'Lucifer'. Bold rodgersia leaves provide a foil without masking the maple's stem.

Recommended partners: *Berberis thunbergii* 'Atropurpurea Nana', *B. wilsoniae*, *Ceratostigma plumbaginoides*, *Euphorbia amygdaloides* 'Purpurea', *Stephanandra tanakae*

H: 33ft (10m) S: 23ft (7m)
✿ **Mid-spring**

 ◊◊ □-■ Z5 pH5.5–7

Aralia elata 'Aureovariegata'

How it works: The dramatic foliage of
Aralia elata 'Aureovariegata' harmonizes
with the warm apricot-yellow of *Crocosmia*
× *crocosmiiflora* 'Lady Hamilton'.

Recommended partners: *Agapanthus*
'Loch Hope', *Crocosmia* 'Vulcan',
Dahlia 'Autumn Luster', *D.* 'Glorie
van Heemstede', *Hibiscus syriacus*
'Oiseau Bleu', *Ipomoea tricolor* 'Heavenly
Blue', *Miscanthus sinensis* 'Strictus',
Nepeta sibirica, *Philadelphus coronarius*
'Aureus'

Artemisia 'Powis Castle'

How it works: A filigree cushion of
Artemisia 'Powis Castle', an outstanding
foliage plant, nestles beneath gracefully
arching stems of *Fuchsia magellanica*
'Versicolor', with its elegant, pendent flowers
and grayish leaves flushed red and edged
with white – an association that is especially
charming at close range. The slender
fuchsia flowers set off the silvery artemisia,
while the foliage colors blend agreeably.

Recommended partners: *Ballota
pseudodictamnus*, *Cistus* × *argenteus* 'Silver
Pink', *Convolvulus cneorum*, *Cosmos
bipinnatus* 'Sonata White', *Euphorbia
dulcis* 'Chameleon', *Lavandula* 'Sawyers',
Rosa Surrey ('Korlanum')

H & S: 16ft (5m)
❀ **Late summer Z5 pH5.5–7.5**

H: 24in (60cm) S: 36in (90cm)
❀ **Summer Z6 pH5.5–7.5**

Berberis thunbergii f. *atropurpurea* 'Atropurpurea Nana'

How it works: Used toward the front of the border where it can be clipped formally as an edging or to a billowing shape to restrict its size, *Berberis thunbergii* f. *atropurpurea* 'Atropurpurea Nana' (syn. *B. t. f. t.* 'Crimson Pygmy') provides structure and rich color from spring to autumn. The strappy foliage of *Hemerocallis* 'Missenden' acts as a foil to its fine-textured leaves, while the daylily's flowers harmonize with those of heleniums, lilies, and broom, and with its foliage and that of golden elder. The soft yellow spring flowers of the *Berberis* are a bonus, but its colored leaves are the plant's main asset, suited to combinations with hot-colored flowers in scarlet, orange, or gold. The effect is enhanced in autumn as the leaves color scarlet before they are shed.

Recommended partners: *Agastache* 'Firebird', *Carex oshimensis* 'Evergold', *Convolvulus sabatius*, *Dahlia* 'Bednall Beauty', *D.* 'Moonfire', *Euphorbia myrsinites*, *Helenium* 'Vivace', *Helianthemum* 'Fire Dragon', *Hosta fortunei* var. *albopicta* f. *aurea*, *Lilium pyrenaicum*, *Milium effusum* 'Aureum', *Solenostemon scutellarioides* 'Wizard Scarlet', *Tagetes* 'Sunburst Yellow'

H: 24in (60cm) S: 30in (75cm)
※ **Late spring**

 ◇-◇◇ □-■ Z5 pH5–7.5

Buddleja alternifolia

How it works: The slightly unruly habit of *Buddleja alternifolia* turns to one of exuberance as its garlanded lilac pompons appear. Beneath is purple sage (*Salvia officinalis* 'Purpurascens'), while in front pompons of chives and *Allium hollandicum* 'Purple Sensation' chime in close harmony.

Recommended partners: *Allium* 'Gladiator', *Campanula lactiflora, Delphinium* 'Bruce', *Elaeagnus* 'Quicksilver', *Geranium psilostemon, Philadelphus* 'Belle Etoile', *Rosa* 'Cerise Bouquet'

H & S: 13ft (4m)
❀ **Early summer Z6 pH5.5–7.5**

Buddleja davidii 'Dartmoor'

How it works: *Buddleja davidii* 'Dartmoor' forms a magnificent backdrop for a planting in which the sunflower *Helianthus salicifolius,* with its bottle-brush columns of foliage, is the other main attraction, partnered by the bamboo *Phyllostachys nigra* f. *punctata.* Pale blue *Clematis* 'Praecox' fills the foreground.

Recommended partners: *Cotinus coggygria* 'Royal Purple', *Elaeagnus commutata, Euphorbia schillingii, Lilium* 'Casa Blanca', *L.* Imperial Gold Group, *Rosa* 'Felicia', *R. glauca*

H & S: 10ft (3m)
❀ **Mid-summer to early autumn**
◇·◇◇ ☐-■ **Z5 pH5–7.5**

Cistus × *cyprius*

How it works: The white blooms of *Cistus* × *cyprius* are tempered by salmon-colored *Alstroemeria ligtu* hybrids. The yellow in the center of the cistus flowers is echoed by the flashes on the alstroemeria's upper petals.

Recommended partners: *Ceanothus* 'Blue Mound', *Dianthus* 'Paisley Gem', *Euphorbia seguieriana* subsp. *niciciana*, *Lavandula pedunculata* subsp. *pedunculata*, *Salvia lavandulifolia*

H & S: 5ft (1.5m)
❀ **Early to late summer**
◊-◊◊ ☐-■ Z8 pH6–7.5

Cistus × *purpureus*

How it works: The large crinkled blooms of *Cistus* × *purpureus* are perfectly complemented by the small crimson flowers and loosely branched habit of *Leptospermum scoparium*.

Recommended partners: *Allium* 'Globemaster', *Convolvulus cneorum*, *Dianthus* 'Haytor White', *D.* 'Old Velvet', *Eryngium bourgatii* 'Picos Blue', *Gypsophila* 'Rosenschleier'

H & S: 40in (1m)
❀ **Early to late summer**
◊-◊◊ ☐-■ Z9 pH6–7.5

Cornus alba 'Elegantissima'

How it works: The creamy variegation and bold leaf shape of *Cornus alba* 'Elegantissima' set off the dissected foliage and blue, early summer flowers of *Geranium* × *magnificum*. A longer-flowering cranesbill such as 'Nimbus' or 'Blue Cloud' would prolong the display. A third plant with bold leaves, perhaps strappy or heart-shaped, might add definition and impact.

Recommended partners: *Colocasia esculenta* 'Black Magic', *Gunnera tinctoria*, *Hosta* 'Sum and Substance', *Phormium cookianum* subsp. *hookeri* 'Tricolor', *Phormium tenax*, *Rodgersia pinnata* 'Superba', *Zinnia* 'Chippendale'

H: 6½ft (2m) S: 10ft (3m)
❀ **Late spring to early summer**
 ◊◊-◊◊◊ ■-■ **Z2 pH4.5–7.5**

Cornus controversa 'Variegata'

How it works: The layered habit and cream-edged leaves of *Cornus controversa* 'Variegata' combine well with the looser form and colored leaves of *Philadelphus coronarius* 'Aureus'.

Recommended partners: *Fatsia japonica, Hedera colchica, Hesperis matronalis, Hosta ventricosa, Lilium martagon* var. *album, Phlox divaricata, Stephanandra tanakae*

Coronilla valentina subsp. *glauca* 'Variegata'

How it works: In a subtle essay in color and form, the glaucous cream-edged leaves and yellow flowers of *Coronilla valentina* subsp. *glauca* 'Variegata' are joined by silver-leaved *Teucrium fruticans* and golden hop (*Humulus lupulus* 'Aureus').

Recommended partners: *Ceanothus* × *delileanus* 'Gloire de Versailles', *Choisya* Goldfingers ('Limo'), *Rosmarinus officinalis*

H & S: 26ft (8m)
❀ Early summer
 Z6 pH5–7

H & S: 31in (80cm)
❀ Late winter to mid-spring
 Z9 pH5.5–7

Cotinus coggygria '**Royal Purple**'

How it works: By keeping this smoke bush (*Cotinus coggygria* 'Royal Purple') well furnished with branches to ground level, sprawling and scrambling plants can be encouraged to weave themselves through its stems, creating an attractive tapestry of foliage and flowers. The vigorous cranesbill *Geranium* × *oxonianum* 'Claridge Druce' here provides contrasting leaves and harmonious mauve-pink flowers.

The reddish purple leaves of this smoke bush have a fiery red glow when backlit by the sun. Its coloring blends well with purple, blue, crimson, and carmine-pink flowers, or with scarlet, coral, orange, or flame. Specimen plants can be underplanted with harmonious flowers such as dark-leaved heucheras laced with *Lilium speciosum* cultivars. Other variants include 'Notcutt's Variety'; Purpureus Group, with green leaves and purplish flowers; and Rubrifolius Group, plum-purple, turning red.

Recommended partners: *Agastache* 'Firebird', *Alonsoa warscewiczii*, *Dahlia* 'David Howard', *Hemerocallis* 'Stafford', *Ipomoea lobata*, *Knautia macedonica*, *Ligularia dentata* 'Desdemona', *Lilium* 'Journey's End', *Lonicera caprifolium*

H & S: 16ft (5m)
❀ **Mid-summer**
◊◊ ☐-■ Z5 pH5.5–7.5

Cytisus nigricans

How it works: The sharp yellow flowers of *Cytisus nigricans* harmonize with the yellow-green leaves of *Geranium* 'Ann Folkard' while contrasting strikingly with its magenta flowers.

Recommended partners: *Aconitum* 'Spark's Variety', *Ceanothus* × *delileanus* 'Gloire de Versailles', *Crocosmia* 'Vulcan', *Dahlia* 'Moonfire', *Hemerocallis* 'Marion Vaughn', *Lilium* Imperial Gold Group, *Miscanthus sinensis* 'Pünktchen', *Nicotiana* 'Lime Green'

H: 5ft (1.5m) S: 40in (1m)
❀ **Late summer to early autumn**
◊-◊◊ ☐-■ Z6 pH5–7.5

Deutzia longifolia 'Vilmoriniae'

How it works: Contrasting red valerian (*Centranthus ruber*) and yellow-green *Euphorbia polychroma* provide a foil for *Deutzia longifolia* 'Vilmoriniae'. The deutzia leavens the color scheme and adds height, while white and magenta foxgloves supply punctuation and help unify the scheme.

Recommended partners: *Campanula lactiflora, Hebe* 'Midsummer Beauty', *Iris* 'Cambridge', *I. orientalis, Lupinus arboreus, Potentilla fruticosa* 'Vilmoriniana', *Rosa* 'Fantin-Latour'

H: 6½ft (2m) S: 10ft (3m)
❀ Early to mid-summer
▰▰▱ ◊◊ ▢-▪ Z6 pH5–7.5

Elaeagnus × *ebbingei* 'Gilt Edge'

How it works: Brightly variegated *Elaeagnus* × *ebbingei* 'Gilt Edge' harmonizes with *Rubus cockburnianus* 'Goldenvale'. In winter the bramble's white stems make a striking contrast.

Recommended partners: *Aconitum* 'Ivorine', *Berberis julianae, Euphorbia sikkimensis, Forsythia ovata* 'Tetragold', *Kerria japonica* 'Golden Guinea', *Physocarpus opulifolius* 'Dart's Gold', *Rosa* 'Chinatown', *Syringa vulgaris* 'Primrose'

H & S: 13ft (4m)
❀ Mid-autumn
▰▰▱ ◊◊ ▪ Z7 pH5–7.5

Elaeagnus 'Quicksilver'

How it works: Leaving the lower stems on *Elaeagnus* 'Quicksilver' allows its softly silver foliage to blend attractively with herbaceous plants such as *Symphytum caucasicum*. Although grown mainly for its dainty foliage, this plant also produces small, sweet-scented, creamy flowers.

Recommended partners: *Aconitum hemsleyanum*, *Clematis* 'Huldine', *C.* 'Prince Charles', *Delphinium* Summer Skies Group, *Ipomoea tricolor* 'Heavenly Blue', *Rosa* 'Sander's White Rambler'

Fuchsia 'Checkerboard'

How it works: The nodding flowers of *Fuchsia* 'Checkerboard', their red tubes and corollas harmonizing with the reddish purple foliage of *Acer palmatum* Dissectum Atropurpureum Group, are enlivened by white sepals. *Dryopteris affinis* 'Cristata' provides a pleasing contrast of foliage form.

Recommended partners: *Anemone* × *hybrida* 'Elegans', *Berberis thunbergii* 'Red Chief', *Rosa* 'Mevrouw Nathalie Nypels', *Schizostylis coccinea* 'Sunrise', *Watsonia* 'Stanford Scarlet'

H & S: 13ft (4m)
※ **Early summer**
 ◊-◊◊ ☐-■ Z3 pH5–7.5

H: 36in (90cm) S: 30in (75cm)
※ **Early summer to mid-autumn**
◊◊ ☐-■ Z8 pH5–7.5

Genista hispanica
SPANISH GORSE

How it works: The small, yellow pea-shaped flowers of *Genista hispanica*, evenly spaced over a dense mound, create a fine-textured effect, which contrasts with the large heads and layered habit of *Viburnum plicatum* 'Mariesii'. The neat habit and bright coloring of this gorse also complement silver-leaved plants.

Recommended partners: *Convolvulus cneorum, C. sabatius, × Halimiocistus wintonensis, Phlomis chrysophylla, Rosmarinus officinalis* 'Aureus', *Salvia officinalis* 'Icterina'

Halimium ocymoides

How it works: In this scheme, *Halimium ocymoides* provides plentiful golden flowers, which are matched by the yellow-edged foliage of *Salvia officinalis* 'Icterina'. Both plants favor a Mediterranean climate and are of comparable stature with a similar growth rate.

Recommended partners: *Cistus × hybridus, Helianthemum* 'Boughton Double Primrose', *Lavandula angustifolia* 'Nana Alba', *Phlomis fruticosa, Potentilla fruticosa* 'Maanelys', *Rosa* 'Golden Wings', *Spartium junceum, Stachys citrina*

H: 30in (75cm) **S: 5ft** (1.5m)
❀ **Early summer**
◊ ☐ **Z7 pH5.5–7.5**

H: 24in (60cm) **S: 40in** (1m)
❀ **Early to mid-summer**
◊ ☐ **Z8 pH6–7.5**

Hebe 'Midsummer Beauty'

How it works: A mature plant of *Hebe* 'Midsummer Beauty', an outstandingly showy evergreen shrub, is large enough to be draped with a late-flowering Texensis or Viticella clematis. Here, the harmonious but much deeper color of Viticella 'Etoile Violette' and its contrasting floral shape make a successful combination.

Recommended partners: *Buddleja* 'Pink Delight', *Lavandula pedunculata* subsp. *pedunculata*, *Lavatera* × *clementii* 'Barnsley', *Penstemon* 'Burgundy', *P.* 'Evelyn', *Perovskia* 'Blue Spire', *Rosa* Iceberg ('Korbin')

H & S: 6½ft (2m)
✿ **Mid-summer to late autumn**
▬▬ ◊◊ ▦ **Z8 pH5–7.5**

Hebe 'Nicola's Blush'

How it works: This combination of *Hebe* 'Nicola's Blush' and *Euonymus fortunei* 'Emerald 'n' Gold' would work equally well with a rich lavender-blue hebe or a white-variegated euonymus. This is one of the most popular smaller hebes, hardier than larger cultivars and easy to grow in an open site.

Recommended partners: *Artemisia* 'Powis Castle', *Festuca glauca* 'Blaufuchs', *Lavandula angustifolia* 'Hidcote', *Salvia officinalis* 'Purpurascens', *Sedum* 'Vera Jameson', *Senecio viravira*

H & S: 30in (75cm)
❀ Late summer to late autumn
 ◊◊ ▨ Z8 pH5–7.5

Hebe ochracea

How it works: *Hebe ochracea* combines with other hummock-forming plants that have leaves of contrasting shapes and sizes to form a subtle patchwork at the front of a border. Its white flowers echo the pale-edged leaves of *Astrantia major* 'Sunningdale Variegated'; purple sage (*Salvia officinalis* 'Purpurascens') and heucheras add to the display.

Recommended partners: *Celmisia semicordata*, *Euphorbia rigida*, *Helianthemum* 'Wisley White', *Hypericum cerastioides*, *Juniperus communis* 'Depressa Aurea', *Salvia officinalis* 'Icterina'

H: 40in (1m) S: 30in (75cm)
❀ Late spring to early summer
◊◊ ▢-▨ Z7 pH5–7.5

Hebe stenophylla

How it works: *Hebe stenophylla*, like other hebes that are not too dense and remain furnished to the ground, is an attractive host for plants of contrasting floral form or color. Here, its spikes of lilac-tinted white flowers combine with pink *Geranium* × *oxonianum*, which scrambles through its lower branches.

Recommended partners: *Artemisia ludoviciana*, *Buddleja davidii* 'Nanho Petite Indigo', *Geranium* 'Brookside', *Lavandula lanata*, *Penstemon* 'Sour Grapes', *Phygelius aequalis* 'Sani Pass'

Hebe 'Watson's Pink'

How it works: The success of this pretty combination with *Hebe* 'Watson's Pink', one of the showiest pink hebes, depends on a contrast of foliage, rather than of flower form or color. The silvery, slightly invasive *Artemisia ludoviciana* lingers at the outer fringes of the hebe rather than scrambling into it.

Recommended partners: *Argyranthemum* 'Summer Melody', *Campanula* 'Van-Houttei', *Helictotrichon sempervirens*, *Lavandula angustifolia* 'Bowles's Early', *Penstemon* 'Cherry'

H & S: 40in (1m)
❀ Mid- to late summer
 ◊◊ ☐-■ Z8 pH5–7.5

H & S: 40in (1m)
❀ Early to mid-summer
■■ ◊◊ ☐-■ Z8 pH5–7.5

Helianthemum 'Fire Dragon'

How it works: Gently invasive *Euphorbia cyparissias* weaves through two sun roses: coral *Helianthemum* 'Fire Dragon' and scarlet 'Ben Hope' to make an effective contrast. The flowers of 'Fire Dragon' are less strongly colored than those of 'Ben Hope', making them suited to combinations with peach or salmon flowers as well as with bronze, purple, or glaucous foliage.

Recommended partners: *Dianella revoluta* Little Rev ('Dr5000'), *Dianthus* 'Doris', *Diascia* Apricot Delight ('Codicot'), *Heuchera* 'Fireworks', *Rosa* Sweet Dream ('Fryminicot')

H: 12in (30cm) **S: 18in** (45cm)
❀ **Early summer**

 ◊-◊◊ ☐-■ **Z6 pH6–7.5**

Helianthemum 'Mrs C. W. Earle'

How it works: Sun roses (*Helianthemum* cvs) are spreading plants that can scramble into other open and low-growing shrubs. In this planting scheme, *Helianthemum* 'Mrs C. W. Earle' pushes its way through *Juniperus communis* 'Depressa Aurea', resulting in a striking contrast of scarlet flowers and yellow-green plumes of foliage.

Recommended partners: *Acaena caesiiglauca*, *Anthemis* 'Beauty of Grallagh', *Briza maxima*, *Carex comans* (bronze), *Euphorbia seguieriana* subsp. *niciciana*

H: 12in (30cm) **S: 18in** (45cm)
❀ **Early summer**

◊-◊◊ ☐-■ **Z6 pH6–7.5**

Hippophae rhamnoides
SEA BUCKTHORN

A large plant or group of sea buckthorn (*Hippophae rhamnoides*) is a useful component of a white garden, where it can readily be draped with a Viticella clematis such as *C.* 'Alba Luxurians'. Beneath, a white Shasta daisy (*Leucanthemum* × *superbum* 'Wirral Pride') continues the color theme.

Recommended partners: *Clematis* 'Błękitny Anioł', *Ipomoea tricolor* 'Heavenly Blue', *Lavatera* × *clementii* 'Barnsley', *Miscanthus sinensis* 'Morning Light', *Pittosporum* 'Garnettii', *Rosa* 'Prosperity'

Hydrangea arborescens

How it works: The solid outline of *Hydrangea arborescens* and its bold flowerheads act as a full stop at the end of a white border. Beyond, not part of the white-flowered theme, the emphatically vertical variegated yellow flag (*Iris pseudacorus* 'Variegata') terminates the vista, acting equally as a full stop but of contrasting form, flanked by the deep peach-pink plumes of *Filipendula rubra*.

Recommended partners: *Aconitum* 'Ivorine', *Cortaderia richardii*, *Hemerocallis* 'Marion Vaughn', *Hosta plantaginea*, *Lilium regale*, *Phlox maculata* 'Omega'

H & S: 20ft (6m)
❀ Mid-spring

◇-◇◇ □-■ Z4 pH6–7.5

H & S: 8ft (2.5m)
❀ **Mid- to late summer Z5 pH5.5–7.5**

◇◇-◇◇◇ □-■ ■

Hydrangea aspera Villosa Group

How it works: Lacy flowerheads of *Hydrangea aspera* Villosa Group contrast with the more solid inflorescences of a *Phlox paniculata* cultivar, accompanied by *Berberis thunbergii* 'Rose Glow', its purple-red leaves splashed with pink. This hydrangea combines well with pink, mauve, lilac, lavender, blue, and crimson flowers.
Recommended partners: *Aconitum* 'Newry Blue', *Clematis* 'Madame Julia Correvon', *C.* 'Prince Charles', *Fargesia nitida*, *Fuchsia* 'Riccartonii', *Lilium* 'Marie North', *Phlox maculata*

H & S: 10ft (3m)
Mid- to late summer Z7 pH4.5–7.5

Hydrangea macrophylla 'Générale Vicomtesse de Vibraye'

How it works: *Hydrangea macrophylla* 'Générale Vicomtesse de Vibraye', one of the most reliably floriferous Hortensia hydrangeas, contrasts with the Lacecap hydrangea *H. serrata* 'Rosalba'. The boldly striped *Hosta undulata* var. *univittata* furnishes the front of the planting scheme.
Recommended partners: *Aconitum × cammarum* 'Bicolor', *Astilbe chinensis* var. *taquetii*, *Miscanthus sinensis* 'Gracillimus', *Monarda* 'Beauty of Cobham', *Potentilla fruticosa* 'Maanelys'

H: 40in–6½ft (1–2m) **S: 4–10ft** (1.2–3m)
Mid- to late summer Z6 pH4.5–7.5

Hydrangea macrophylla 'Mariesii Perfecta'

How it works: *Hydrangea macrophylla* 'Mariesii Perfecta' is perhaps the most popular of the Lacecap Group of hydrangeas. Here, it combines attractively with cool colors and silver foliage, such as *Artemisia absinthium* 'Lambrook Silver'. Lacecaps are the most suitable hydrangeas for semi-natural conditions.

Recommended partners: *Aconitum* × *cammarum* 'Bicolor', *Astilbe chinensis* var. *taquetii*, *Miscanthus sinensis* 'Gracillimus', *Monarda* 'Beauty of Cobham', *Potentilla fruticosa* 'Maanelys'

H: 40 in–6½ft (1–2m) S: 4–10ft (1.2–3m)
❀ Mid- to late summer Z6 pH4.5–7.5
◊◊-◊◊◊ □-■ ■

Hydrangea paniculata

How it works: An elegant, fairly upright shrub, *Hydrangea paniculata* has conical, creamy white, attractively lacy flowerheads. Its color mixes particularly well with pale green, blue, or white, and with glaucous or white- or gold-variegated foliage. Here, it makes a boldly emphatic statement, with the glaucous foliage of the giant reed (*Arundo donax*) providing contrast behind.

Recommended partners: *Agapanthus caulescens* subsp. *caulescens*, *Ipomoea tricolor* 'Heavenly Blue', *Lathyrus latifolius* 'Blushing Bride', *Lilium* 'Casa Blanca', *Nicotiana* 'Lime Green'

H: 10–16ft (3–5m) S: 6½–13ft (2–4m)
❀ Mid- to late summer
◊◊ □-■ ■ Z5 pH5–7.5

Hydrangea paniculata 'Grandiflora'

How it works: The contrast in the flower-head shapes, conical *Hydrangea paniculata* 'Grandiflora' set against round agapanthus, is striking and perhaps most appealing when the hydrangea blooms are young, before they assume their eventual pink shading.

Recommended partners: *Actaea racemosa*, *Buddleja* 'Lochinch', *Ceanothus × delileanus* 'Gloire de Versailles', *Lilium regale*, *L.* 'Sterling Star', *Potentilla fruticosa* 'Tilford Cream'

H: 10ft (3m) S: 6½ft (2m)
❀ Mid- to late summer
◊◊ ☐-☐ ■ Z5 pH5–7.5

Hydrangea paniculata 'Greenspire'

How it works: Combining one plant with large inflorescences and another with small individual flowers often results in a very successful close-range partnership, as shown here with *Hydrangea paniculata* 'Greenspire' and *Nicotiana langsdorffii*, both in subtle shades of green.

Recommended partners: *Fuchsia magellanica* 'Versicolor', *Hosta* 'Sum and Substance', *Ilex × altaclerensis* 'Golden King', *Rosa* 'Ballerina', *R.* Iceberg ('Korbin')

H: 6½ft (2m) S: 13ft (4m)
❀ Mid- to late summer
◊◊ ☐-☐ ■ Z5 pH5–7.5

Hydrangea serrata 'Rosalba'

How it works: *Hydrangea serrata* 'Rosalba', its relatively small Lacecap flowerheads assuming shadings of red as they age, is gracefully draped with the flame flower (*Tropaeolum speciosum*) and studded with its scarlet blooms.

Recommended partners: *Buddleja* 'Pink Delight', *Deutzia setchuenensis* var. *corymbiflora*, *Hydrangea macrophylla*, *Perovskia* 'Blue Spire', *Rosa* Bonica ('Meidomonac'), *R.* 'Yesterday'

H & S: 4ft (1.2m)
❋ **Mid- to late summer Z6 pH4.5–7.5**

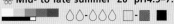

Hypericum forrestii

How it works: Hard annual pruning restricts the height of *Hypericum forrestii* to about 24 in (60cm), which allows it to be combined with herbaceous plants of similar height – as with the contrasting foliage and flowers of *Crocosmia* × *crocosmiiflora* shown here.

Recommended partners: *Agapanthus* 'Blue Moon', *Crocosmia* × *crocosmiiflora* 'Lady Hamilton', *Hosta* 'August Moon', *Miscanthus sinensis* 'Strictus', *Rosa* Elina ('Dicjana'), *R.* Graham Thomas ('Ausmas')

H: 4ft (1.2m) S: 5ft (1.5m)
❋ **Late summer**

Z6 pH5.5–7

Ilex aquifolium 'Myrtifolia Aurea Maculata'

How it works: The common holly (*Ilex aquifolium*) is available in hundreds of cultivars. Compact cultivar *I. a.* 'Myrtifolia Aurea Maculata', its relatively small leaves generously splashed with yellow on a bush well furnished to ground level, provides a support for scrambling *Potentilla* 'Flamenco' in fiery scarlet. This is a non-fruiting holly.

Recommended partners: *Clematis potaninii, Forsythia suspensa* 'Nymans', *Holodiscus discolor, Miscanthus sinensis* 'Strictus', *Parthenocissus tricuspidata* 'Lowii', *Rosa* 'Climbing Paul Lédé'

H: 6½–65ft (2–20m) S: 5–26ft (1.5–8m)
✽ Late spring to early summer
 ◊◊ ☐-▧ Z6 pH4.5–7.5

Lavandula angustifolia 'Hidcote'

How it works: *Lavandula angustifolia* 'Hidcote' makes a popular combination both visually and for its fragrance with gold-variegated sage (*Salvia officinalis* 'Icterina'). The partnership is useful equally in a herb garden, at the front of a border, or alongside a path, where passers-by will brush against the plants, releasing their aromatic scent.

Recommended partners: *Anthemis* Susanna Mitchell ('Blomit'), *A. tinctoria* 'E. C. Buxton', *Cistus* × *lenis* 'Grayswood Pink', *Convolvulus cneorum, Dianthus* 'Haytor White', *Sedum* 'Vera Jameson'

H: 24in (60cm) S: 30in (75cm)
✽ Mid- to late summer Z6 pH5.5–7.5
 ◊-◊◊ ☐-▧

Lavandula lanata

How it works: The appeal of *Lavandula lanata* lies in its purple flowers and the broad, intensely silver foliage. This is perhaps never more effective than when set against rich blue. Here, *Ceanothus* 'Puget Blue', kept furnished with branches down to ground level, is a perfect companion in a sunny border backed by a wall. This lavender is also an asset in rock or gravel gardens.

Recommended partners: *Anthemis punctata* subsp. *cupaniana*, *Artemisia schmidtiana*, *Halimium* 'Susan', *Phlomis chrysophylla*, *Salvia chamaedryoides*, *S. officinalis* 'Purpurascens'

Lavandula pedunculata subsp. *pedunculata*

How it works: *Lavandula pedunculata* subsp. *pedunculata* combines agreeably with many alliums, whose round flowerheads provide a contrast of form, while their colors are usually harmonious. In this informal patchwork of plants, the dying leaves of *Allium cristophii* are hidden by young shoots of gypsophila, with chives (*Allium schoenoprasum*) in the foreground.

Recommended partners: *Cistus* 'Grayswood Pink', *Crambe cordifolia*, *Dianthus* 'Becky Robinson', *D.* 'Musgrave's Pink', *Helianthemum* 'Wisley White', *Rosa* Pink Flower Carpet ('Noatraum')

H: 30in (75cm) S: 36in (90cm)
✿ **Late summer**
 ◇ ☐ Z7 pH5.5–7.5

H & S: 24in (60cm)
✿ **Late spring to early summer**
 ◇ ☐ Z8 pH5.5–7.5

Lavatera × *clementii* 'Barnsley'

How it works: Later clematis such as C. 'Perle d'Azur' make an ideal backcloth for *Lavatera* × *clementii* 'Barnsley'. Planted nearby, the odd trail of clematis, perhaps a Viticella or Texensis cultivar in carmine, crimson, or sumptuous burgundy, can be allowed to weave itself through the lavatera.

This floriferous, long-flowering, deciduous mallow rapidly develops into a medium to large shrub, useful for quickly filling gaps in a border. There it blends with cool colors and purple, silver, or glaucous foliage. Its slightly amorphous habit is best combined with architectural plants, or those with flower spikes or plates or other equally contrasting floral forms. As long as it is not severely frosted, it will regenerate from the roots, although it does then tend to revert to the original clone, the deeper-colored 'Rosea'. Protecting the base of the plant over winter usually averts this danger.

Recommended partners: *Aconitum* × *cammarum* 'Bicolor', *Buddleja davidii* 'Nanho Petite Purple', *Cistus* × *argenteus* 'Blushing Peggy Sammons', *Dahlia* 'Gerrie Hoek', *Hebe* 'Midsummer Beauty', *Romneya californica*, *Rosa* Iceberg ('Korbin'), *Thalictrum delavayi* 'Hewitt's Double'

H & S: 6½ft (2m)
❋ **Early to late summer**
△△ ☐-■ Z8 pH5.5–7.5

Lupinus arboreus
TREE LUPIN

How it works: Purple smoke bush makes a striking contrast to the vertical spikes of this soft yellow tree lupin (*Lupinus arboreus*), furnished in front with cushions of lady's mantle (*Alchemilla mollis*). A single white-flowered rose provides the background.

Recommended partners: *Anchusa azurea*, *Aquilegia canadensis*, *Cistus* × *hybridus*, *Nigella damascena* 'Miss Jekyll', *Paeonia lactiflora* 'Jan van Leeuwen', *Papaver orientale* 'Black and White', *P. o.* 'May Queen', *Rosa* 'Frühlingsgold', *Thalictrum flavum* subsp. *glaucum*

H & S: 5ft (1.5m)
❋ **Early summer**
◇-△△ ☐-■ Z8 pH5.5–7

Nandina domestica
SACRED BAMBOO

How it works: In this scheme of Japanese plants designed principally for foliage effect, the mahogany coloring of *Acer palmatum* Dissectum Atropurpureum Group is echoed by the fruits and some bronze-flushed leaves of *Nandina domestica*.

Recommended partners: *Acer palmatum* 'Seiryû', *Cercidiphyllum japonicum*, *Cornus alba* 'Kesselringii', *Fatsia japonica*, *Miscanthus sinensis* 'Zebrinus', *Physalis alkekengi*, *Pleioblastus viridistriatus*, *Rhus typhina* 'Dissecta', *Sorbus vilmorinii*, *Xanthorhiza simplicissima*

Neillia thibetica

How it works: After flowering, the rose-pink inflorescences of *Neillia thibetica* take on brickish tints as its seeds ripen, and the same hues are echoed along its leaf veins and margins. The mauve-pink flowers of the vigorous cranesbill *Geranium* × *oxonianum* 'Claridge Druce' scrambling

H: 6ft (1.8m) S: 5ft (1.5m)
❀ Mid-summer

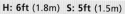

⬦⬦ ☐-■ Z7 pH5–7.5

H & S: 6½ft (2m)
❀ Early summer

⬦⬦ ☐-■ Z6 pH5–7.5

Philadelphus 'Beauclerk'

How it works: Scrambling among the lower branches and flowers of *Philadelphus* 'Beauclerk', the mauve-pink cranesbill *Geranium* × *oxonianum* 'Claridge Druce' proves itself an agreeable invader. When both plants are in bloom, the effect is pretty and informal.

Recommended partners: *Anthriscus sylvestris* 'Ravenswing', *Aruncus dioicus*, *Campanula latifolia* 'Gloaming', *Chaerophyllum hirsutum* 'Roseum', *Kolkwitzia amabilis*, *Rosa elegantula* 'Persetosa', *R.* 'Nevada', *Syringa* × *prestoniae* 'Elinor', *Thalictrum aquilegiifolium*

through its stems clash slightly but not disagreeably. With its quiet charm and gracefully arching habit, *N. thibetica* is more at home in wilder parts of the garden.

Recommended partners: *Chaerophyllum hirsutum* 'Roseum', *Philadelphus* 'Belle Etoile', *Rhododendron viscosum*, *Rosa glauca*, *Spiraea cantoniensis*, *Viburnum opulus* 'Roseum'

H & S: 6½ft (2m)
❀ **Early summer**

◊◊ ▢-◼ Z5 pH5.5–7.5

Philadelphus 'Belle Etoile'

How it works: Covered in headily fragrant, pink-stained white flowers in early summer, *Philadelphus* 'Belle Etoile' combines charmingly with *Spiraea canescens*, whose tiny, creamy white florets are massed along arching sprays.

Recommended partners: *Ammi majus, Aquilegia vulgaris* var. *stellata* 'Nora Barlow', *Campanula lactiflora, Clematis montana* var. *wilsonii, Geranium sylvaticum* 'Baker's Pink', *Hesperis matronalis, Paeonia lactiflora* 'White Wings', *Papaver orientale* 'Black and White', *Rosa* 'New Dawn'

H & S: 6½ft (2m)
❀ **Early summer**

 ◊◊ ▢-■ Z5 pH5.5–7.5

Philadelphus intectus

How it works: The creamy plumes of handsome *Aruncus dioicus* contrast in form with *Philadelphus intectus*, here unpruned and so remaining furnished to ground level with flowering stems. One of the larger, more vigorous mock oranges, this shrub has strong, arching stems. The flowers are short-lived but prolific and very fragrant.

Recommended partners: *Lonicera periclymenum* 'Graham Thomas', *Rosa* 'Cerise Bouquet', *R. nutkana* 'Plena', *Styrax japonicus* 'Pink Chimes', *Syringa* × *josiflexa* 'Bellicent'

H: 20ft (6m) **S:** 16ft (5m)
❀ **Early summer**

 ◊◊ ■ Z5 pH5–7.5

Phlomis fruticosa
JERUSALEM SAGE

How it works: In this combination, the bright flowers of *Phlomis fruticosa* harmonize with cream-variegated *Ligustrum sinense* 'Variegatum' and are set off by purple smoke bush (*Cotinus coggygria* 'Royal Purple').

Recommended partners: *Artemisia stelleriana* 'Boughton Silver', *Festuca glauca* 'Blaufuchs', *Geranium* 'Johnson's Blue', *Hakonechloa macra* 'Aureola', *Iris* 'Jane Phillips', *Nepeta* 'Six Hills Giant', *Salvia lavandulifolia*

Photinia × fraseri '**Birmingham**'

How it works: The coppery red spring shoots of *Photinia × fraseri* 'Birmingham' have here lost their initial brilliance but still remain in perfect harmony with *Euphorbia griffithii* 'Dixter'. The species and its cultivars are primarily used as foliage plants.

Recommended partners: *Fritillaria imperialis* 'Aurora', *Geum* 'Beech House Apricot', *G. chiloense*, *Rhododendron* 'Coccineum Speciosum', *Tulipa* 'Prinses Irene'

H: 40in (1m) S: 5ft (1.5m)
✿ **Early summer**
 ◊ ▢ Z7 pH5.5–7.5

H & S: 16ft (5m)
✿ **Early summer**
 ◊◊ Z7 pH5–7

Phygelius aequalis 'Yellow Trumpet'

How it works: The soft yellow florets of *Phygelius aequalis* 'Yellow Trumpet', borne along one side of the stem, contrast dramatically in color and form with *Geranium psilostemon*.

Recommended partners: *Argyranthemum maderense*, *Euphorbia seguieriana* subsp. *niciciana*, *Felicia amelloides* 'Santa Anita', *Geranium* 'Ann Folkard', *Nicotiana* 'Lime Green', *Petunia* Surfinia Purple ('Shihi Brilliant'), *Salvia greggii*, *S. patens*

H: 40in (1m) S: 20in (50cm)
❀ **Mid-summer to early autumn**

 Z8 pH5.5–7.5

Physocarpus opulifolius 'Dart's Gold'

How it works: When in flower, *Physocarpus opulifolius* 'Dart's Gold' has dazzlingly bright yellow-green leaves, which make a striking contrast here with purple filbert (*Corylus maxima* 'Purpurea'). The leaves become greener as the season advances.

Recommended partners: *Agapanthus* 'Loch Hope', *Clematis* 'Frances Rivis', *Cotinus coggygria* 'Royal Purple', *Ipomoea tricolor* 'Heavenly Blue', *Miscanthus sinensis* 'Strictus'

H & S: 5ft (1.5m)
❀ **Early summer**

Z3 pH5–6.5

Pleioblastus viridistriatus

How it works: At the front of a border filled primarily with herbaceous plants, the slightly invasive, brightly variegated bamboo *Pleioblastus viridistriatus* provides an attractive contrast with the soft orange flowers of *Geum* 'Dolly North'. The bamboo's foliage is at its brightest in late spring and early summer when the geum is in full bloom.

This evergreen bamboo spreads slowly to form a large clump that looks effective towards the front of a shrub border or in a woodland garden, mixed with hot colors, blue flowers, and glaucous foliage. In a woodland garden it is best grown in an open glade to ensure it receives partial sun.

Recommended partners: *Corydalis flexuosa, Euphorbia griffithi* 'Dixter', *Helleborus foetidus, Hosta* (Tardiana Group) 'Halcyon', *Hydrangea arborescens* subsp. *discolor* 'Sterilis', *H. macrophylla* 'Blue Bonnet', *Meconopsis grandis, Ophiopogon planiscapus* 'Nigrescens', *Phormium* 'Dark Delight', *Rhododendron augustinii, R.* 'Coccineum Speciosum', *R.* 'Narcissiflorum'

H: 4ft (1.2m) S: 5ft (1.5m)
✺ **Summer**

Z7   pH5–7

Potentilla fruticosa 'Primrose Beauty'

How it works: *Potentilla fruticosa* 'Primrose Beauty' is a shrubby cinquefoil with silvery leaves and pale flowers that blend with most colors. Here, it is planted with *Rosa* 'Felicia', purple-leaved *Actaea simplex* Atropurpurea Group, blue *Polemonium foliosissimum*, coral kniphofias, and white violas.

Recommended partners: *Agapanthus* 'Donau', *Caryopteris* × *clandonensis*, *Eryngium* × *tripartitum*, *Hakonechloa macra* 'Aureola', *Helictotrichon sempervirens*, *Hemerocallis* 'Corky', *Hosta* 'Big Daddy', *Lavandula angustifolia* 'Hidcote', *Nepeta* × *faassenii*, *Perovskia* 'Blue Haze', *Rosa* 'Sally Holmes', *Sedum* 'Herbstfreude'

H: 1–6½ft (30cm–2m) S: 40in–6½ft (1–2m)
�֍ **Late spring to mid-autumn**

◊◊ ☐-■ Z3 pH5–7.5

Rhus × *pulvinata* Autumn Lace Group

How it works: The sumacs are most striking in autumn, when their attractively feathered deciduous leaves assume glorious seasonal tints of rich yellow, orange, and red, but they are extremely handsome for the rest of the year, too. In this planting, the distinctive foliage of *Rhus* × *pulvinata* Autumn Lace Group provides a backcloth for *Geranium* 'Ann Folkard', *Salvia officinalis* 'Purpurascens', and *Artemisia abrotanum*.

Recommended partners: *Acer palmatum* 'Sango-kaku', *Cortaderia selloana* 'Sunningdale Silver', *Helianthus* 'Monarch', *Rudbeckia fulgida* var. *sullivantii* 'Goldsturm'

H: 10ft (3m) S: 16ft (5m)
✖ **Mid-summer**

◊◊ ■ Z3 pH5–7.5

Rosmarinus officinalis 'Roseus'

How it works: Pink-flowered rosemaries such as *Rosmarinus officinalis* 'Roseus' combine well with silver, purple, red, or glaucous foliage, as here with purple sage *Salvia officinalis* 'Purpurascens', and with flowers in cool colors. They also associate happily with other plants from dry, sunny climates such as the European maquis and plants of the North American chaparral.

Recommended partners: *Artemisia ludoviciana, Cistus* × *hybridus, Convolvulus cneorum, C. sabatius, Iris* 'Jane Phillips', *Lavandula* 'Fathead', *L. pedunculata* subsp. *pedunculata* 'James Compton', *Salvia canariensis, Santolina chamaecyparissus*

H: 36in (90cm) S: 20in (50cm)
❀ **Mid-spring to early summer**
 ◊◊ ☐-■ **Z8 pH5.5–7.5**

Rubus cockburnianus 'Goldenvale'

How it works: *Rubus cockburnianus* 'Goldenvale' is combined here with lady's mantle (*Alchemilla mollis*) – the leaves of the two plants contrast markedly in shape, while the flowers of the alchemilla harmonize with the rubus foliage. Both are deciduous, allowing underplanting with early bulbs.

Recommended partners: *Ajuga reptans* 'Catlin's Giant', *Bergenia cordifolia* 'Purpurea', *Elaeagnus* × *ebbingei* 'Gilt Edge', *Erica carnea* 'Vivellii', *Galanthus nivalis, Gentiana asclepiadea, Hosta sieboldiana* var. *elegans, Muscari latifolium, Ranunculus ficaria* 'Brazen Hussy', *Viburnum tinus* 'Eve Price'

H: 6ft (1.8m) S: 4ft (1.2m)
❀ **Mid-summer**
◊-◊◊ ☐-■ **Z6 pH5–7.5**

Ruta graveolens 'Jackman's Blue'

How it works: The yellow-green flowers of *Ruta graveolens* 'Jackman's Blue' perfectly match the foliage of *Choisya ternata* Sundance ('Lich'), while the rue's foliage provides a gentle and pleasing contrast. Larger cream flowers would be effective for leavening the scheme, while strong blue could be used for contrast.

Recommended partners: *Ajuga reptans* 'Atropurpurea', *Cistus* × *cyprius*, *Euphorbia myrsinites*, *Halimium ocymoides*, *Iris* 'Joyce', *Nepeta* 'Six Hills Giant', *Rosmarinus officinalis* Prostratus Group, *Salvia officinalis* 'Icterina', *Symphytum* × *uplandicum* 'Variegatum'

Sambucus nigra f. *porphyrophylla* 'Guincho Purple'

How it works: Horizontal creamy white flowerheads of the elder *Sambucus nigra* f. *porphyrophylla* 'Guincho Purple', among the showiest common elders, match exactly the

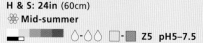

H & S: 24in (60cm)
✿ Mid-summer
◊-◊◊ ☐-■ Z5 pH5–7.5

H & S: 20ft (6m)
✿ Early summer Z5 pH4.5–7.5
◊◊ ☐-■

color of upright foxgloves *Digitalis purpurea* 'Sutton's Apricot', leavened by white *D. p.* f. *albiflora*. The elder's dark foliage adds depth. **Recommended partners:** *Acer shirasawanum* 'Aureum', *Ammi majus*, *Berberis* × *ottawensis* f. *purpurea* 'Superba', *Lonicera nitida* 'Baggesen's Gold', *Prunus spinosa* 'Purpurea'

Santolina chamaecyparissus

LAVENDER COTTON

How it works: In this Mediterranean planting, santolinas occupy the foreground, contrasting silver *S. chamaecyparissus* with deep green *S. rosmarinifolia*. A pale lavender and an upright rosemary fill the border by the wall. The attractive billowing masses of santolina will need occasional pruning to prevent them becoming gappy. **Recommended partners:** *Cerinthe major* var. *purpurascens*, *Cistus* 'Silver Pink', *Dianthus* 'Haytor White', *Euphorbia myrsinites*, *Festuca glauca* 'Blaufuchs', *Helianthemum* 'Rhodanthe Carneum', *Nepeta* × *faassenii*, *Phlomis fruticosa*

H: 20in (50cm) **S: 36in** (90cm)
Mid-summer
Z7 pH6–7.5

Spiraea nipponica 'Snowmound'

How it works: Grown in a narrow border and crowded with blooms from top to toe, the arching stems of *Spiraea nipponica* 'Snowmound' contrast with billowing masses of *Ceanothus* 'Puget Blue'. The yellow-green foliage beyond contrasts equally effectively with the ceanothus.

Given a wider border, adding a shorter, yellow-flowered shrub or another with yellow-green leaves would bring unity to the scheme.

Recommended partners: *Berberis thunbergii* 'Aurea', *Geranium* 'Mavis Simpson', *Iris* 'Cambridge', *Lathyrus latifolius* 'Rosa Perle', *Lilium pyrenaicum* var. *pyrenaicum*, *Potentilla fruticosa* 'Beesii'

H & S: 4ft (1.2m)
✿ **Early summer**
◊◊ ☐-■ Z5 pH5.5–7.5

Ulmus minor '**Dicksonii**'
DICKSON'S GOLDEN ELM

How it works: Adding dramatic height to a deep border, *Ulmus minor* 'Dicksonii' is contrasted with silver willow (*Salix alba* var. *sericea*); lavender *Hebe* 'Jewel' furnishes the front. A lavender-blue Viticella clematis could also be included to drape the willow and elm, further unifying the design.

Recommended partners: *Clematis viticella* 'Flore Pleno', *Delphinium* 'Alice Artindale', *Helianthus decapetalus* 'Soleil d'Or', *Pyrus salicifolia* 'Pendula', *Rosa* 'Frensham'

Weigela '**Florida Variegata**'

How it works: *Weigela* 'Florida Variegata', its leaves edged in creamy yellow, is furnished in front with *Berberis thunbergii* 'Atropurpurea Nana', whose reddish purple foliage harmonizes with the weigela's rose-pink flowers, while contrasting strikingly with its leaves.

Recommended partners: *Choisya ternata* Sundance ('Lich'), *Euphorbia* × *martini*, *Geranium albanum*, *Potentilla fruticosa* 'Tilford Cream', *Rosa* 'Carmenetta', *Tulipa* 'Elegant Lady'

H: 33ft (10m) S: 20ft (6m)
✿ **Early to mid-spring**
 Z4 pH5–8

H & S: 5ft (1.5m)
✿ **Early summer**
Z5 pH5.5–7.5

Climbers

Climbers add an extra dimension to the garden. They have the ability to clothe walls, trellises, and pillars, which makes them especially useful for providing height in small gardens. Their need for something on or through which to climb means that they can be planted with trees, shrubs, other climbers, and herbaceous perennials with great success.

Introducing climbers

In the wild, climbers have adapted to scrambling through other plants to reach the sun. It is vital to understand how these plants climb if they are to be used successfully in the garden: a wisteria planted at the base of a stout pergola pillar will writhe forever on the ground unless it is tied to a support, such as a horizontal wire. It is also important to match the vigor of the plant to its situation. Eccremocarpus will be satisfied with a bamboo cane measuring 6½–10ft (2–3m) high, while *Vitis coignetiae* and *Clematis montana* will eventually climb to the top of the tallest tree. Finally, it makes sense to position those climbers that have scented flowers – jasmines, honeysuckles, sweet peas – in sheltered situations where both their scent and those who appreciate it will be inclined to linger.

How do climbers climb?

- Some climbers, such as clematis, sweet peas, or vines, climb by tendrils or leaf stalks, which curl tightly around any convenient support.
- Others twine their whole stem spirally around thin supports – such as honeysuckles, morning glories, and summer jasmine.
- Aerial roots or suckers adhere to and sometimes penetrate rough brick, stone, timber, or bark. Ivy climbs like this.
- A few plants, roses and bougainvilleas among them, are scramblers rather than climbers, with long stems clothed with sharp thorns to hook on to their supports. Such plants are never secure until their stems can intertwine and form a self-supporting structure.

- Wall plants – figs, flowering quinces, and cotoneaster – are naturally shrubs but are often fastened to a wall because they are decorative or benefit from the shelter and warmth offered by the wall. They can be held in place on a trellis or with wires.

Because they take up very little space, climbers can be used in a variety of ways around even the smallest garden to disguise and decorate house walls, garages, sheds, fences, and eyesores. They can be trained on purpose-built trellises, arches, pergolas, and pillars to provide a lighter and more colorful vertical emphasis than trees or walls. It is also possible to grow plants in combination: dark red clematis through purple-leaved vines, for example, or interwoven strands of early and late

Above: This spring combination of *Clematis* 'Ruby', an Atragene Group cultivar, with *Malus* × *zumi* var. *calocarpa* shows the value of contrasting floral form, especially when colors are harmonious, a principle that applies equally in summer.

Left: Annual climbers such as nasturtiums and sweet peas are valuable for quick effect and can either be trained upward or allowed to tumble down.

honeysuckles. Of course, with such mixtures, great care has to be taken to prevent the plants from growing into an unruly mass.

Climbers in pots and borders

In a border, the wigwams, obelisks, or single posts up which many climbers like to grow will add height while occupying minimal ground area, and the lighter-stemmed climbers can be used, without artificial support, to scramble through shrubs or over robust perennials to give a second period of interest.

Annual climbers, in particular, are excellent in large pots. A tripod of canes will support sweet peas, eccremocarpus, canary creepers, or morning glories. These can also be allowed to trail down over the edge of the container.

Actinidia kolomikta

How it works: The boldly splashed leaves of *Actinidia kolomikta* harmonize with the pink and red in the flowers of the honeysuckle *Lonicera* × *italica*, both supported by wires against a moderately sunny wall. The actinidia will remain colorful after the honeysuckle has finished flowering.

Many of the leaves of this vigorous, deciduous twining climber have a white zone tipped with pink. This leaf coloring is most pronounced on male specimens (the white male and female flowers being borne on separate plants) and develops maximum intensity in full sun. Plants with pink, white, or crimson flowers and those with purple foliage make excellent associates. In areas with fairly cool summers, actinidia benefits from being grown against a wall. With careful training it is possible to combine it with two or more other climbers quite uniformly, but for this to be effective at long range, the coloring of companion plants should not be too close to that of the actinidia.

Recommended partners: *Clematis florida* var. *sieboldiana*, *C.* 'Madame Julia Correvon', *Jasminum* × *stephanense*, *Rosa* 'Madame Grégoire Staechelin', *Vitis vinifera* 'Purpurea'

H: 16ft (5m)
❀ **Early summer**
◊◊ ☐-■ Z5 pH5.5–7.5

Ampelopsis brevipedunculata var. *maximowiczii* 'Elegans'

How it works: This subtle tapestry of foliage owes much of its charm to the different leaf shapes – palmate in *Ampelopsis brevipedunculata* var. *maximowiczii* 'Elegans', pinnate in *Jasminum officinale* 'Aureum', and peltate in nasturtium. The mottled variegation lightens the leaf color, making this scheme more effective at close range.

Recommended partners: *Billardiera longiflora fructu-albo*, *Ceanothus* 'Autumnal Blue', *Clematis* 'Duchess of Albany', *Ipomoea lobata*, *Jasminum beesianum*, *Maurandya barclayana*, *Tropaeolum tricolor*

H: 13ft (4m)
❀ **Summer**
◊◊ ☐-■ Z9 pH6–7.5

Clematis

The genus *Clematis* is immensely diverse, with flowers, from large to tiny, of almost every color except pure blue, always presented with poise and elegance. Most are moderately vigorous and easy to keep in balance with other plants, producing slender stems that can drape themselves over or through their companions without suppressing them. Along with roses, they are the most useful climbers for plant associations. Yet clematis are often grown in isolation, without any attempt to allow them to interact with their neighbors. It is true that the most vigorous sorts – like *Clematis montana* var. *rubens* – create such large areas of color that any interaction is apparent only around the fringes of the plant; and on a pillar or obelisk, a single clematis of reasonable vigor allows little space for a companion, except for wispy climbers such as morning glories or perennial peas. A clematis "balloon," however, gives scope for two cultivars to be interwoven, perhaps with another slender scrambler.

On a wall, different clematis can be used to carry upward the color scheme of the border beneath, possibly mixed with a bold-leaved vine or *Actinidia kolomikta* to compensate for their lack of good foliage, and enhanced by using clematis with flowers of differing sizes.

Small-flowered *C.* × *triternata* 'Rubromarginata' or *C.* 'Praecox', for example, can be mixed with medium-sized Viticella and larger Early Large-flowered cultivars.

Clematis may also be draped over shrubs, to contrast with gold or silver foliage or harmonize with purple, or to add interest to shrubs that are dull after flowering. A number of species and almost all clematis in the Tangutica Group have decorative seedheads, some persisting through winter, and these are particularly effective if sited in the open garden, rather than on walls. Texensis cultivars have upward-facing blooms, which are an asset if grown across a carpet of ground cover. Shorter clematis, such as *C.* × *bonstedtii*, *C.* × *durandii*, *C. heracleifolia*, and *C. recta*, can be grown as border plants with the help of brushwood stakes.

Clematis climb by means of their twining leaf-stalks. They may be deciduous or evergreen, although all those described in this book are deciduous. Early-flowering kinds with axillary flowers (for example Alpina Group cultivars and *C. montana*) are pruned after flowering, while large- or

Summer-flowering Early Large-flowered and Viticella clematis (purple *C.* 'Jackmanii Superba', crimson 'Ville de Lyon', and pink 'Comtesse de Bouchaud') mingle harmoniously here against a dry stone wall.

later small-flowered cultivars are pruned in late winter or early spring. Regular tying-in of new shoots, ideally at least semi-monthly, helps to spread out the stems for maximum floral display and prevent them kinking at the base, which encourages clematis wilt disease. If the rootball is set 3in (8cm) or so below the soil surface, the plant will usually regrow after an attack by wilt. Mildew can be a problem for groups such as Early Large-flowered, Texensis, and some Viticellas, particularly if grown on a wall. Bare stems at the base of the clematis are best hidden by other plants, casting the roots into the shade they prefer.

Clematis flowers are most frequently more or less round in outline, less commonly starry, cross-shaped, or like nodding lanterns. It helps to contrast them with partners that have a different floral form. Perhaps the most telling are spires such as delphiniums, lupins, verbascums, or buddlejas. The flat plates of flowers such as achilleas are also effective, though taller sorts are usually needed to reach up high enough to interact with the clematis. To these can be added flowers of more diffuse form such as thalictrums or *Crambe cordifolia*. Roses and clematis form a popular combination, most successful if the clematis is distinct in color from its partner.

A large expanse of clematis foliage and flower can be relatively structureless, so a boldly architectural plant can make a good companion. This might be a fastigiate conifer, a fountain of an early-flowering *Cortaderia*, or a large-leaved plant such as *Tetrapanax papyrifer*.

The vigorous nature of most clematis makes them unsuited to ground cover, though some of more modest growth can be very effective if planted at the top of a small wall and allowed to tumble downward.

Combining clematis of different flower size and distinct colors can add sparkle, as here with red Texensis 'Gravetye Beauty', soft lavender Early Large-flowered 'Perle d'Azur', and white Viticella 'Huldine'.

Clematis **'Alba Luxurians'**

How it works: *Clematis* 'Alba Luxurians' scrambles among pretty blue periwinkle (*Vinca major*) and arching white *Lysimachia clethroides*, while spiky-leaved *Astelia chathamica* stands tall at the back of the border.

Recommended partners: *Buddleja* 'Lochinch', *B.* 'Pink Delight', *Ceanothus* × *delileanus* 'Gloire de Versailles', *Clematis* 'Prince Charles', *Hippophae rhamnoides*, *Prunus spinosa* 'Purpurea', *Salix elaeagnos* subsp. *angustifolia*

H: 13ft (4m)
✿ Mid-summer to early autumn
▬▬▭▬ ◊◊ ▭-▬ Z5 pH5–8

Clematis **'Comtesse de Bouchaud'**

How it works: Grown with *Clematis* 'Jackmanii', *C.* 'Comtesse de Bouchaud' gives a good color contrast, while erect stems of white *Actaea cordifolia* and magenta lythrum provide variety of form.

Recommended partners: *Clematis* × *triternata* 'Rubromarginata', *C. viticella* 'Flore Pleno', *Ipomoea batatas* 'Blackie', *Lathyrus rotundifolius* 'Albus', *Maurandya barclayana*, *Prunus cerasifera* 'Nigra', *Rosa* 'Brenda Colvin'

H: 13ft (4m)
✿ Early summer to early autumn
▬▬▭▬ ◊◊ ▭-▬ Z5 pH5–8

Clematis × *diversifolia* 'Blue Boy'

How it works: *Clematis* × *diversifolia* 'Blue Boy' presents its flowers with poise when allowed to scramble freely over bright yellow-green *Choisya ternata* Sundance ('Lich'). The rich, dark leaves and flowers of *Bupleurum fruticosum* provide an excellent foil, while the whole is leavened by creamy white *Anthemis tinctoria* 'Sauce Hollandaise'.

Although this clematis is as near to true blue as *C.* × *durandii* (facing page),

it differs from it in its strongly recurved sepals and paler tone, which give it an altogether daintier appearance. This and its smaller flower size make it suitable for smaller-scale groupings to be seen at closer range. If allowed to scramble over ground cover or shrubs, the flowers will display themselves more elegantly.

Recommended partners: *Achillea* 'Lucky Break', *Brachyglottis* 'Sunshine', *Calluna vulgaris* 'Gold Haze', *Crocosmia* 'Honey Angels', *Philadelphus coronarius* 'Aureus', *Rosa* Iceberg ('Korbin')

H: 6½ft (2m)
✤ **Mid-summer to early autumn**
 ◊◊ ☐-◼ Z5 pH5–8

Clematis × *durandii*

How it works:

Below: *Clematis* × *durandii* looks effective trained over gold-leaved shrubs such as *Lonicera nitida* 'Baggesen's Gold'.

Right: Grown as a herbaceous perennial on tall brushwood stakes, *Clematis* × *durandii* harmonizes with purplish red *Knautia macedonica*, violet *Nepeta sibirica*, and pinkish purple *Stachys macrantha*, with vivid *Rosa* News ('Legnews') making its presence known behind.

Recommended partners: *Achillea* 'Lucky Break', *Atriplex halimus*, *Berberis temolaica*, *Calluna vulgaris* 'Gold Haze', *Lonicera periclymenum* 'Graham Thomas', *Philadelphus coronarius* 'Aureus', *Rosa* 'Leverkusen', *R. multiflora*, *Verbascum* 'Gainsborough'

H: 6½ft (2m)

✿ Early summer to mid-autumn

 ◊◊ ☐-■ Z5 pH5–8

Clematis 'Etoile Rose'

How it works: The mix of *Clematis* 'Etoile Rose' and *Buddleja* 'Lochinch' benefits from the excellent contrast of flower form, size, and color, as well as from the buddleia's silver foliage.

Most Texensis cultivars have upward-facing blooms, making them ideal for growing across ground-covering plants, but the flowers of 'Etoile Rose' nod downward so that they are perhaps best seen from beneath. As with *C.* × *diversifolia* 'Blue Boy' (page 80), the grace with which the flowers are borne can be lost if the plant is trained too tightly against a wall; it is also more prone to mildew here than in an open situation. A much more pleasing effect is obtained if the clematis can arrange itself loosely over a wall plant or a tall, freestanding shrub. 'Etoile Rose' works well with silver or purple foliage, or with mauve, purple, crimson, or pale pink flowers, including larger-flowered Viticella clematis.

Recommended partners: *Ceanothus* × *pallidus* 'Marie Simon', *Clematis* 'Hagley Hybrid', *C.* 'Prince Charles', *Cotinus coggygria* 'Royal Purple', *Hibiscus syriacus* 'Hamabo', *H. s.* 'Red Heart', *Prunus spinosa* 'Purpurea', *Rosa* Super Dorothy ('Heldoro'), *Salix alba* var. *sericea* (pollarded)

H: 8ft (2.5m)
✿ **Mid-summer to mid-autumn**
 ◊◊ ☐-■ Z5 pH5–8

Clematis 'Etoile Violette'

How it works: The sumptuous but recessive tone of *Clematis* 'Etoile Violette' provides a good foil for honeysuckles such as *Lonicera* × *americana*. Although their flower shape is very different, they have similar foliage texture; contrasting daylily leaves beneath help to prevent monotony.

Recommended partners: *Buddleja davidii* 'Dartmoor', *Ceanothus* × *delileanus* 'Gloire de Versailles', *Clematis* 'Perle d'Azur', *Hebe* 'Midsummer Beauty', *Hosta* 'August Moon', *Lathyrus latifolius, Lophospermum erubescens, Passiflora caerulea, Robinia pseudoacacia* 'Frisia'

H: 13ft (4m)
✿ **Mid-summer to early autumn**
 ◊◊ ☐-■ Z5 pH5–8

Clematis florida var. *sieboldiana*

How it works: *Clematis florida* var. *sieboldiana* is flattered here by the bold pink-tipped foliage of *Actinidia kolomikta*. Such a vigorous companion could overwhelm it unless regularly curbed.

Recommended partners: *Fuchsia magellanica* var. *gracilis*, *Lathyrus odoratus* 'Matucana', *Rosa* 'Climbing Pompon de Paris', *R.* 'Leverkusen', *R.* 'Reine Victoria'

H: 8ft (2.5m)
✽ Early summer to early autumn
▪▬▭▮ ◊◊ ▢-▪ Z8 pH5.5–7.5

Clematis 'Gravetye Beauty'

How it works: The combination of *Clematis* 'Gravetye Beauty' with summer-flowering heathers is a classic one – although white or deepest red-purple heathers might be more agreeable than the mauve-pink *Calluna vulgaris* cultivar used here. Heaths with colored foliage, groups of bergenias, or carpeting conifers, such as some of the junipers, could also be attractively draped with the clematis.

H: 16ft (5m)
✽ Mid-summer to early autumn
▪▬▭▮ ◊◊ ▢-▪ Z6 pH5.5–7.5

With their pinched sepals, the cross-shaped flowers of this crimson clematis are extremely effective seen from above but not from below, making it best suited to growing across ground cover.

Recommended partners: *Bergenia* 'Sunningdale', *Calluna vulgaris* 'Beoley Gold', *Clematis* 'Huldine', *C.* 'Perle d'Azur', *Erica carnea* 'Vivellii', *E. cinerea* 'Pentreath', *Juniperus horizontalis* 'Wiltonii', *J. sabina* var. *tamariscifolia*

Clematis integrifolia

How it works: *Clematis integrifolia* is similar in height to *Rosa gallica* var. *officinalis* and sets off the rich carmine color of its blooms as well as providing a contrast of flower shape.

Recommended partners: *Achillea* 'Credo', *Artemisia ludoviciana* 'Silver Queen', *Iris* 'Jane Phillips', *Nepeta sibirica* 'Souvenir d'André Chaudron', *Stachys macrantha* 'Robusta'

H: 27in (70cm)
❋ **Mid- to late summer**

 ◊-◊◊ ☐-▨ **Z3 pH5–8**

Clematis 'Jackmanii'

How it works: Arching gracefully above a wrought-iron gate, *Clematis* 'Jackmanii' contrasts dramatically with the gold-variegated ivy *Hedera colchica* 'Sulphur Heart'. Each flower of 'Jackmanii' usually has four rhomboid violet sepals.

Recommended partners: *Acer platanoides* 'Drummondii', *Buddleja* 'Lochinch', *Ceanothus* × *pallidus* 'Perle Rose', *Clematis* 'Comtesse de Bouchaud', *C.* 'Purpurea Plena Elegans', *Rosa* 'Lavender Lassie', *R.* Super Dorothy ('Heldoro'), *Salix alba* var. *sericea*, *Vitis vinifera* 'Incana'

H: 13ft (4m)
❀ **Early summer to early autumn**

 ◊◊ □-■ **Z4 pH5–8**

Clematis 'Jackmanii Superba'

How it works: *Luma apiculata* 'Variegata' makes an effective pale backdrop for *Clematis* 'Jackmanii Superba'. The clematis is a shade deeper than 'Jackmanii', making it slightly less punchy in contrasts and less visible from a distance, though still sumptuous when seen at close range.

Recommended partners: *Buddleja* 'Pink Delight', *Clematis* 'Prince Charles', *C.* 'Praecox', *Lonicera periclymenum* 'Graham Thomas'

H: 13ft (4m)
Early summer to early autumn
Z4 pH5–8

Clematis 'Kermesina'

How it works: The gently nodding blooms of *Clematis* 'Kermesina' mingle easily with the old, richly scented sweet pea *Lathyrus odoratus* 'Matucana'. The sweet pea has been sown in spring to make its flowering coincide with that of the clematis.

Recommended partners: *Clematis* 'Victoria', *Eccremocarpus scaber*, *Humulus lupulus* 'Aureus', *Lathyrus odoratus* 'Noel Sutton', *Rosa* 'Climbing Madame Caroline Testout', *R.* 'Mermaid', *R.* Super Dorothy ('Heldoro')

H: 13ft (4m)
Mid-summer to early autumn
Z5 pH5–8

Clematis 'M. Koster'

How it works: The contrasting form and soft peach coloring of old glory rose (*R.* 'Gloire de Dijon') make a telling combination with *Clematis* 'M. Koster'. Its flowers face outward and slightly upward, suiting it to use over shrubs and ground cover as well as on a wall.

Recommended partners: *Ceanothus* × *delileanus* 'Gloire de Versailles', *C.* × *pallidus* 'Perle Rose', *Cercis canadensis* 'Forest Pansy', *Clematis* 'Prince Charles', *Euphorbia schillingii*

H: 10ft (3m)
 Mid-summer to early autumn
  ◊◊ ☐-▨ **Z4 pH5–8**

Clematis montana var. *rubens*

How it works: A fence clothed with a pale selection of *Clematis montana* var. *rubens* provides an effective background for purple and white honesty (*Lunaria annua*).

Sweet-scented *C. montana* typically has white flowers, but most of its cultivars are pink, derived from var. *rubens*. Free-flowering and easy to grow, it is admirably suited to bold planting on the largest scale. It is almost uncontrollably vigorous, tending to form a large sheet of growth that is covered in bloom in late spring; the white var. *wilsonii* flowers about two weeks later, allowing different planting combinations with the first of the summer flowers. Although *C. montana* can produce the most exquisite late spring partnerships, its vigor is its greatest limitation in achieving them. Stunning combinations are sometimes seen, but the chances of achieving a successful balance without careful management of the clematis – and often its partner, too – are very small.

Recommended partners: *Choisya ternata*, *Malus × zumi* 'Golden Hornet', *Prunus cerasifera* 'Nigra', *P.* 'Shirotae', *P.* 'Shôgetsu', *Rosa* 'Cooperi', *Syringa vulgaris* 'Congo', *S. v.* 'Krasavitsa Moskvy', *Wisteria floribunda* 'Alba'

Clematis 'Perle d'Azur'

How it works: *Clematis* 'Etoile Violette' makes a good match for 'Perle d'Azur', although here both are so large that the supporting obelisk is hidden beneath them. With a bigger support, the clematis could produce a more spectacular display.

Recommended partners: *Clematis* 'Ville de Lyon', *C.* 'Purpurea Plena Elegans', *Hemerocallis* 'Hyperion', *Lavatera × clementii* 'Barnsley', *Lonicera sempervirens* f. *sulphurea*, *Prunus spinosa* 'Purpurea', *Rosa* 'Sander's White Rambler', *Vitis vinifera* 'Purpurea'

H 33ft (10m)
✽ Late spring to early summer
 ◊◊ ☐-■ Z6 pH5–8

H: 13ft (4m)
✽ Mid-summer to late autumn
◊◊ ☐-■ Z5 pH5–8

Clematis 'Praecox'

How it works: *Clematis* 'Praecox' is too
vigorous for draping shrubs, but it can
be trained on a wall with other clematis
and climbers. Here, it acts as a foil for
C. 'Victoria', toning down its possible
excess of gorgeousness. *C.* 'Praecox' can
also be used as a ground-covering carpet.

Recommended partners: *Buddleja davidii*
'Dartmoor', *Caryopteris* × *clandonensis*
'Pershore', *Ipomoea tricolor* 'Heavenly Blue',
Monarda 'Beauty of Cobham', *Pulmonaria
saccharata*

Clematis 'Prince Charles'

How it works: *Clematis* 'Prince Charles'
is shorter than most other Early Large-
flowered or Viticella cultivars, allowing it
to be draped over shrubs of moderate size,
such as *Berberis thunbergii* 'Golden Ring'.
The rich color of the berberis is not a
true purple and contrasts with the gentle
lavender of the clematis.

Compared with 'Perle d'Azur' (page 89),
this Early Large-flowered cultivar has slightly
paler, smaller, more delicate flowers with
four or six sepals, making it perhaps more

H: 20ft (6m)
�֎ **Mid-summer to mid-autumn**

 ◊◊ ☐-☐ **Z4 pH5–8**

H: 8ft (2.5m)
�֎ **Early summer to early autumn**

◊◊ ☐-☐ **Z5 pH5–8**

interesting in flower shape and better suited to smaller-scale plantings seen at closer range. 'Prince Charles' is best in gentle schemes with white, soft pinks, mauves, and blues, or with smoky purple or silver foliage.

Recommended partners: *Buddleja* 'Lochinch', *Ceanothus* × *delileanus* 'Gloire de Versailles', *Clematis* 'Alba Luxurians', *C.* × *triternata* 'Rubromarginata', *Hydrangea aspera* Villosa Group, *Lavatera* × *clementii* 'Barnsley', *Prunus spinosa* 'Purpurea', *Rosa* 'Climbing Iceberg', *Salix elaeagnos* subsp. *angustifolia*

Clematis 'Venosa Violacea'

How it works: *Clematis* 'Venosa Violacea' provides a contrast of floral form with *Lonicera tragophylla*. After its spring pruning, the clematis should be trained out into the honeysuckle, with care being taken to maintain a balance between the two, neither plant being allowed to crowd out the other.

Recommended partners: *Clematis* 'Purpurea Plena Elegans', *C.* × *triternata* 'Rubromarginata', *Lonicera nitida* 'Baggesen's Gold', *Prunus spinosa* 'Purpurea', *Rosa glauca*, *R.* 'Karlsruhe'

H: 13ft (4m)
✿ **Mid-summer to mid-autumn**
◊◊ ☐-■ Z5 pH5–8

Clematis 'Victoria'

How it works: This harmonious mixture of *Clematis* 'Victoria' (right), an unnamed Viticella (center), and *C.* 'Kermesina' (left), also of the Viticella Group, offers blooms of varying size. It is chosen so that all three plants flower together.

Recommended partners: *Clematis* 'Huldine', *C.* 'Praecox', *C.* × *triternata* 'Rubromarginata', *C.* 'Venosa Violacea', *Lathyrus grandiflorus*, *L. latifolius*, *Maurandya barclayana*, *Prunus cerasifera* 'Nigra', *P. spinosa* 'Purpurea', *Rosa* Super Dorothy ('Heldoro'), *R.* Super Excelsa ('Helexa'), *Vitis vinifera* 'Purpurea'

H: 13ft (4m)
Mid-summer to early autumn

Z4 pH5–8

Clematis 'Ville de Lyon'

How it works: The combination of *Clematis* 'Ville de Lyon', *C.* 'Comtesse de Bouchaud', and *C.* 'Jackmanii Superba' provides an eye-catching display of sumptuous crimson, pink, and purple. Greater variety of flower size might give even more impact.

The rather solid outline of the 'Ville de Lyon' flower is alleviated by the gradation of color within each sepal, dark at the edge with a bright crimson center, and the contrasting central boss of creamy yellow stamens. Its color is just light enough to show against deep purple foliage, and it goes well with pink, mauve, or lavender-blue flowers. Acid contrasts with chartreuse flowers or foliage are also good. 'Ville de Lyon' can be trained over shrubs of moderate size or against a wall with tall herbaceous plants in front. This helps hide the bareness of the lower parts of the stems by late summer.

Recommended partners: *Aconitum* 'Newry Blue', *Cercis canadensis* 'Forest Pansy', *Clematis* 'Hagley Hybrid', *C.* 'Minuet', *C.* 'Prince Charles', *C.* 'Victoria', *Eupatorium purpureum*, *Filipendula rubra*, *Foeniculum vulgare*, *Humulus lupulus* 'Aureus', *Prunus cerasifera* 'Nigra'

H: 10ft (3m)
Mid-summer to mid-autumn

Z4 pH5–8

Clematis viticella, double-flowered derivatives

How it works: The colors, sizes, and growth habits of *Clematis* 'Purpurea Plena Elegans' and *C.* 'Perle d'Azur' are ideally suited to each other. After pruning, both cultivars need careful training and tying in to their supports to ensure that they are well blended and balanced.

Doubles derived from *C. viticella* share flowers with four outer sepals surrounding successively smaller sepals, the innermost ones curled over to show a paler reverse and make a contrasting button center. Although the flowers are relatively small, their doubleness makes them long lasting, so many may bloom at once. They provide a very different, more intricate effect than the large-flowered hybrids. *C. v.* 'Flore Pleno' (syn. 'Mary Rose') has flowers of a bluer purple on a rather weaker plant.

Recommended partners: *Actinidia kolomikta*, *Clematis* 'Hagley Hybrid', *C.* 'Little Nell', *C.* 'Prince Charles', *C.* 'Victoria', *Hydrangea aspera* Villosa Group, *Ipomoea purpurea*, *I. tricolor* 'Crimson Rambler', *Jasminum officinale*, *Lophospermum erubescens*, *Mutisia oligodon*, *Rosa* Super Dorothy ('Heldoro'), *Salix alba* var. *sericea*, *S. elaeagnos* subsp. *angustifolia*, *Vitis vinifera* 'Purpurea'

H: 13ft (4m)
✿ Mid-summer to early autumn
◌◌ ☐-■ Z5 pH5–8

Hedera helix 'Buttercup'

How it works: In this combination, *Hedera helix* 'Buttercup', rather pale through being grown in sun, and white-variegated *H. algeriensis* 'Gloire de Marengo' show the shrubby habit characteristic of mature ivies, producing attractively billowing branches. Such a partnership could serve as an effective backdrop for blue flowers or dark foliage.

Recommended partners: *Anemone blanda*, *Calluna vulgaris* 'Robert Chapman', *Ceanothus* 'Cascade', *Galanthus elwesii* var. *monostictus*, *Lonicera caprifolium*, *Parthenocissus quinquefolia*, *P. tricuspidata*, *Schizophragma hydrangeoides* 'Roseum'

H: 16ft (5m)
✿ Autumn
◌◌ ☐-■ Z5–7 pH5–8

Ipomoea lobata
SPANISH FLAG

How it works: *Ipomoea lobata* can be used
to weave through much shorter herbaceous
plants or shrubs. Here, its flowers create a
brilliant contrast of color and form with
a rose-pink cultivar of *Phlox paniculata*. For
a more subtle effect, a cream phlox could
be used; for more pizzazz, a magenta one.

Recommended partners: *Atriplex
hortensis* var. *rubra, Berberis thunbergii*
f. *atropurpurea, Dahlia* 'Bishop of Llandaff',
Lychnis coronaria, Nicotiana 'Lime Green',
Parthenocissus tricuspidata, Rosa
'Frensham', *Tropaeolum speciosum*

H: **10ft** (3m)
❀ **Mid-summer to mid-autumn**
▰▱ ◊◊ ▨ **Z10 pH6–7.5**

Ipomoea tricolor
'Heavenly Blue'

How it works: A cascade of *Ipomoea tricolor*
'Heavenly Blue' tumbles through a *Plumbago
auriculata* in matching azure. Broad-leaved
Fatsia japonica and pots of agapanthus
provide a contrast of foliage and form.

Recommended partners: *Argyranthemum*
'Jamaica Primrose', *Artemisia ludoviciana,
Coronilla valentina* subsp. *glauca, Elaeagnus*
'Quicksilver', *Fremontodendron californicum,
Hedera helix* 'Buttercup', *Hemerocallis*
'Golden Chimes', *Hippophae rhamnoides,
Kniphofia* yellow cultivars, *Lonicera
caprifolium, Philadelphus coronarius* 'Aureus'

H: **10ft** (3m)
❀ **Mid-summer to mid-autumn**
▰▱ ◊◊ ▨ **Z10 pH6–7.5**

Lathyrus odoratus 'Noel Sutton'

How it works: Sweet peas, such as *Lathyrus odoratus* 'Noel Sutton', combine well with clematis flowers or seedheads, as here with the silvery heads of *Clematis macropetala*, although the seeds tend to lose their silky sheen before the pea stops blooming. Sweet peas may be grown on supports such as trellises, wigwams, or pea sticks, or be allowed to scramble over shrubs.

Recommended partners: *Clematis* 'Kermesina', *Crambe maritima*, *Gypsophila paniculata*, *Lathyrus rotundifolius*, *Lophospermum erubescens*, *Verbena bonariensis*

H: 2–8ft (60cm–2.5m)
Early summer to early autumn
Z6 pH5.5–7.5

Lathyrus rotundifolius

PERSIAN EVERLASTING PEA

How it works: The rather small flowers of *Lathyrus rotundifolius* provide subtle variety when scrambling together with those of a sweet pea (*L. odoratus*) cultivar. Beneath, the imposing flowerheads of spider flowers (*Cleome hassleriana*), in a mixture of perfectly harmonious colors, offer a more striking contrast of form.

Recommended partners: *Achillea* 'Lachsschönheit', *Berberis thunbergii* f. *atropurpurea*, *Cotinus coggygria* 'Royal Purple', *Rosa* 'Buff Beauty', *R.* Sweet Dream ('Fryminicot')

H: 6ft (1.8m)
Early to late summer
Z5 pH5.5–7.5

Lonicera × americana

How it works: Like most deciduous climbing honeysuckles, *Lonicera × americana* can be draped over a large shrub or small tree, or mingled with other climbers on a wall. In this scheme, its dainty blooms mingle freely with those of *Clematis montana* var. *wilsonii*. Maintaining a balance between two such vigorous climbers is difficult unless they are planted some distance apart and trained toward each other. Hard pruning will be needed every few years, being more severe on the dominant climber. Instead, each could be trained to horizontal wires on a wall, but an unnatural effect, with honeysuckle and clematis alternating evenly, is best avoided.

Recommended partners: *Clematis* 'Etoile Violette', *C.* 'Kermesina', *Cotinus coggygria* 'Royal Purple', *Prunus cerasifera* 'Nigra', *Rosa* 'Climbing Iceberg', *R.* 'Goldfinch'

H: 30ft (9m)
✿ **Early summer to autumn**
 ◊◊ ☐-■ **Z6 pH5–8**

Lonicera × heckrottii '**Gold Flame**'

How it works: *Lonicera × heckrottii* 'Gold Flame' contrasts with golden hop (*Humulus lupulus* 'Aureus'). The hop dies back in winter, allowing the honeysuckle to be pruned or retrained. The hop's new shoots need to be trained out sideways when they emerge and thinned occasionally later.

Recommended partners: *Berberis × ottawensis* f. *purpurea* 'Superba', *Cotinus coggygria* 'Royal Purple', *Philadelphus coronarius* 'Aureus', *Rosa* 'Buff Beauty', *R.* 'François Juranville'

Lonicera periclymenum '**Belgica**'

How it works: The common honeysuckle or woodbine, *Lonicera periclymenum* 'Belgica', in its second flush of flower, is featured here with Viticella clematis 'Polish Spirit'. The clematis does not show up well from a distance, so this combination is best seen at close range.

Recommended partners: *Ceanothus × delileanus* 'Gloire de Versailles', *Clematis* 'Kermesina', *Rosa* 'Cerise Bouquet', *R.* 'Climbing Iceberg', *R.* 'François Juranville'

H: 13ft (4m)
❀ Early to late summer
◊◊ ☐-▧ Z6 pH5–8

H: 23ft (7m)
❀ Early summer to autumn
◊◊ ☐-▧ Z5 pH4–8

Schizophragma hydrangeoides 'Roseum'

How it works: The large, pink-tinted flowerheads of *Schizophragma hydrangeoides* 'Roseum', grown at the foot of a sunny wall, contrast in form with the tiny stars of *Trachelospermum jasminoides*. The grassy leaves of *Iris unguicularis* add foliage contrast and promise a winter display.

Recommended partners: *Ampelopsis brevipedunculata* var. *maximowiczii* 'Elegans', *Hedera algeriensis* 'Gloire de Marengo', *H. helix* 'Buttercup', *Sambucus nigra* 'Guincho Purple'

H: 40ft (12m)
※ Mid- to late summer Z5 pH5.5–7.5

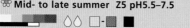

Tropaeolum speciosum
FLAME FLOWER

How it works: Spectacular trails of *Tropaeolum speciosum*, the perennial relative of the annual nasturtium, drape themselves across a somber hedge of common yew (*Taxus baccata*). The surface of the hedge is angled toward the sun, encouraging the flame flower to bloom profusely.

Recommended partners: *Acer palmatum* (purple-leaved), *Amelanchier lamarckii*, *Hydrangea serrata* 'Rosalba', *Ilex aquifolium*, *Rhododendron luteum*, *Tropaeolum tuberosum*

H: 13ft (4m)
※ Mid-summer to mid-autumn

Z7 pH5–6.5

Tropaeolum tuberosum var. *lineamaculatum* 'Ken Aslet'
AÑU

How it works: *Tropaeolum tuberosum* var. *lineamaculatum* 'Ken Aslet' flowers from mid-summer, coinciding with the season of *T. speciosum* (left). Its trumpet-shaped blooms and peltate leaves harmonize with those of its companion but differ sufficiently to create a most effective combination.

Recommended partners: *Berberis* × *ottawensis* f. *purpurea* 'Superba', *Humulus lupulus* 'Aureus', *Rosa* Geranium', *Sambucus nigra* 'Aurea', *Vitis vinifera* 'Purpurea'

H: **13ft** (4m)
✿ **Mid-summer to mid-autumn**

■■■ ◊◊ □-■ ■ Z8 pH5.5–7

Vitis vinifera 'Purpurea'

How it works: When *Clematis* 'Perle d'Azur' starts to bloom in mid-summer, the leaves of *Vitis vinifera* 'Purpurea' are downy gray, becoming gradually less so but more flushed with purple as the season advances. At all stages, the color of the vine and its handsome leaves flatter the clematis and punctuate its solid sheet of bloom.

Recommended partners: *Acanthus spinosus*, *Buddleja fallowiana*, *Celastrus orbiculatus* Hermaphrodite Group, *Clerodendrum bungei*, *Parthenocissus henryana*, *Rosa* 'Albertine', *R. rugosa*, *Vitis coignetiae*

H: **23ft** (7m)
✿ **Early summer**

■■■ ◊-◊◊ □-■ Z6 pH5–7.5

Roses

The most versatile of
garden plants, roses are
capable of climbing boldly
to the top of a tall tree
or decorating a small pot
with elfin charm. Their
popularity is ensured by
their ability to blend
subtly with other shrubs
and climbers or to be the
focal point of a display
that includes less
flamboyant companions.

Introducing roses

For centuries the rose has intrigued gardeners and plant breeders alike. As a result of this fascination and the untiring work of the plant breeders, there are now roses for almost every garden situation: swooning shrubs laden with scented flowers for borders and shrubberies, elegant climbers to festoon pergolas and arches, rampant ramblers to adorn trees and walls, neat and tidy bushes to use as bedding, and minute patio plants to fill pots, window boxes, and raised beds.

Rose flowers come in an enormous variety of colors and forms, and many are beautifully fragrant. Some rose plants flower only once a year, while others bloom sparsely but more or less continuously over a long period or produce several flushes of blooms. While the leaves are rarely the reason they are grown, plenty of roses do have attractive and healthy foliage. A few species and varieties also have brightly colored hips that extend the interest.

Because the rose genus is so large, horticulturalists have divided it into different categories according to habit of growth and the form and presentation of the flowers. These categories include:

- Climbing and Rambler roses
- Old and modern Shrub roses
- Hybrid Teas
- Floribundas
- Groundcover roses

Many of the categories are further subdivided. All this can make choosing a rose seem a difficult task. However, it simplifies matters to consider the two main ways that roses are used in gardens: the shrubby roses and many of the climbers are perfect for integrating into the garden as a whole, while the larger-flowered roses, such as the Hybrid Teas and Floribundas, are suitable for more formal presentations.

Roses in beds and borders

The type of rose that is ideal for growing in mixed borders or in shrubberies tends to produce large trusses of somewhat informal, softly colored flowers on plants with ample foliage. Apart from the modern "old" roses, most of these are shrubs that have one main flush of bloom with perhaps a second sprinkling later in the season.

All these roses will complement a wide variety of herbaceous plants, as well as each other, and they are very versatile because they may be left to

grow into large masses or pruned regularly to produce small plants with more blooms.

Although often used for formal arrangements (see below), some of the larger-flowered roses with their clear colors and freedom of flowering can be invaluable in mixed borders.

A trio of trained roses – the white Rambler *R.* 'Wedding Day' and the sumptuous purple Rambler *R.* 'Bleu Magenta', along with the shorter Climbing Hybrid Tea 'Bantry Bay' – decorate a pergola above lower shrub roses.

Formal rose beds

Roses suitable for planting alone or in geometric beds usually produce large flowers of exquisite shape in a steady trickle over long periods. Unlike many of their forebears, most of the recent introductions have compact growth, numerous flowers, and good resistance to disease. However, their habit of growth is gaunt and their foliage is sparse and, therefore, formal rose

Left: *Rosa* Pretty Polly ('Meitonje') has the perfect combination of dense, shrubby but informal habit and outstanding flower color to be a success in a container.

gardens require careful complementary planting if they are to be attractive for more than a few weeks of the year.

Edging the beds with boxwoods or lavenders or, less formally, with stachys or other low-growing evergreens will provide a longer season of interest and emphasize the geometry of the beds in a way that the roses cannot. In the summer, carpets of violas or cranesbills will furnish the garden more fully at ground level and will harmonize with most rose colors. As in mixed borders, standard roses can be used to introduce greater height, and climbers – roses or others – can be grown up pillars, over arches, or on trellises to ensure year-round structure.

Planting notes

Roses are grown for their flowers, so they are always best where these can be fully appreciated, especially if they are fragrant. Even the taller shrubs should be planted near the front of borders, where they will also produce a useful variation in height. Where roses are grown over arches, careful tying in is necessary to keep the thorns away from eyes, skin, and clothes.

Right: Roses can play an important role as members of a mixed border or shrubbery. Here, Shrub roses, with their soft, fairly informal habit, can come to the fore while in bloom and, if they have little or no recurrence, will then blend in comfortably for the rest of the season.

Climbing and Rambler roses

Climbing roses may be divided into two
main classes: Ramblers and Large-flowered
Climbers (including Climbing Hybrid Teas
and Climbing Floribundas).

Ramblers include hybrids of the fragrant
R. multiflora and glossy-leaved *R. wichurana*,
as well as the stronger-growing species
roses, including rampant kinds like *R. filipes*.
They produce vigorous new shoots near
the base of the plant each year, which
flower the following year. Flowered stems
are normally cut out immediately after
flowering, but this can be difficult if the
rose is closely combined with another
climber; in this case, it is usually possible
to prune both rose and companion in late
winter. Shorter-growing Ramblers are ideal
for pillars and as ground cover or, if grafted
on to tall stems, as weeping standards.
Varieties of middling vigor make stems
long enough to reach over a pergola or
arcade; they can also sprawl into large
shrubs or small trees; some may be trained
against walls. The most vigorous sorts can
be left to scramble unrestrained into trees.

Large-flowered Climbers usually have
fewer main stems, each of which provides
flowering sideshoots for several years.
Pruning, in late winter, consists of cutting
back both main stems and sideshoots, and
removing some older stems to encourage
strong new growth.

Rosa 'Albertine'

How it works: Trained to mingle agreeably against a wall, the double flowers of *Rosa* 'Albertine' and the lobed leaves of the ornamental vine *Vitis vinifera* 'Purpurea' complement each other beautifully in both color and shape. It is unusual for this vine to be so strongly purple-flushed when *R.* 'Albertine' is in full bloom, except when grown in a nutrient-poor soil in a dry, sunny situation or hot climate.

This Wichurana Rambler flowers just once, at the height of summer, but so lavishly that the dark green foliage can disappear beneath the exuberant display. The fully double salmon pink blooms, borne singly or in small sprays, emerge from copper-red buds and are deliciously scented. The rose is vigorous enough to be grown on a pergola or an arcade, and although it succeeds trained against a wall, it is rather prone to mildew where air flow is restricted. It is relatively healthy if allowed to scramble freely into small trees or to develop as a sprawling, rather lax bush in the open garden.

Recommended partners: *Jasminum officinale* 'Aureum', *Lonicera* × *italica* Harlequin ('Sherlite'), *Photinia* × *fraseri* 'Red Robin', *Physocarpus opulifolius* 'Diabolo', *Rosa* 'American Pillar'

H: 16ft (5m) S: 13ft (4m)
✿ **Mid-summer**
 ◊◊ ■-■ Z5 pH5.5–7.5

Rosa 'American Pillar'

How it works: The single, white-eyed, rich carmine flowers of *Rosa* 'American Pillar' are borne in clusters in one exuberant summer display. Here, they are combined with the more delicate pink rose *R.* 'Albertine' and *Helichrysum petiolare*. The helichrysum, with its elegant sprays of gray-green foliage tipped with clusters of creamy flowers, is an ideal companion for the roses in warmer climates, where it can be grown outdoors year-round, trained against a wall for shelter.

Recommended partners: *Acacia baileyana* 'Purpurea', *Cotinus coggygria* 'Royal Purple', *Eucalyptus kybeanensis*, *Euphorbia sikkimensis*, *Knautia macedonica*, *Senecio viravira*

H: 16ft (5m) S: 13ft (4m)
❀ **Mid- to late summer**
◊◊ ▣-■ Z5 pH5–7.5

Rosa 'Brenda Colvin'

How it works: The large-flowered *Clematis* 'Comtesse de Bouchaud' is an excellent partner for *Rosa* 'Brenda Colvin', echoing the rose's pink buds and the palest blush of its young blooms. However, the rose is so vigorous that the clematis will occupy only a part of its spread.

Recommended partners: *Chamaecyparis lawsoniana* 'Pembury Blue', *Lonicera japonica* var. *repens, Prunus cerasifera* 'Pissardii', *Pyrus salicifolia* 'Pendula', *Rosa* 'Seagull'

H: 30ft (9m) S: 20ft (6m)
✿ Mid-summer

 Z5 pH5–7.5

Rosa 'Climbing Paul Lédé'

How it works: *Rosa* 'Climbing Paul Lédé' harmonizes well with the cinnamon pink of *Verbascum* 'Helen Johnson', bronze fennel (*Foeniculum vulgare* 'Purpureum'), and red-leaved Japanese maples. *Cotoneaster simonsii* and white-variegated holly (*Ilex aquifolium* 'Silver Queen') leaven the scheme.

Recommended partners: *Achillea* 'Inca Gold', *Agastache* 'Firebird', *Elaeagnus* 'Quicksilver', *Hemerocallis* 'Penelope Vestey', *Hosta sieboldiana* var. *elegans, Stipa arundinacea*

H: 11ft (3.5m) S: 8ft (2.5m)
✿ Mid-summer to mid-autumn

◊◊ ▣-▢ Z7 pH5.5–7

Rosa 'Constance Spry'

How it works: Although *Rosa* 'Constance Spry' flowers earlier than many of the large-flowered Climbing roses, if moderately pruned (with all sideshoots cut back substantially), it will coincide in season with *R.* 'Rambling Rector'. The small, informal, white florets of 'Rambling Rector' contrast effectively in size and color with the lush and glorious blooms of its partner.

Recommended partners: *Clematis* 'Princess Diana', *C.* 'Venosa Violacea', *Deutzia* × *elegantissima* 'Rosealind', *Philadephus* 'Manteau d'Hermine', *Vitis vinifera* 'Purpurea'

Rosa 'Easlea's Golden Rambler'

How it works: The delicate butter-yellow of *Rosa* 'Easlea's Golden Rambler' is a rare choice to combine with rich pink and red. This partnership with red valerian (*Centranthus ruber*) succeeds only through the sheer size, sumptuousness, and profusion of the rose.

Recommended partners: *Clematis* 'Alba Luxurians', *Cornus alba* 'Spaethii', *Cotinus* 'Grace', *Digitalis purpurea* 'Sutton's Apricot', *Euphorbia griffithii* 'Dixter', *Lonicera periclymenum* 'Belgica', *Paeonia delavayi*, *Philadelphus* 'Innocence', *Potentilla fruticosa* 'Primrose Beauty'

H & S: 10ft (3m)
✿ **Early summer**
◊◊ ■-■ **Z5 pH5–7.5**

H: 20ft (6m) S: 16ft (5m)
✿ **Early summer**
◊◊ ■-■ **Z5 pH5–7.5**

Rosa filipes 'Kiftsgate'

How it works: The dark, richly colored foliage of a purple plum (*Prunus cerasifera* 'Pissardii') makes a dramatic foil for the profuse, creamy white flowers of *Rosa filipes* 'Kiftsgate'. The rose will ultimately suppress even the largest plum unless pruned, although a comparable combination of the rose with a fairly mature, purple-leaved maple or beech, or even a large, dark green conifer, would work well.

Recommended partners: *Acer platanoides* 'Crimson King', *Ampelopsis megalophylla*, *Fagus sylvatica*, *Fraxinus angustifolia* 'Raywood', *Parthenocissus quinquefolia*, *Vitis coignetiae*

H: **33ft** (10m) S: **65ft** (20m)
✺ **Mid-summer**
 ◊◊ ▪-▪ Z5 pH5–7.5

Rosa 'Karlsruhe'

How it works: The rich, recessive purple of the late-flowering *Clematis* 'Venosa Violacea', its blooms enlivened by their star of pale petal centers, makes an attractive foil for *Rosa* 'Karlsruhe', providing a contrast of floral form. They are excellent companions, both remaining in flower for several months. The fully double pink blooms of 'Karlsruhe' are scented and borne in clusters of up to 10.

Recommended partners: *Clematis* 'Rouge Cardinal', *Lilium* Pink Perfection Group, *Phlox paniculata* 'Windsor', *Phygelius × rectus* 'Salmon Leap', *Weigela florida* 'Foliis Purpureis'

H: **8ft** (2.5m) S: **6ft** (1.8m)
✺ **Mid-summer to mid-autumn**
▪▪▪ ◊◊ ▪-▪ Z5 pH5.5–7

Rosa 'Mermaid'

How it works: The bold boss of stamens of each bloom of *Rosa* 'Mermaid' and the hint of yellow in its petals harmonize with the variegation of the ivy *Hedera colchica* 'Sulphur Heart'. Keeping the latter pruned close to the wall with the rose stems held just clear of the ivy facilitates maintenance.

Recommended partners: *Ceanothus* 'Pershore Zanzibar', *Clematis* 'Helios', *Corokia* × *virgata* 'Red Wonder', *Cytisus battandieri*, *Fremontodendron* 'Pacific Sunset', *Jasminum officinale* Fiona Sunrise ('Frojas'), *Lilium lancifolium* 'Flore Pleno', *Phygelius* × *rectus* 'African Queen', *Piptanthus nepalensis*

H & S: 20ft (6m)
❀ **Early summer to mid-autumn**
▰▰▱ ◊◊ ▰-▰ Z6 pH5.5–7

Rosa multiflora

How it works: Left to its own devices to form a mound of stems, powerfully fragrant *Rosa multiflora* is charming in more informal parts of the garden. Here, white foxgloves (*Digitalis purpurea* f. *albiflora*) echo its color and add bold vertical accents, while *Clematis* × *durandii* provides a gentle contrast in flower shape and color.

Recommended partners: *Cotoneaster lacteus*, *Eremurus robustus*, *Lunaria rediviva*, *Paeonia lactiflora* 'Bowl of Beauty', *Philadelphus coronarius* 'Variegatus', *Selinum wallichianum*, *Verbascum* 'Gainsborough', *Viburnum rhytidophyllum*

H: 16ft (5m) S: 10ft (3m)
❀ **Mid-summer**
▰▰▱ ◊◊ ▰-▰ Z5 pH5–7.5

Rosa 'New Dawn'

How it works: In this pleasingly delicate association, the marks at the base of the florets of *Philadelphus* 'Belle Etoile' echo the color of the buds and flowers of *Rosa* 'New Dawn'. This combination would be easier to manage if only a few odd stems of rose were trained in from a nearby wall, rather than allowing the two plants to tangle. The fragrant blooms of 'New Dawn' are often borne singly but also in clusters.

Recommended partners: *Centranthus ruber, Cestrum parqui, Deutzia* × *hybrida* 'Mont Rose', *Lonicera periclymenum* 'Belgica', *Persicaria bistorta* 'Superba', *Viburnum sargentii* 'Onondaga'

H: 10ft (3m) **S: 8ft** (2.5m)
❀ **Early summer to mid-autumn**
◊◊ ■-■ Z5 pH5.5–7

Rosa 'Pink Perpétué'

How it works: Freestanding shrubs often make good companions to roses grown on a wall, as do biennials such as this Scotch thistle (*Onopordum nervosum*), punctuating the rich blooms of *Rosa* 'Pink Perpétué' with a bold structure of pale leaves.

Recommended partners: *Berberis thunbergii* 'Rose Glow', *Clematis* 'Duchess of Albany', *Cotinus coggygria* 'Royal Purple', *Phygelius aequalis* 'Sani Pass', *Rosa* 'Narrow Water'

H: 10ft (3m) S: 8ft (2.5m)
✿ Mid-summer to mid-autumn
◊◊ ■-■ Z5 pH5.5–7

Rosa 'Rambling Rector'

How it works: An intimate combination of three different flowers usually succeeds if each is distinct in at least two of the three major characteristics – size, shape, and color – while achieving pleasing harmonies or contrasts. This combination of *Rosa* 'Rambling Rector', the Chilean potato tree cultivar *Solanum crispum* 'Glasnevin', and *Clematis* 'Hagley Hybrid' meets this criterion, creating an attractive, harmonious effect.

H & S: 20ft (6m)
✿ Mid-summer
◊◊ ■-■ Z5 pH5–7.5

The extraordinary vigor of the once-flowering 'Rambling Rector' makes pruning and training difficult, and it is perhaps best planted where it can be allowed to grow without restraint – scrambling into a small or medium-sized tree, for example, or tumbling over an unsightly wall.

Recommended partners: *Clematis* 'Perle d'Azur', *Lonicera periclymenum* 'Graham Thomas', *Parthenocissus henryana*, *Rosa* 'Constance Spry', *Vitis vinifera* 'Purpurea'

Rosa 'Sander's White Rambler'

How it works: *Rosa* 'Sander's White Rambler' makes a dome of cascading white blooms, surrounded by a contrasting carpet of lavender (*Lavandula angustifolia*).

Recommended partners: *Acanthus mollis*, *Campanula lactiflora*, *Catananche caerulea*, *Clematis* 'Silver Moon', *Delphinium* 'Blue Nile', *Lupinus arboreus* (blue), *Miscanthus sinensis* var. *condensatus* 'Cosmopolitan', *Rhamnus alaternus* 'Argenteovariegata'

H & S: 13ft (4m)
❀ **Mid- to late summer**
◊◊ ▪-▪ Z5 pH5–7.5

Rosa 'Seagull'

How it works: *Rosa* 'Seagull', growing
along a catenary swag from the left of the
picture, makes a charming combination
where it meets the luscious pink blooms
of the Climbing Bourbon rose *R.* 'Blairii
Number Two', growing from the right.

Recommended partners: *Campanula
latifolia* 'Gloaming', *Elaeagnus* 'Quicksilver',
Eryngium × oliverianum, *Humulus lupulus*
'Aureus', *Jasminum officinale* Fiona Sunrise
('Frojas'), *Ligustrum lucidum* 'Excelsum
Superbum', *Lonicera periclymenum*
'Belgica', *Philadelphus* 'Innocence'

H: 20ft (6m) S: 13ft (4m)
❀ Mid-summer

 ◊◊ ◼-◼ Z5 pH5-7.5

Rosa 'Sophie's Perpetual'

How it works: The deliciously fragrant,
vibrant cerise blooms of *Rosa* 'Sophie's
Perpetual' glow against the dusky purple
of the Viticella clematis *C.* 'Venosa
Violacea'. The pruning of the clematis,
cutting it almost to the ground in late
winter, is easier than that of a woody
climber intertwined with the rose.

Recommended partners: *Buddleja
fallowiana* var. *alba*, *Cotinus coggygria*
'Royal Purple', *Geranium × oxonianum*
'Winscombe', *Liatris spicata*, *Ruta
graveolens*, *Weigela* 'Victoria'

H: 8ft (2.5m) S: 4ft (1.2m)
❀ Early summer to mid-autumn

 ◊◊ ◼-◼ Z6 pH5.5–7

Old Shrub roses

No group of garden plants has a greater power for evoking the romance of the past than the old Shrub roses. Their intricately shaped blooms, heady fragrance, and petals with sumptuous textures of satin or velvet are exquisite at close range, yet borne in enough profusion for grand effect. Although some do have a short flowering season – just a few glorious weeks at the height of summer – the beauty and quality of these plants offer more than adequate compensation.

Hard annual pruning is seldom necessary; removal of weak, old, or spindly stems and shortening the longest ones will usually suffice, although occasionally removing large old branches helps to ensure a succession of vigorous flowering stems. However, where smaller bushes are needed, many respond to harder pruning, giving a later, longer flush of larger blooms. Those with long, whippy stems benefit from training, either to a frame or by building up a structure from their own branches. If the flowers nod, higher training ensures that they face the viewer.

Their foliage is generally indifferent, and tedious when they are planted *en masse*; their appearance is much improved by combining them with plants of boldly contrasting leaf form or color.

Rosa 'Charles de Mills'

How it works: The superlative rich crimson blooms of *Rosa* 'Charles de Mills' contrast in size and color with the pale-leaved white rose campion (*Lychnis coronaria* 'Alba'), which is echoed in the distance by a white Rambler rose. Harmonious crimson Texensis Group clematis *C.* 'Gravetye Beauty' winds around the nearby post.

Recommended partners: *Allium hollandicum* 'Purple Sensation', *Aquilegia* 'Apple Blossom', *Knautia macedonica*, *Salvia nemorosa* 'Rose Queen', *S. officinalis* 'Purpurascens', *Sambucus nigra* 'Gerda'

H & S: 4ft (1.2m)
❀ **Early to mid-summer**
◊◊ ☐-■ **Z4 pH5.5–7**

Rosa 'De Rescht'

How it works: The exquisitely scented, purplish crimson *Rosa* 'De Rescht' clashes gently with Shirley poppies, most of which are a bright scarlet color. A hedge of dwarf boxwood (*Buxus sempervirens* 'Suffruticosa') furnishes the front of the border, adding a touch of crisp formality lacking in the other plants.

Recommended partners: *Cleome hassleriana* 'Cherry Queen', *Geranium phaeum*, *Monarda* 'Prärienacht', *Stachys macrantha*, *Teucrium hircanicum*, *Veronica spicata* 'Rotfuchs'

H: 36in (90cm) **S: 24in** (60cm)
✻ **Mid-summer to mid-autumn**

◊◊ ☐-■ **Z5 pH5.5–7**

Rosa 'Fantin-Latour'

How it works: The soft pink blooms of *Rosa* 'Fantin-Latour' contrast in size and form with the slender spires of the perennial toadflax *Linaria purpurea* 'Canon Went' while matching its color exactly. Mixed foxgloves (*Digitalis purpurea*) echo the shape of the toadflax, which weaves itself through the rose, integrating the whole scheme perfectly.

Recommended partners: *Alchemilla mollis*, *Eremurus robustus*, *Euphorbia palustris*, *Geranium* × *oxonianum* 'Laura Skelton', *Lychnis coronaria* Oculata Group, *Rosa* 'Impératrice Joséphine'

H: 5ft (1.5m) **S: 4ft** (1.2m)
✻ **Early to mid-summer**

◊◊ ☐-■ **Z5 pH5–7.5**

Rosa gallica 'Versicolor'

ROSA MUNDI

How it works: The large, informal blooms of Rosa Mundi (*Rosa gallica* 'Versicolor'), extravagantly splashed and striped with palest pink, contrast in size with the slightly taller cranesbill *Geranium psilostemon*, its magenta flowers veined and eyed with glistening black.

Recommended partners: *Campanula latiloba* 'Hidcote Amethyst', *Dianthus* 'Pink Mrs Sinkins', *Galega* 'His Majesty', *Geranium sylvaticum*, *Lilium candidum*, *Viola cornuta*

H: 31in (80cm) **S:** 40in (1m)

Early to mid-summer

Z4 pH5.5–7

Rosa 'Impératrice Joséphine'

How it works: Sumptuous blooms of *Rosa* 'Impératrice Joséphine' are set above a sea of silvery rose campion (*Lychnis coronaria* 'Alba' and pink-eyed *L. c.* Oculata Group), with a bush of the paler pink *R.* 'Fantin-Latour' behind. A yellow-green-leaved shrub in the background provides piquancy, saving the scheme from potential blandness.

Recommended partners: *Centaurea* 'John Coutts', *Hosta* 'Buckshaw Blue', *Hyssopus officinalis* 'Roseus', *Lonicera nitida* 'Red Tips', *Salvia sclarea*, *Viburnum sargentii* 'Onondaga'

H & S: 4ft (1.2m)

Early to mid-summer

Z4 pH5.5–7

Rosa × *odorata* '**Mutabilis**'

How it works: The chameleon colors of *Rosa* × *odorata* 'Mutabilis' embrace the soft yellow, pink, and red found in the blooms of *Alstroemeria* 'Charm', creating a perfect harmony. Both contrast gently with the lilac blooms of the herbaceous *Clematis* 'Arabella' and spires of the perennial toadflax *Linaria purpurea*.

Recommended partners: *Asclepias curassavica, Canna* 'Phasion', *Eccremocarpus scaber, Fuchsia magellanica* 'Versicolor', *Penstemon barbatus, Phygelius* × *rectus* 'African Queen'

Rosa '**Prince Charles**'

How it works: The purplish crimson blooms of *Rosa* 'Prince Charles' blend perfectly with the pink Damask rose *R.* 'La Ville de Bruxelles' and the large amethyst flowerheads of *Allium cristophii*, backed by white *Crambe cordifolia*. Adding another relatively tall allium between the roses would help break up their undistinguished foliage and unify the scheme.

Recommended partners: *Centaurea montana, Geranium sanguineum* 'Cedric Morris', *Linaria purpurea, Malva moschata, Phuopsis stylosa, Verbascum* 'Megan's Mauve'

H: 40in–4ft (1–1.2m) S: 24–36in (60–90cm)
❀ **Early summer to mid-autumn**
 ◊◊ ☐-■ **Z7 pH5–7**

H: 5ft (1.5m) S: 4ft (1.2m)
❀ **Early to mid-summer**
 ◊◊ ☐-■ **Z5 pH5–7**

Rosa 'Reine des Centifeuilles'

How it works: The intricately pleated, clear pink blooms of *Rosa* 'Reine des Centifeuilles' harmonize perfectly with the pink toadflax *Linaria purpurea* 'Canon Went'. The toadflax contrasts in shape, as does the lavender goat's rue (*Galega orientalis*), which adds a second harmonious color.

Recommended partners: *Cirsium rivulare* 'Atropurpureum', *Corylus maxima* 'Purpurea', *Erigeron* 'Quakeress', *Eryngium giganteum*, *Salvia verticillata* 'Purple Rain', *Silybum marianum*

H & S: 5ft (1.5m)
❀ **Early to mid-summer**
◊◊ ☐-☐ Z5 pH5–7.5

Rosa 'Tuscany Superb'

How it works: The bright blooms of white rose campion (*Lychnis coronaria* 'Alba'), and its silvery stems and leaves, help lift the sumptuous but recessive colors of *Rosa* 'Tuscany Superb'. The velvety blooms of this once-flowering Gallica rose merit inspection at close range, and combine particularly well with pink, purple, lilac, and mauve flowers, and purple foliage.

Recommended partners: *Aquilegia vulgaris* var. *stellata* 'Royal Purple', *Astrantia major* 'Ruby Wedding', *Galactites tomentosa* 'Alba', *Geranium* 'Sirak', *Rosa gallica* 'Versicolor'

H & S: 4ft (1.2m)
❀ **Early to mid-summer**
◊◊ ☐-☐ Z4 pH5–7.5

Rosa 'Zéphirine Drouhin'

How it works: The thornless and sweetly fragrant *Rosa* 'Zéphirine Drouhin', variable in color and here almost at the palest end of its potential color range, blends perfectly with the rich crimson blooms of the Viticella clematis *C.* 'Madame Julia Correvon', which also provides a contrast of flower shape.

Recommended partners: *Cotinus coggygria* 'Royal Purple', *Lupinus* 'Blueberry Pie', *L.* 'Plummy Blue', *Nicotiana sylvestris*, *Persicaria bistorta*, *Phlox paniculata* 'Mother of Pearl'

H 10ft (3m) **S: 6½ft** (2m)
✿ Mid-summer to mid-autumn
▬▬▭ ◊◊ ▭-▨ Z5 pH5–7

Larger species and larger modern Shrub roses

Apart from their size, the roses in this section have no shared characteristics but fall into a number of categories, each with its own distinct traits and uses.

The species and their primary hybrids tend to be more elegant than the highly bred cultivars. Many are single-flowered and often attractive also for their hips and autumn color. Some, such as *R. moyesii* and *R. glauca* and their hybrids, have a vase-shaped habit, with tall, arching stems that are bare at the base.

The Rugosa roses have glistening parsley-green foliage. They are immensely useful for their hardiness, fragrance, continual blooming, and autumn color.

Hybrid Musk roses, their rich fragrance derived not from the musk rose but mainly from *R. multiflora* (page 114), usually have loosely double blooms in clusters borne continually from summer to autumn. Their colors include peach, apricot, and soft yellow, rare in old roses but gentle enough to blend with them, as well as vibrant carmines and scarlets.

David Austin's English roses were bred to combine the floral form of the old roses with the colors and continual flowering of modern varieties. Selected for the English climate, many perform better in hotter areas such as California or the Mediterranean.

Rosa Bonica ('Meidomonac')

How it works: The large, loosely but charmingly informal pink flowers of *Rosa* Bonica contrast effectively with the dark, dusky pincushion blooms of *Knautia macedonica*, which furnish the rose's stems.
Recommended partners: *Cosmos bipinnatus* 'Daydream', *Nepeta* 'Six Hills Giant', *Penstemon* 'Alice Hindley', *Phlox paniculata* 'Eventide', *Verbena bonariensis*, *Vernonia noveboracensis*

H: 3ft (90cm) S: 4ft (1.2m)
❀ **Mid-summer to mid-autumn**

◊◊ ■-■ Z5 pH5–7.5

Rosa 'Buff Beauty'

How it works: The buff-apricot blooms of
Rosa 'Buff Beauty' are here complemented
by the contrasting flower and leaf shape of
the bright yellow columbine *Aquilegia
chrysantha*. Several other columbines have
warm-colored flowers for combining with
soft yellow, peach, or apricot roses.

Recommended partners: *Alchemilla
mollis*, *Amaranthus hybridus* 'Hot Biscuits',
Bupleurum fruticosum, *Carex testacea*,
Eupatorium rugosum 'Chocolate',
Foeniculum vulgare 'Purpureum',
Hemerocallis 'Cynthia Mary', *Iris* 'Elixir'

Rosa 'Carmenetta'

How it works: The bare stems of *Rosa*
'Carmenetta' can be dramatic in informal
settings, lifting a cloud of smoky foliage
and pink flowers above the carpet of plants
beneath. This display includes pinkish purple
alliums (*Allium cristophii*), a variegated
weigela, and the upright *Campanula
latiloba* and *C. l.* 'Hidcote Amethyst'.

Recommended partners: *Clematis
× durandii*, *Geranium phaeum* 'Rose Air',
G. pyrenaicum 'Bill Wallis', *Hesperis
matronalis*, *Hosta sieboldiana* 'Blue Angel',
Miscanthus sinensis 'China'

H & S: 5ft (1.5m)
❀ **Early summer to mid-autumn**
 Z5 pH5–7.5

H: 8ft (2.5m) S: 6½ft (2m)
❀ **Early to mid-summer**
Z4 pH5–7.5

Rosa 'Cerise Bouquet'

How it works: *Crambe cordifolia* is one of relatively few herbaceous plants that can match the gigantic scale of *Rosa* 'Cerise Bouquet', particularly if several plants are grouped together. Here, the vibrant blooms of the rose are contrasted with the crambe's clouds of tiny white flowers against an azure sky.

Recommended partners: *Achillea* 'Summerwine', *Atriplex hortensis* var. *rubra*, *Lychnis coronaria*, *Malva sylvestris* 'Zebrina', *Persicaria amplexicaulis*, *Weigela florida* 'Foliis Purpureis'

Rosa 'Excellenz von Schubert'

How it works: The sturdy stems of *Rosa* 'Excellenz von Schubert' arch down to meet snow-in-summer (*Cerastium tomentosum*), its silver foliage and white flowers contrasting with the rich coloring of the rose. The ground-covering snow-in-summer could be underplanted with bulbs.

Recommended partners: *Dianthus* 'Laced Monarch', *Galtonia candicans*, *Heuchera* 'Magic Wand', *Lamium maculatum* 'Beacon Silver', *Lavandula angustifolia* 'Hidcote Pink'

H & S: 13ft (4m)
❀ Early summer to mid-autumn
 ◊◊ ▣-▣ Z5 pH5–7.5

H & S: 5ft (1.5m)
❀ Mid-summer to late autumn
◊◊ ▣-▣ Z5 pH5.5–7

Rosa 'Felicia'

How it works: Extended groups of roses are often more pleasing and effective than singletons dotted around the garden. Here, a simple scheme depends on the repetition of delicate pink *Rosa* 'Felicia' and the contrasting green seedheads of *Allium hollandicum*. These draw the eye along the group toward the bright Hybrid Musk rose 'Vanity'. 'Felicia' makes a sturdy, weather-proof hedge, even on light, dry soils where other classes of rose might become thin and unthrifty.

Recommended partners: *Eupatorium capillifolium* 'Elegant Feather', *Iris* 'Jane Phillips', *Nepeta grandiflora* 'Dawn to Dusk', *Potentilla nepalensis* 'Miss Willmott'

H: **5ft** (1.5m) S: **6½ft** (2m)
✿ **Mid-summer to late autumn**
 ◊◊ ■-■ **Z5 pH5–7.5**

Rosa Graham Thomas ('Ausmas')

How it works: Rich blue, columnar flowerheads, such as the vertical spikes of *Delphinium* 'Cristella', make a highly effective contrast with the large, round blooms of the yellow rose *Rosa* Graham Thomas, while the horizontal plates of *Achillea* 'Coronation Gold' provide another contrast of form in a harmonious color.

Graham Thomas is one of David Austin's English roses. The fully double blooms have a good Tea rose fragrance and are borne singly and in clusters, from early summer through to autumn, in a color that varies from light to mid butter-yellow, occasionally taking on amber tints. It creates excellent harmonies with warm colors – soft orange, peach, apricot, and cream – and makes a fine contrast with blue. It combines well with yellow-green flowers and foliage, and with silver or glaucous foliage. Vigorous and freely branching as a specimen shrub, it may also be trained against a fence or trellis. In warm climates it can produce very long stems.

Recommended partners: *Aquilegia vulgaris* 'Mellow Yellow', *Eschscholzia californica* 'Apricot Flambeau', *Hemerocallis* 'Golden Chimes', *Nigella damascena* 'Oxford Blue', *Salvia patens*

H: **4ft** (1.2m) S: **5ft** (1.5m)
✿ **Early summer to mid-autumn**
◊◊ ■-■ **Z5 pH5–7.5**

Rosa 'Highdownensis'

How it works: *Rosa* 'Highdownensis' displays its rich pink blooms on a gracefully arching bush, while *Artemisia arborescens* furnishes the foot of the rose with silvery foliage. The double red campion *Silene dioica* 'Flore Pleno' has blooms that match those of the rose, unifying the scheme.

Recommended partners: *Chrysanthemum* 'Mary Stoker', *Crocosmia × crocosmiiflora* 'Queen of Spain', *Kniphofia* 'Royal Standard', *Rudbeckia fulgida* var. *sullivantii* 'Goldsturm', × *Solidaster luteus*, *Stokesia laevis*, *Strobilanthes atropurpurea*

H: 10ft (3m) S: 6½ft (2m)
❀ **Early to mid-summer**
Z4 pH5–7.5

Rosa 'Maigold'

How it works: The soft amber-yellow, loosely informal blooms of *Rosa* 'Maigold', borne on an arching bush, here contrast effectively with the blue flowers of *Iris sibirica*. The subdued blooms of the allium relative *Nectaroscordum siculum*, naturalized throughout the area, neither add to nor detract from the color scheme but provide a quiet charm.

The strong, upright growth of this climbing Spinosissima hybrid rose is useful for training against a fence or wall or around a pillar. Without support, it is also an attractive shrub, its prickly stems arching gracefully to form a large sprawling bush, well furnished with healthy foliage. Its large amber-yellow blooms are semi-double or loosely double and very fragrant, most of them borne in clusters in a single flush in late spring or early summer. Their gentle color and a relaxed growth habit make 'Maigold' suitable for less formal areas of the garden, even for a wild garden, where it can scramble through other shrubs or over a hedge.

Recommended partners: *Euphorbia sikkimensis*, *Geranium himalayense*, *Iris* 'Blenheim Royal', *I.* 'Butter and Sugar', *Lupinus arboreus*, *Scrophularia buergeriana* 'Lemon and Lime'

H & S: 8ft (2.5m)
❀ **Late spring to early summer**
Z5 pH5–7.5

Rosa 'Nevada'

How it works: Newly opened blooms of *Rosa* 'Nevada', each with a central boss of golden anthers, retain a hint of yellow in their petals, contrasting here with a cloud of lavender catmint *Nepeta* 'Six Hills Giant'. Boldly shaped foliage, either in front or farther back in the border, might be added to provide structure. The lightly scented blooms of 'Nevada' open palest yellow, fading in cool climates to white, while in hot situations they take on pinkish tints.

Recommended partners: *Eucalyptus gunnii*, *Hemerocallis* 'Prairie Sunset', *Lupinus* 'African Sunset', *Potentilla fruticosa* 'Abbotswood', *Rhamnus alaternus* 'Argenteovariegata'

Rosa Peach Blossom ('Ausblossom')

How it works: In this pleasingly subtle combination, the delicate pink of *Rosa* Peach Blossom is echoed in the pink-flushed leaves of *Fuchsia magellanica* 'Versicolor'. A carpet of silver-green lamb's ears (*Stachys byzantina*) furnishes the front of the bed, while a cloud of *Crambe cordifolia* fills the background. The flowers of this David Austin rose have a light almond fragrance.

Recommended partners: *Achillea* 'Apfelblüte', *Astrantia maxima*, *Lavatera* 'Pavlova', *Malva moschata* f. *alba*, *Phlox maculata* 'Rosalinde', *Saponaria officinalis* 'Rosea Plena'

H & S: 6½ft (2m)
✳ **Early summer to early autumn**
 ◊◊ ▫-◾ **Z4 pH5–7**

H: 3ft (90cm) S: 4ft (1.2m)
✳ **Mid-summer to mid-autumn**
◊◊ ▫-◾ **Z5 pH5–7.5**

Rosa 'Penelope'

How it works: Trained to cover a post-and-wire fence, creamy yellow *Rosa* 'Penelope' is seen here in a classic partnership with a columnar flower, the relatively short foxglove *Digitalis purpurea* Foxy Group. This shorter variant interacts with the rose more effectively than if a taller sort, such as *D. p.* 'Sutton's Apricot', had been used.

Recommended partners: *Berberis thunbergii* 'Pink Queen', *Carex comans* (bronze), *Hemerocallis* 'Ruffled Apricot', *Iris* 'Champagne Elegance', *Persicaria virginiana* Compton's form, *Stokesia laevis* 'Peach Melba', *Uncinia egmontiana*

H & S: 5ft (1.5m)
✿ Mid-summer to late autumn
◇◇ ☐-■ Z5 pH5–7.5

Rosa 'Robin Hood'

How it works: Cranesbills are effective plants for carpeting in front of and beneath roses. Here, *Geranium clarkei* 'Kashmir Purple' – a useful cultivar flowering from early to late summer – weaves itself through the arching stems of the cherry-red Hybrid Musk rose 'Robin Hood'. This rose is wonderful as a flowering hedge, and it looks attractive planted in tubs and other large containers

Recommended partners: *Cotinus coggygria* Golden Spirit ('Ancot'), *Geranium* 'Lydia', *Hypericum androsaemum* 'Albury Purple', *Leycesteria formosa* Golden Lanterns ('Notbruce'), *Sidalcea* 'Mrs Borrodaile'

H: 4ft (1.2m) S: 3ft (90cm)
✿ Mid-summer to late autumn
◇◇ ■-■ Z5 pH5–7.5

Rosa 'Roseraie de l'Haÿ'

How it works: If *Rosa* 'Roseraie de l'Haÿ' is pruned only lightly or not at all, it will bloom in late spring, making possible dazzling combinations such as this with tree lupin (*Lupinus arboreus*), the young leaves of *Lysimachia ciliata* 'Firecracker', and a richly colored broom. Each brings its own contrasting texture and structure to the ensemble.

Recommended partners: *Atriplex hortensis* var. *rubra*, *Clematis* 'Princess Diana', *C. recta* 'Velvet Night', *Hypericum androsaemum* 'Albury Purple', *Lathyrus grandiflorus*, *Nepeta govaniana*

H & S: 6½ft (2m)
✿ **Early summer to late autumn**
◊◊ ☐-■ Z4 pH5.5–7

Rosa 'Sally Holmes'

How it works: *Rosa* 'Sally Holmes' is here pruned hard, as for a Floribunda, keeping it compact and spectacularly floriferous. *Potentilla fruticosa* 'Goldfinger' furnishes the rose's base and harmonizes with its golden yellow anthers. Deadheading the rose encourages plentiful later bloom.

'Sally Holmes' is an outstanding Shrub rose for the second or third rank of a border. Its flowers, creamy white and single with a central boss of golden anthers, are borne in large clusters in summer and autumn and make a strong visual impact. Its parentage is similar to that of the Hybrid Musk roses, hence its rich fragrance. If pruned fairly hard, it may be treated as a Floribunda, whereas lighter pruning allows it to achieve more substantial size. This versatile rose looks especially effective with silver or glaucous foliage. Dramatic combinations can be made with yellow flowers that reflect the golden centers of the rose blooms or with blue flowers to create a contrast to the anthers.

Recommended partners: *Campanula lactiflora* 'Prichard's Variety', *Clematis* × *durandii*, *Consolida ajacis*, *Convolvulus tricolor* 'Royal Ensign', *Coreopsis verticillata* 'Grandiflora', *Geranium* 'Brookside', *Geum* 'Lady Stratheden'

H: 6½ft (2m) S: 40in (1m)
✿ **Mid-summer to late autumn**
◊◊ ■-■ Z5 pH5–7.5

Hybrid Teas and Floribundas

Hybrid Teas (Large-flowered roses), popular for the size and often superb shape of their blooms, and the very floriferous Floribundas (Cluster-flowered roses) are the largest and most commonly grown classes of bush rose, both of them available in a wide range of colors. Generally, bush roses are best combined with plants of other genera rather than planted in the traditional way – massed in beds or as a series of sentry singletons in clashing colors, with their usually coarse foliage and stiff habit on view.

Large blooms, particularly if brightly colored, can look far too big in a tiny garden. A single bush, or a whole bed of them, might not match the scale of planting of the rest of the garden: three, five, or more bushes, perhaps loosely grouped, and with other plants woven through them, might provide a more fitting scale.

Hybrid Teas are traditionally pruned in late winter: remove weak or spindly shoots, shorten the main stems and sideshoots to outward-facing buds, and remove occasional older main stems to ensure a constant supply of vigorous flowering wood. For Floribundas, the main stems are pruned more severely to encourage larger new shoots, each of which will provide a cluster of blooms in early summer, followed later in the season by smaller sprays on the sideshoots.

Rosa Anne Harkness ('Harkaramel')

How it works: The tall Floribunda *Rosa* Anne Harkness blooms a little later than others of its group, continuing into the autumn. Its habit makes it eminently suitable for use in a mixed border, where it can be combined with mid-summer or later flowers in warm or hot colors, ideally using several bushes of the rose to relate the scale of the group to that of other planting and to avoid a spotty effect. Here, it is partnered by vermilion sprays of *Crocosmia paniculata* and the acid yellow-green buds of goldenrod; it would also combine well with dahlias.

Renowned for its generous sprays of well-spaced blooms, the upright habit and extra height of this rose, to 5ft (1.5m) or more if only lightly pruned, suit it to narrow borders where the planting has to be steeply banked. However, in such situations it helps to furnish the base of the roses with a companion that covers the bottom half of the bush.

Recommended partners: *Amaranthus cruentus* 'Foxtail', *Canna* 'Wyoming', *Choisya* Goldfingers, *Dahlia* 'Tally Ho', *Miscanthus sinensis* 'Strictus', *Patrinia scabiosifolia*, *Pennisetum setaceum* 'Rubrum', *Phlomis chrysophylla*, *P. fruticosa*, *Potentilla fruticosa* 'Primrose Beauty', *Tagetes patula* 'Cinnabar'

H: 4½ft (1.4m) S: 24in (60cm)
❀ Mid-summer to late autumn
◊◊ ☐-◼ Z5 pH5–7.5

Rosa Avalanche ('Jacay')

How it works: *Rosa* Avalanche is here combined with the charming annual umbellifer *Orlaya grandiflora*, its lacy flowers and fern-like foliage contrasting with the altogether more solidly substantial rose. Other annual umbellifers such as *Ammi majus* could be used in the same way with roses. The cream flowers of this Floribunda fade to white, and often reveal the yellow anthers at the center of the bloom.

Recommended partners: *Achillea* 'Hella Glashoff', *A.* 'Hoffnung', *Artemisia* 'Powis Castle', *Eschscholzia californica* 'Alba', *Hakonechloa macra* 'Alboaurea', *Verbascum* (Cotswold Group) 'Gainsborough'

H: 4ft (1.2m) S: 3ft (90cm)
❀ **Mid-summer to late autumn**
▬▬▬ ░░ ◊◊ ☐-▪ **Z5 pH5–7.5**

Rosa 'Chinatown'

How it works: Pruned hard, *Rosa* 'Chinatown' is compact, with a prolific first flush of flowers produced at an ideal height to contrast with those of the catmint *Nepeta* 'Six Hills Giant'. Deadheading the rose will encourage blooming into the autumn. The catmint will also produce later flowers if cut back after its first flush.

Recommended partners: *Achillea* 'Lucky Break', *Delphinium* Summer Skies Group, *D.* 'Sungleam', *Hosta* 'Sum and Substance', *Iris* 'Cambridge', *I. orientalis*, *Miscanthus sinensis* 'Strictus', *Nigella damascena* 'Miss Jekyll', *Verbascum* (Cotswold Group) 'Cotswold King'

H: 4ft (1.2m) S: 3ft (90cm)
❀ **Early summer to late autumn**
▬▬▬ ░░ ◊◊ ☐-▪ **Z5 pH5–7.5**

Rosa 'Europeana'

How it works: The flat, formal, rich red flowers of *Rosa* 'Europeana' and its red-flushed young leaves combine perfectly with the salmon and scarlet, dark-centered blooms of sprawling *Potentilla nepalensis* 'Roxana'. For impact at a distance, the colors of *R.* 'Europeana' are a little dusky and do not show up as well as lighter reds, but its attractive formation is very striking at close range.

Recommended partners: *Alchemilla mollis, Dahlia* 'Tally Ho', *Lychnis* × *arkwrightii* 'Vesuvius', *Narcissus* 'Ambergate', *Nicotiana* 'Lime Green', *Primula* Cowichan Venetian Group, *Tulipa* 'Couleur Cardinal'

H & S: **24in** (60cm)
✿ Mid-summer to late autumn
▰▰▰▰▰ ◊◊ ▰-▰ Z5 pH5–7.5

Rosa Evelyn Fison ('Macev')

How it works: The orange flowers of *Crocosmia* 'Vulcan' and its bold, pleated leaves contrast in form with the rich scarlet, double blooms of *Rosa* Evelyn Fison, with golden *Ligularia dentata* adding further warmth. Its even, compact habit makes this slightly fragrant Floribunda rose suitable to places at the front of a border, perhaps behind a rank of mounded, sprawling plants.

Recommended partners: *Cosmos sulphureus* 'Polidor', *Eupatorium capillifolium* 'Emerald Feather', *Potentilla* 'Monsieur Rouillard', *Tagetes patula* 'La Bamba', *Tithonia rotundifolia*

H: **27in** (70cm) S: **24in** (60cm)
✿ Mid-summer to late autumn
▰▰▰▰▰ ◊◊ ▰-▰ Z5 pH5–7.5

Rosa 'Frensham'

How it works: In this border of red, yellow, and creamy white flowers combined with dusky foliage, the rich scarlet *Rosa* 'Frensham' and the dark-leaved loosestrife *Lysimachia ciliata* 'Firecracker' are leavened by the sulphur-yellow candelabra of *Verbascum* 'Vernale' and the fluffy yellow panicles of the meadow rue *Thalictrum flavum* subsp. *glaucum*.

Recommended partners: *Dahlia* 'Bednall Beauty', *Hemerocallis* 'Root Beer', *Kniphofia* 'Green Jade', *Nicotiana langsdorffii* 'Cream Splash', *Persicaria microcephala* 'Red Dragon'

H: **4ft** (1.2m) S: **30in** (75cm)
�֍ **Mid-summer to late autumn**
◊◊ ▪-▪ Z5 pH5–7.5

Rosa 'Gruss an Aachen'

How it works: *Rosa* 'Gruss an Aachen' can vary a little in color according to climate and situation and is here pale pink, rather than its usual pale apricot-blush, allowing it to combine even more harmoniously with the foxglove *Digitalis purpurea* Foxy Group. Because the foxglove is relatively short, its spires can be seen in close conjunction with the rose, providing a contrast of form.

Recommended partners: *Campanula punctata* 'Bowl of Cherries', *Dianthus* 'Doris', *Geranium* 'Mavis Simpson', *Lavandula angustifolia* 'Miss Katherine'

H & S: **18in** (45cm)
✤ **Mid-summer to late autumn**
◊◊ ▫-▪ Z6 pH5.5–7

Rosa Iceberg ('Korbin')

How it works: The large white blooms of *Rosa* Iceberg and deep pink *R*. Mary Rose ('Ausmary') and the dense flowerheads of red valerian (*Centranthus ruber*) contrast in form with the more diffuse pink blooms of *Kolkwitzia amabilis* and *Gypsophila elegans* 'Giant White'. The cranesbill *Geranium* 'Johnson's Blue' carpets the foreground.

Recommended partners: *Echinops sphaerocephalus* 'Arctic Glow', *Hemerocallis* 'Gentle Shepherd', *Lobelia* × *speciosa* 'La Fresco', *Lupinus* 'Storm', *Salvia nemorosa* 'Ostfriesland', *Sidalcea candida*

H: 4–6ft (1.2–1.8m) S: 3ft (90cm)
✿ Mid-summer to late autumn
◊◊ ☐-■ Z5 pH5–7.5

Rosa Lilli Marlene ('Korlima')

How it works: *Rosa* Lilli Marlene is here combined with other red flowers, including bold-leaved *Crocosmia* 'Lucifer' (behind), its red tending slightly toward orange, and in front a carpet of sprawling *Potentilla* 'Gibson's Scarlet', with the foliage of purple plum (*Prunus cerasifera* 'Pissardii') providing a strong, dusky background.

Recommended partners: *Anthemis tinctoria* 'Sauce Hollandaise', *Coreopsis verticillata* 'Moonbeam', *Hemerocallis* 'Golden Chimes', *Hypericum frondosum*, *Lathyrus chloranthus*

H: 30in (75cm) S: 24in (60cm)
✿ Mid-summer to late autumn
◊◊ ■-■ Z5 pH5–7.5

Rosa Purple Simplicity ('Jaclav')

How it works: Pruned hard to give a concentrated flush of bloom on long stems, the burgundy blooms of *Rosa* Purple Simplicity, with their paler backs, harmonize with the mauve flowers of *Tulbaghia violacea*. The rose is about to stop blooming for a while but will produce a second flush if deadheaded. The combination could be further enhanced by adding plants to cover the ground: a dark-leaved *Heuchera* could be used in the part shade at the foot of the roses, while a silver-leaved plant in front of the *Tulbaghia* would harmonize with its rather grayish leaves. A simple dark background, perhaps a yew hedge, would also flatter the ensemble. Purple Simplicity combines well with cool colors, perhaps with purple, silver, or glaucous foliage, but is strong enough in hue to be contrasted with yellow-green or sulphur.

Recommended partners: *Achillea* 'Lucky Break', *Alchemilla mollis*, *Artemisia ludoviciana* 'Valerie Finnis', *Cleome* 'Señorita Rosalita', *Dianella caerulea* Cassa Blue ('Dbb03'), *Euphorbia seguieriana* subsp. *niciciana*, *Heuchera* 'Molly Bush', *Lavandula angustifolia* 'Loddon Blue', *Stachys byzantina* 'Cotton Boll', *Verbascum* 'Christo's Yellow Lightning'

H: 4ft (1.2m) S: 40in (1m)
✿ Mid-summer to late autumn
 ◊◊ ☐-■ Z6 pH5–7.5

Rosa 'The Fairy'

How it works: A cascading mound of *Rosa* 'The Fairy', with its large clusters of lightly fragrant, pink blooms, here harmonizes perfectly with the blooms of *Alstroemeria* 'Charm'. The combination would be further enhanced by the addition of some handsome foliage, perhaps in darkest red or silvery green.

Recommended partners: *Carex muskingumensis* 'Ice Fountains', *Diascia barberae* 'Blackthorn Apricot', *Hosta* 'Krossa Regal', *Scabiosa* 'Chile Pepper', *Senecio cineraria*, *Stachys coccinea*

H: 24in (60cm) **S: 4ft** (1.2m)
✽ **Mid-summer to late autumn**
� ◇◇ ☐-■ **Z5 pH5–7.5**

Rosa Westerland (**'Korwest'**)

How it works: The soft apricot blooms of *Rosa* Westerland are borne on a bush tall enough to overtop the other, scarlet-flowered border plants in this scheme, which includes opium poppy (*Papaver somniferum*), Jerusalem cross (*Lychnis chalcedonica*), and a climbing nasturtium (*Tropaeolum majus*).

Recommended partners: *Hemerocallis* 'Lemon Bells', *Hypericum androsaemum* 'Albury Purple', *Lilium henryi*, *Miscanthus sinensis* 'Zebrinus', *Rosa* Molineux ('Ausmol'), *R.* Pat Austin ('Ausmum')

Rosa **'Yesterday'**

How it works: In this scheme, depending for its success solely on flowers in soft magenta, ruby, and white, *Rosa* 'Yesterday' overtops the exotic-looking *Rehmannia elata* behind a carpet of *Diascia barberae* 'Ruby Field' and *Viola cornuta* Alba Group. The rehmannia and diascia would need to be treated as annuals in cooler climates.

Recommended partners: *Indigofera amblyantha*, *Lavandula* 'Pukehou', *Lupinus* 'Storm', *Lysimachia ephemerum*, *Physostegia virginiana* 'Summer Snow'

H: 6ft (1.8m) S: 4ft (1.2m)
� Mid-summer to late autumn
◊◊ ☐-■ Z5 pH5–7.5

H: 5ft (1.5m) S: 4ft (1.2m)
✿ Mid-summer to late autumn
◊◊ ☐-■ Z5 pH5–6.5

Smaller species and smaller modern Shrub roses

In tiny gardens, conventional bush and Shrub roses can sometimes seem oversized, and roses that are smaller in height and spread, and often in flower and leaf, may look more appropriate. Among these are the Scotch or Burnet roses, slender Shrubs with tiny flowers borne in great profusion in early summer, sometimes followed by rounded hips. Thriving in light soil and tolerant of some shade, they are ideal plants for a natural garden. *R.* 'Cécile Brünner' is entirely different in form, a diminutive China rose with perfect, high-pointed buds unfurling to pale pink flowers on frail-looking stems. Many of the Miniature and Patio roses follow in its train. These are hybrids between the very tiny sports of China roses and the more robust and free-flowering modern Floribunda roses.

The smallest of the Miniatures, only 9–18in (23–45cm) tall, are best used in pots so that they may be most easily appreciated at close range – and in colder climates be moved to shelter in winter inasmuch as the roots are intolerant of freezing. The somewhat larger Patio roses look more like plants than scale models or toys and can be used effectively in raised beds or containers, or perhaps along the outer edge of a terrace so that their small flowers and fine-textured foliage can be viewed in detail from below.

Rosa 'Raubritter'

How it works: The sprawling habit of *Rosa* 'Raubritter' allows other flowers to be woven through its outer fringes. Here, dainty blue love-in-a-mist (*Nigella damascena*) mingles with the globular blooms of the rose.

Recommended partners: *Achillea* 'Apfelblüte', *Hebe* 'Pink Pixie', *Iris* 'Pacific Mist', *I.* 'Dreaming Spires', *Lavatera* × *clementii* 'Kew Rose', *Nicotiana langsdorffii*, *Physostegia virginiana* 'Bouquet Rose', *Ruta graveolens*

H: 40in (1m) S: 6ft (1.8m)
❀ **Early to mid-summer**
◊◊ ■-■ **Z4 pH5.5–7.5**

Rosa Sweet Dream ('Fryminicot')

How it works: *Rosa* Sweet Dream blends harmoniously with a carpet of *Diascia* 'Salmon Supreme' and the loose, greenish cream panicles of dark-leaved *Heuchera villosa* 'Palace Purple'. Deadheading the rose and shearing over the diascia after it has completed its first flush of flowers will ensure that the display continues into the autumn. Winner of numerous awards, this Patio rose is among the most popular rose varieties of all time. Like all Patio roses, its flowers and foliage are proportionately smaller than those of Hybrid Teas or Floribundas, making it especially useful for smaller gardens, intimate plantings, and containers.

Recommended partners: *Diascia barberae* 'Blackthorn Apricot', *Heuchera* 'Chocolate Ruffles', × *Heucherella* 'Chocolate Veil', *Hosta* 'Buckshaw Blue', *Lavandula* × *chaytoriae* 'Sawyers', *Persicaria microcephala* 'Red Dragon', *Stokesia laevis* 'Peach Melba'

H: 16in (40cm) S: 14in (35cm)
❀ **Mid-summer to late autumn**
◊◊ ▢-▮ **Z5 pH5–7.5**

Ground-cover roses

There are two main kinds of Ground-cover roses. Some are vigorous, decidedly prostrate plants, most flowering only once, in the summer. Others are neater and more compact, and rather like low, spreading modern Shrub roses; many of the more recent cultivars bloom repeatedly, producing showy flowers over a long season from summer into autumn.

The more prostrate types have trailing stems that often root where they touch the ground and usually form dense mats or hummocks of cover. Some may be too strongly horizontal to associate well with border plants, but are excellent for clothing banks or slopes, especially in more naturalistic parts of the garden.

The shrubby types have arching stems, giving a rather mounded or dome-shaped habit. These roses are particularly pleasing when allowed to tumble over a bank or low wall, or over the edge of a large container.

Perhaps the main point to bear in mind when using Ground-cover roses is that most are too open to be really effective in smothering weeds. It is therefore vital to ensure there are no perennial weeds in the soil before planting and to control annual weeds meticulously in the first year.

These roses don't need regular pruning, but they can be cut back severely every few years using loppers or a brush cutter.

Rosa 'Nozomi'

How it works: *Rosa* 'Nozomi' here spreads itself gracefully across a carpet of yellow-green-leaved heather (*Calluna vulgaris*), creating a pleasingly uneven mix of the two plants and a contrast of foliage and form. The rose will have almost completed its flowering before the heather starts to bloom.

'Nozomi' is a versatile Ground-cover or Miniature Climbing rose that can be trained against a low wall or fence, or as a weeping standard for use as a focal point or repeated accent in a border. It is effective draped over a bank and in containers. The single, unscented flowers, which open palest blush-pink, take on grayish tints as they age, and the anthers turn black, giving the blooms a slightly subdued tone that blends pleasingly with white and muted colors, such as old rose or dusky mauve, and complements silver, purple, or red-flushed foliage. Its trailing stems can be pegged down to improve coverage, and these will often root, extending the spread.

Recommended partners: *Achillea* 'Apfelblüte', *Astrantia maxima*, *Geranium* 'Emily', *Salvia nemorosa* 'Amethyst', *S. officinalis* 'Purpurascens', *Stachys byzantina*, *Veronica* 'Ellen Mae'

H: **3ft** (90cm) S: **6ft** (1.8m)
❀ **Mid-summer**

 Z5 pH5–7.5

Rosa Pink Bells ('Poulbells')

How it works: The sprawling habit of Ground-cover roses allows them to mingle more effectively than bush roses, such as Floribundas, with neighbouring plants. In this scheme, *Rosa* Pink Bells blends harmoniously with a white musk mallow (*Malva moschata* f. *alba*) and a lavender-blue peach-leaved bellflower (*Campanula persicifolia*).

Recommended partners: *Lavandula angustifolia* 'Imperial Gem', *Monarda* 'Aquarius', *Nepeta* 'Six Hills Giant', *Penstemon* 'Evelyn', *Salvia verticillata* 'Purple Rain', *Sidalcea candida*

H: **30in** (75cm) S: **5ft** (1.5m)
❀ **Mid-summer to early autumn**

Z5 pH5–7.5

Perennials

Providing beauty and
interest through their often
showy flowers and diverse
foliage, herbaceous
perennials play an essential
role in furnishing the
garden. Their ability to
change dramatically through
the seasons makes them an
invaluable component of
borders, while many can also
be used for ground cover,
for naturalizing in a wild
garden, or for containers.

Introducing perennials

Strictly defined, perennials are any plants that live for two or more years and flower each year. Gardeners use the word for herbaceous, non-woody plants that die back to an overwintering rootstock. Gertrude Jekyll, an early-twentieth-century British garden designer, was perhaps the first to advocate borders based on a limited color range, with flowers of a single color, two pleasantly contrasting ones such as blue and yellow, or a spectrum of colors shifting gradually along the border's length. Miss Jekyll was also an early advocate of the use of foliage color and form, both to enhance color schemes and to add structure to planting. She also favored the "drift," a long, narrow group of plants running at a shallow oblique angle to the border's front. This is especially useful in borders that are 10–13ft (3–4m) deep and planted with groups that gradually rise in height from front to back.

Mixing form and color

Whatever the color scheme, a variety of flower form generally gives the most pleasing effect. Flowers borne in spikes, such as those of lupins, delphiniums, verbascums, and hardy salvias, provide useful vertical accents and can be contrasted with the flat plates of achilleas and clouds of crambe, gypsophila, or thalictrum. Using varied foliage helps: fine-textured grasses, straps of daylilies, spiky sword-shaped leaves of crocosmias, or handsomely architectural acanthus, for example. Foliage color can also be used to complement a color scheme: silver, glaucous, or purple leaves blend well with cool shades, while red, bronze, or yellow-green leaves are effective with hot ones.

Contrasts of form are easy to achieve and often successful. Harmonies are harder. A border planted solely with daylilies or hostas may become tedious, yet the gentle textures found in a grass garden can be immensely pleasing, the result of the most subtle variations of leaf color and form, particularly telling when they soften a formal pattern of beds.

Even if we love a particular genus of perennials to the exclusion of all others, growing them in mixed company usually gives more satisfying results than a monoculture. Even plants with a strong definite form, such as daylilies, lupins, or delphiniums, benefit from two or three different companions to provide a foil. Many more than this, however, would risk diluting the essential character of the preferred genus and result in something like any other border.

Year-round appeal

The main challenge in designing a traditional herbaceous border is to ensure that it performs for as much of the year as possible. There are two factors that will help achieve this:

- Make the most of foliage, not just for architecture and structure but for color, too.
- Incorporate tender perennials such as dahlias, cannas, penstemons or argyranthemums. These come from climates where frost does not curtail their yearly cycle; they do not have to rush to produce seed before the weather cuts them down, and they often flower incessantly. Some annuals can also be used in this way.

When it comes to creating a large and imposing display with a long season of interest, a mixed border is especially invaluable. Combining herbaceous perennials mainly with shrubs, it is potentially the most attractive synthesis of garden plants.

Numbers and spacing

There is a general convention among gardeners that perennials are best grouped in odd numbers, and it is

In this border, blue echinops, perovskias, eryngiums, and salvias are leavened by white cosmos, phlox, anemones, and tall cream antirrhinums. Foliage plays an important role.

indeed difficult to avoid, say, a block of four or six plants looking self-consciously regular. Some, however, consider that this is a rule made to be broken. An irregularly shaped group with odd plants of the same sort a little distance from it gives a more natural effect, and groups of the same sort of perennial can be repeated at intervals along the length of a border to provide a unifying theme.

Many books on perennials, as well as any number of nursery catalogs, give a recommended spacing for plants within a group. Adjacent groups need spacing further apart than this if they are not to appear cramped. A rule of thumb is that the spacing between two groups should be three-quarters the sum of their spacings: in other words, if one group has plants spaced at 16in (40cm) and its neighbor has plants spaced at 24in (60cm), the gap between the outermost plants of the two groups should be 30in (75cm).

In this simple color scheme, the planting is improved during the summer months by variations in height and flower shape.

Frontline candidates

The choice of perennials for the front of beds and borders is perhaps the most crucial. Generally they should be of neat habit and/or should have attractive foliage. Spacious and gently rising borders can have low carpeters such as alpine pinks or lamb's ears in front, with mound-forming plants in the second rank to hide the stems of taller plants behind. If the border is steeply banked, the carpeters must be dispensed with and the mounds must come to the fore. Some bold foliage, such as that of hostas, toward the front can help define the border, anchoring it and giving it gravitas. Fluffs such as catmint and gypsophila can set a tone of amorphous anonymity if used to excess, although they have ethereal charm when used in moderation with bolder plants.

Rebels may wish to flout the convention of designing the border as an evenly graded bank of flowers, gradually rising in height, and allow some tall plants to grow well forward of others of their size. By contouring the heights of perennials more irregularly and dramatically, it is possible to create bays within the planting whose innermost recesses are hidden when the border is viewed obliquely from a distance – their contents will be revealed as a delightful surprise as the viewer moves along the border.

This striking planting includes *Crocosmia* 'Lucifer', *Heuchera villosa* 'Palace Purple', and *Achillea* 'Fanal'. Longer-lasting color is added by annual antirrhinums and tender perennial *Dahlia* 'Bishop of Llandaff', with shrubby *Rosa glauca* adding height and structure.

Acanthus spinosus

How it works: The handsome, architectural leaves and bold flower spikes of *Acanthus spinosus* act as a focal point in a sunny border, backed by the shrubby, pale mauve-pink *Lavatera* × *clementii* 'Barnsley' and furnished in front by contrasting golden feverfew (*Tanacetum parthenium* 'Aureum') and the yellow-green flowerheads of lady's mantle (*Alchemilla mollis*).

Recommended partners: *Allium cristophii, Geranium* 'Johnson's Blue', *G.* 'Mavis Simpson', *Philadelphus coronarius* 'Aureus', *Rosa glauca*

H: 5ft (1.5m) S: 36in (90cm)
❀ Early to late summer
 ◊-◊◊ ☐-■ Z7 pH5–7.5

Achillea 'Coronation Gold'

How it works: The horizontal plates of *Achillea* 'Coronation Gold' contrast with the vertical spires of a verbascum hybrid, while the red flowers of *Lychnis chalcedonica*, feathery heads of bronze fennel (*Foeniculum vulgare* 'Purpureum'), and orange-yellow *Ligularia dentata* fill the gap between the two.

Recommended partners: *Artemisia ludoviciana, Campanula persicifolia, Coreopsis* 'Baby Gold', *Delphinium* 'Sabrina', *Kniphofia* 'David', *Onopordum nervosum, Salvia nemorosa* 'Lubecca', *Stipa capillata, Viola cornuta*

H: 36in (90cm) S: 18in (45cm)
❀ Early to late summer
◊◊ ☐-■ Z4 pH5–7.5

Achillea 'Fanal'

How it works: The flowerheads of *Achillea* 'Fanal' open rich scarlet and turn to terra-cotta before aging through salmon to chamois. Here, the terra-cotta tones with the distant wall, while the scarlet chimes with the flowers of bold-leaved *Crocosmia* 'Lucifer'. The curious spherical seedheads of *Allium cristophii* are just tall enough to appear behind the achillea.

Recommended partners: *Dahlia* 'Bishop of Llandaff', *Diascia* 'Salmon Supreme', *Elymus magellanicus, Foeniculum vulgare* 'Purpureum', *Monarda* 'Cambridge Scarlet'

H: 30in (75cm) **S: 18in** (45cm)
✽ **Early summer to mid-autumn**
▬▬ ◊-◊◊ ▢-▧ Z3 pH5–7.5

Achillea filipendulina 'Gold Plate'

How it works: Borne near eye level, the flat heads of *Achillea filipendulina* 'Gold Plate' appear as narrow yellow lines, creating a distinctive pattern. The bold leaves of *Canna indica* 'Purpurea', *Dahlia* 'Blaisdon Red', orange heleniums, and the tall sunflower *Helianthus* 'Velvet Queen' add exotic richness.

Recommended partners: *Crocosmia* 'Lucifer', *Delphinium* 'Alice Artindale', *Eryngium × tripartitum, Hemerocallis* 'Stafford', *Salvia pratensis* 'Indigo'

H: 5ft (1.5m) **S: 24in** (60cm)
✽ **Early to late summer**
▬▬ ◊-◊◊ ▢-▧ Z4 pH5–7.5

Achillea 'Lachsschönheit'

How it works: After opening rose-pink, the flowers of *Achillea* 'Lachsschönheit', a delightful yarrow, age to pale biscuit tints, harmonizing with the bronze leaves of *Heuchera villosa* 'Palace Purple', which furnishes in front. Removing the heuchera's flowers ensures fresh and healthy foliage.

Recommended partners: *Berberis thunbergii* f. *atropurpurea*, *Delphinium* 'Sungleam', *Diascia barberae* 'Blackthorn Apricot', *Foeniculum vulgare* 'Purpureum', *Iris pallida* 'Variegata'

Achillea millefolium 'Cerise Queen'

How it works: The profuse blooms of *Achillea millefolium* 'Cerise Queen' provide the mainstay of this display, aided by crimson *Knautia macedonica*, bold heads of agapanthus, and a carpet of pansies. An additional bold-leaved plant at the front, perhaps one with glaucous or silver foliage, would give structure and anchor the design.

Recommended partners: *Artemisia schmidtiana* 'Nana', *Berberis thunbergii* 'Atropurpurea Nana', *Ruta graveolens* 'Jackman's Blue', *Salvia* × *superba* 'Superba'

H: 30in (75cm) **S: 18in** (45cm)
❀ **Early to late summer**
◊-◊◊ ☐-■ **Z3 pH5–8**

H: 24in (60cm) **S: 18in** (45cm)
❀ **Mid-summer to early autumn**
◊-◊◊ ☐-■ **Z3 pH5–8**

Achillea '**Moonshine**'

How it works: The blooms of *Achillea* 'Moonshine', opening sharp lemon before ageing to more gentle sulfur, contrast here in form and color with *Campanula lactiflora*. The achillea needs regular replanting to encourage free blooming.

Recommended partners: *Crambe maritima*, *Delphinium* (Belladonna Group) 'Volkerfrieden', *Dianella caerulea* Cassia Blue ('Dbb03'), *Miscanthus sinensis* 'Gracillimus', *Ruta graveolens* 'Jackman's Blue', *Salvia × superba* 'Superba'

H: 24in (60cm) **S: 18in** (45cm)
✿ **Early to late summer**
◊-◊◊ □-■ **Z4 pH5–7.5**

Achillea 'Terra-cotta'

How it works: *Achillea* 'Terra-cotta' is partnered with *Acanthus hungaricus* and the fine-textured grass *Stipa tenuissima* in this prairie-like planting. The vertical accents of the acanthus contrast effectively with the horizontal plates of the achillea, which emerge a soft orange and age through biscuity tints to creamy fawn. The color of the achillea is seldom strong enough to suit the hottest combinations or fiercest contrasts, and bright or strong colors, including white, can make it seem grubby in comparison. However, it harmonizes with the muted mauve of the acanthus and with warm hues such as peach, apricot, sulphur, and cream, as well as with bronze-leaved plants and yellow-green foliage or flowers.

Recommended partners: *Agastache* (Acapulco Series) 'Acapulco Orange', *Alchemilla mollis*, *Allium paniculatum* 'Valerie Finnis', *Calamagrostis brachytricha*, *Carex comans* (bronze-leaved), *Diascia barberae* 'Blackthorn Apricot', *Helenium* 'Goldreif', *Heuchera villosa* 'Palace Purple', *Hypericum androsaemum* 'Albury Purple', *Kniphofia* 'Timothy', *Potentilla fruticosa* 'Limelight', *Rosa* Sweet Dream ('Fryminicot'), *Stipa gigantea*, *Verbascum* 'Cotswold Beauty', *V.* 'Gainsborough'

H: 40in (1m) S: 18in (45cm)
❀ **Early summer to mid-autumn**
◊-◊◊ □-■ **Z3 pH5–7.5**

Aconitum napellus
MONKSHOOD

How it works: The sumptuous, deep purplish blue flowers of monkshood (*Aconitum napellus*), borne on a tall and slender plant, provide a contrast with the dainty pink flowers of *Astrantia major* var. *rosea* in a steeply planted narrow border.

Recommended partners: *Anemone* × *hybrida* 'Honorine Jobert', *A.* × *h.* 'Elegans', *Aster* × *frikartii* 'Mönch', *Choisya ternata* Sundance ('Lich'), *Digitalis purpurea* f. *albiflora*, *Hosta* 'August Moon', *Miscanthus sinensis* 'Sarabande', *Stipa capillata*

H: 5ft (1.5m) S: 12in (30cm)
❀ **Mid- to late summer**
◊◊ ▨ Z5 pH5–7.5

Agapanthus 'Loch Hope'

How it works: Blue flowers and creamy yellow variegation can provide a pleasing contrast, as shown here with *Agapanthus* 'Loch Hope', the variegated pampas grass *Cortaderia selloana* 'Aureolineata', and *Helichrysum petiolare* 'Roundabout', each supplying a distinctive foliage effect.

'Loch Hope' has tall, upright stems and deep blue flowers, held well above the leaves, which do not develop the reddish tints that mar some hybrids as they age. It goes easily with grasses such as miscanthus, with silver foliage, and with blue, mauve, purple, or pink flowers, and contrasts well with soft yellow flowers and gold foliage, such as that of golden hostas (in situations where some midday shade can protect the hosta leaves from scorching).

Agapanthus need space on all sides for their magnificent foliage and flower stems to have maximum impact, so they should stand a little forward in the bed and not be near plants of their own height.

Recommended partners: *Elaeagnus* 'Quicksilver', *Euphorbia schillingii*, *Hosta* 'Sum and Substance', *Iris pallida* 'Variegata', *Miscanthus sinensis* 'Variegatus', *Sambucus nigra* 'Aurea', *Sisyrinchium striatum* 'Aunt May'

H: 5ft (1.5m) S: 24in (60cm)
❀ **Late summer to early autumn**
  ◊◊ ☐-◼ Z7 pH5–7.5

Agastache 'Black Adder'

How it works: *Agastache* 'Black Adder' is a neat, long-flowering hybrid producing lavender flowers over a long period. Here, it harmonizes with mauve-pink *Echinacea purpurea* and salvia, while clashing gently with *Helenium* 'Rubinzwerg', in a planting akin to the prairie or New Perennial style. The ensemble is helped by being arranged in bold, flowing drifts, and the flower shapes form an effective contrast, the repeated verticals of agastache and salvia establishing both rhythm and texture. The flower color of 'Black Adder' is effective, with cool colors and white, lemon, or primrose yellow and yellow-green, and with purple, silver, or glaucous foliage.

Recommended partners: *Achillea* Anthea ('Anblo'), *A.* 'Summerwine', *Aconitum* × *cammarum* 'Eleanora', *Agapanthus* 'Torbay', *Anaphalis margaritacea* var. *yedoensis*, *Anemone* × *hybrida* 'Honorine Jobert', *Anthemis* 'Tinpenny Sparkle', *Artemisia ludoviciana* 'Valerie Finnis', *Calamagrostis brachytricha*, *Dahlia* (Mystic Ladies Series) Candy Stripe ('Ham02'), *Cosmos bipinnatus* 'Sonata White', *Euphorbia seguieriana* var. *niciciana*, *Hemerocallis* 'Marion Vaughn', *Miscanthus sinensis* 'Hinjo', *Potentilla recta* var. *sulphurea*, *Sidalcea* 'Elsie Heugh', *Verbascum* 'Gainsborough', *V.* 'Merlin'

H: 24in (60cm) S: 18in (45cm)
✽ **Early summer to mid-autumn**
◖ ◗-◖◗ ☐-▮ **Z7 pH5–7.5**

Agastache 'Firebird'

How it works: The gentle coloring of *Agastache* 'Firebird', with its grayish foliage and slightly diffuse heads of flowers of almost indefinable color, somewhere between deep salmon-pink, coral, and soft orange, matches perfectly the variegation of *Berberis thunbergii* 'Rose Glow', whose darker tints and red stems add richness.
Recommended partners: *Argyranthemum* 'Jamaica Primrose', *Artemisia* 'Powis Castle', *Crocosmia* × *crocosmiiflora* 'Lady Hamilton', *Dahlia* 'Bishop of Llandaff', *Diascia barberae* 'Ruby Field', *Foeniculum vulgare* 'Purpureum'

H: 24in (60cm) **S:** 12in (30cm)
❀ **Mid-summer to late autumn**
Z7 pH5–7.5

Ajuga reptans 'Atropurpurea'
COMMON BUGLE

How it works: *Ajuga reptans* 'Atropurpurea' is an excellent foil beneath summer foliage and flowers. Here, it contrasts dramatically with *Hedera helix* 'Schäfer Three', effective in showing off the single stems of the ivy and the poise with which every leaf is placed. It is also a good foil for summer bulbs and clump-forming smaller grasses and sedges.
Recommended partners: *Acorus gramineus* 'Ōgon', *Colchicum byzantinum*, *Dianthus* Allwoodii Alpinus Group, *Impatiens namcharwabensis*, *Iris pallida* 'Argentea Variegata', *Origanum vulgare* 'Aureum'

H: 6in (15cm) **S:** 24–36in (60–90cm)
❀ **Late spring to early summer** Z3 pH5–7.5

Alchemilla mollis
LADY'S MANTLE

How it works: Mounds of *Alchemilla mollis*
flowers anchor the design at the front of
the border. *Cornus alba* 'Aurea' provides
matching yellow-green behind, while the
bold crocosmia leaves form a focal point.
The pale foliage of *Rhamnus alaternus*
'Argenteovariegata' offers a lighter tone.

Recommended partners: *Calendula
officinalis, Elymus magellanicus, Festuca glauca*
'Elijah Blue', *Geranium* 'Ann Folkard',
Lupinus arboreus, Penstemon 'Chester
Scarlet', *Rosa* Graham Thomas ('Ausmas'),
Rubus cockburnianus 'Goldenvale'

H: 16in (40cm) **S: 24in** (60cm)
❄ **Early summer Z3 pH4–8**
 ◊◊-◊◊◊ ▢-▪

Alstroemeria 'Apollo'

How it works: *Hydrangea arborescens*
provides bulk and solidity next to a group
of *Alstroemeria* 'Apollo'. The hydrangea
flowerheads will mature to pure white
while the alstroemeria remains in flower,
harmonizing with its beautifully marked
blooms. 'Apollo', soft white with a yellow
throat, is an excellent choice for any
border; it may also be used for cutting.

Recommended partners: *Aconitum
napellus, Campanula persicifolia, Delphinium*
'Sabrina', *Hydrangea paniculata*
'Grandiflora', *Rosa* 'Albertine', *R.* 'Felicia',
R. 'Frensham'

H: 36in (90cm) **S: 30in** (75cm)
❄ **Mid-summer**
 ◊◊ ▢-▪ **Z7 pH5.5–7.5**

Alstroemeria aurea

How it works: *Alstroemeria aurea* looks best with hot colors and bronze foliage. This scheme, with *Alstroemeria aurea* and harmonious *Crocosmia* 'Vulcan', is given greater depth by the recessive purplish blue tints of *Aconitum* 'Spark's Variety' in the background.

Recommended partners: *Achillea* 'Moonshine', *Cotinus coggygria* 'Royal Purple', *Geranium* 'Johnson's Blue', *Kniphofia* 'David', *Lychnis* × *arkwrightii* 'Vesuvius', *Rosa* 'Prince Charles'

H: **36in** (90cm) S: **24in** (60cm)
✳ **Mid-summer**

Z7 pH5.5–7.5

Alstroemeria ligtu **hybrids**

How it works: The color of *Penstemon* 'Andenken an Friedrich Hahn' in the foreground is close enough to primary red to blend agreeably with the salmon flowers of the *Alstroemeria ligtu* hybrids beyond. They themselves harmonize with the color of the brick wall behind. With their relatively short stature, these hybrids are well suited to the front ranks of a border.

Recommended partners: *Cistus* × *cyprius*, *Geranium renardii*, *Heuchera villosa* 'Palace Purple', *Macleaya microcarpa*

H: **30in** (75cm) S: **24in** (60cm)
✳ **Early summer**

Z7 pH5.5–7.5

Alstroemeria psittacina

How it works: *Alstroemeria psittacina* is not a showy plant, but it looks very appealing at close range. Its florets have their own internal contrast provided by the green tips to their rich rust-red blooms. This makes them particularly effective with lime green flowers. The stems are slender and can produce a slightly tousled effect, so plants often make the best impression when they are positioned next to something of more solid habit and with bolder foliage. In this scheme, mixing the alstroemeria with *Nicotiana* 'Lime Green', its flowers harmonizing with the tips but contrasting with the predominant red, creates a striking combination. A background of *Berberis thunbergii* 'Rose Glow', its rich leaf color enlivened by splashes of pink, completes the picture.

Recommended partners: *Alonsoa warscewiczii, Cotinus coggygria* 'Royal Purple', *Euphorbia schillingii, Heuchera* 'Plum Pudding', *Phygelius* × *rectus* 'Salmon Leap'

H: 36in (90cm) **S: 18in** (45cm)
✿ **Mid-summer to early autumn**
■–■ ◊◊ ■–■ **Z7 pH5.5–7.5**

Anemone × *hybrida* 'Elegans'

How it works: *Anemone* × *hybrida* and its cultivars are perhaps the most beautiful and useful of the Japanese anemones. In this planting scheme, the cross-banded *Miscanthus sinensis* 'Zebrinus' is of the right height to provide excellent contrast of form with the late *A.* × *hybrida* 'Elegans', whose mid-pink flowers become paler with age.

Recommended partners: *Arundo donax* var. *versicolor*, *Aster novi-belgii* 'Marie Ballard', *Chrysanthemum* 'Clara Curtis', *Clematis* 'Alba Luxurians', *Rosa* 'Penelope'

H: **40in** (1m) S: **20in** (50cm)
✾ **Late summer to mid-autumn**
 ◊◊ ▨ ■ Z6 pH5–8

Anthemis punctata subsp. *cupaniana*

How it works: The cypress spurge (*Euphorbia cyparissias*) is slightly invasive, enabling it to grow through a carpet of white, yellow-centered *Anthemis punctata* subsp. *cupaniana*, punctuating it with its acid yellow-green flowerheads.

Recommended partners: *Festuca glauca* 'Elijah Blue', *Helleborus foetidus*, *Iris* 'Curlew', *Kniphofia* 'Goldelse', *Lavandula angustifolia* 'Hidcote', *Myosotis alpestris*, *Salvia* × *sylvestris* 'Mainacht', *Stipa tenuissima*, *Tulipa* 'Ballerina', *T.* 'Fantasy'

H: **12in** (30cm) S: **36in** (90cm)
✾ **Early summer**
■▬ ▨ ◊ ☐ Z7 pH5.5–7.5

Anthemis sancti-johannis

How it works: *Anthemis sancti-johannis* is an outstanding source of hot color for the front of a border. In this richly colored combination, orange *A. s.-j.* and its companions – light magenta *Stachys macrantha*, purplish blue *Campanula latiloba* 'Highcliffe Variety', and dusky pinkish crimson *Astrantia major* 'Rubra' – are allowed to flop forward over the adjoining path.

Recommended partners: *Alonsoa warscewiczii, Calendula officinalis* 'Gitana Orange', *Campanula glomerata* 'Joan Elliott', *Geum* 'Lady Stratheden', *G.* 'Mrs J. Bradshaw', *Hemerocallis* 'Golden Chimes', *Heuchera villosa* 'Palace Purple', *Lychnis* × *arkwrightii* 'Vesuvius'

Anthemis tinctoria 'E. C. Buxton'

How it works: The soft yellow flowers of *Anthemis tinctoria* 'E. C. Buxton' contrast with the spires of purple toadflax (*Linaria purpurea*) and the magenta blooms of the cranesbill *Geranium* 'Ann Folkard'. The cranesbill's yellowish green foliage harmonizes with the camomile's lemon daisy-like flowerheads while contrasting with its own flowers and those of the toadflax.

Recommended partners: *Achillea* 'Moonshine', *Aconitum* 'Spark's Variety', *Bidens ferulifolia, Centaurea macrocephala, Clematis* × *diversifolia* 'Blue Boy', *Lavandula angustifolia* 'Hidcote', *Mimulus cardinalis, Rosa* 'Buff Beauty', *R.* Graham Thomas ('Ausmas'), *Tanacetum parthenium*

H & S: **24in** (60cm)
❀ **Early to mid-summer**
◯ ☐ Z5 pH5.5–7.5

H: **24in** (60cm) S: **24in** (60cm)
❀ **Early to mid-summer Z4 pH5.5–7.5**
 ◯-◯◯ ☐-■

Arrhenatherum elatius subsp. *bulbosum* 'Variegatum'
VARIEGATED BULBOUS OAT GRASS

How it works: Linear foliage, including the white-striped *Arrhenatherum elatius* subsp. *bulbosum* 'Variegatum', sword-shaped crocosmia, and arching, gold-banded pampas grass (*Cortaderia selloana* 'Aureolineata'), is contrasted with clouds of the goldenrod *Solidago* 'Goldenmosa' in a scheme for a broad, informally planted bed.
Recommended partners: *Allium cristophii*, *Artemisia stelleriana* 'Boughton Silver', *Crocosmia* 'Lucifer', *Hemerocallis* 'Stafford', *Ophiopogon planiscapus* 'Nigrescens'

Artemisia ludoviciana 'Valerie Finnis'

How it works: Though usually used with cool colors, this attractive wormwood is here used to leaven the strong and hot hues of *Verbascum* (Cotswold Group) 'Cotswold Queen', *Knautia macedonica* and *Geum* 'Dolly North'. Cutting back

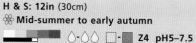

H & S: 12in (30cm)
☸ Mid-summer to early autumn
�○-�○�○ ☐-■ Z4 pH5–7.5

H: 4ft (1.2m) **S: 24in** (60cm)
☸ Mid-summer to early autumn
�○-�○�○ ☐-■ Z4 pH5.5–7.5

Artemisia ludoviciana var. *latiloba*

How it works: A subtle interplay of leaf shapes in silvery gray-green is achieved by combining *Artemisia ludoviciana* var. *latiloba*, whose leaves are largely uncut, and filigree *Senecio cineraria*, interlaced with bronze-tinged umbels of dill (*Anethum graveolens*), giving a delicate association best appreciated at close range.

Recommended partners: *Cistus × purpureus*, *Geranium tuberosum*, *Hebe* 'Watson's Pink', *Iris* 'Nightfall', *Penstemon* 'Chester Scarlet', *Rosa* 'Carmenetta', *Tulipa* 'Palestrina'

the stems by about one-third in late May (the "Chelsea chop") will help keep the foliage bright throughout summer and discourage flopping.

Recommended partners: *Cistus × purpureus*, *Geranium tuberosum*, *Hebe* 'Watson's Pink', *Iris* 'Nightfall', *Penstemon* 'Chester Scarlet', *Rosa* 'Carmenetta'

H: 4ft (1.2m) S: 24in (60cm)
❀ **Mid-summer to early autumn**
◊·◊◊ ☐·☐ **Z4 pH5.5–7.5**

Artemisia schmidtiana 'Nana'

How it works: A carpet of compact silvery *Artemisia schmidtiana* 'Nana' spreads before tussocks of bronze sedge (*Carex flagellifera*), in front of the handsome spurge *Euphorbia characias*.

Recommended partners: *Berberis thunbergii* 'Atropurpurea Nana', *Cistus* × *purpureus*, *Dianthus* Allwoodii Alpinus Group, *Lavandula lanata*, *Rosmarinus officinalis* Prostratus Group, *Rosa* Pink Bells ('Poulbells'), *Salvia officinalis* 'Purpurascens'

H: 12in (30cm) **S: 18in** (45cm)
❀ Mid- to late summer **Z4** **pH5.5–7.5**

Artemisia stelleriana 'Boughton Silver'

How it works: Although *Artemisia stelleriana* 'Boughton Silver' is far less vigorous than *Geranium* 'Ann Folkard', planting the artemisia near to the limit of the cranesbill's spread prevents it being overwhelmed by its neighbor and allows an attractive intermingling of the two.

Sometimes known as dusty miller, this semi-evergreen artemisia is a sprawling, prostrate plant with deeply indented, silvery leaves, and flowers of similar color borne in sprays. It is ideal for the front of a border, for a gravel or rock garden, or for softening the edge of a path. A good partner for cool-colored flowers and silver or glaucous foliage, it is attractive when fronting mound-forming plants such as rue, lavenders, rosemaries, helichrysums, smaller cistus, perovskias, lavender cottons, and other artemisias, together with dianthus, marjorams, and smaller irises. It also mixes well with other sprawling plants that grow at a similar rate.

Recommended partners: *Dianthus* Allwoodii Alpinus Group, *Hebe pinguifolia* 'Pagei', *Lavandula angustifolia* 'Hidcote', *Origanum vulgare* 'Aureum', *Perovskia* 'Blue Spire', *Salvia officinalis* 'Kew Gold', *Sedum spectabile* 'Brilliant'

H: 6in (15cm) **S: 16in** (40cm)
❀ Mid-summer to early autumn **Z4** **pH5.5–7.5**

Aruncus dioicus
GOAT'S BEARD

How it works: The splendid architectural form of goat's beard (*Aruncus dioicus*) makes it a good choice where a specimen plant is needed, as here where it contrasts with a formal opening through a hedge of beech (*Fagus sylvatica*). A pair of clipped box (*Buxus sempervirens*) in containers, one on either side, echoes the formality of the beech.

Recommended partners: *Achillea* 'Lachsschönheit', *Astilbe* 'Red Sentinel', *Heuchera* 'Pewter Moon', *Ligularia dentata* 'Desdemona', *Philadelphus intectus*, *Rosa* 'Highdownensis'

H: 6ft (1.8m) S: 4ft (1.2m)
❀ Early to mid-summer Z3 pH4.5–7.5

Asclepias tuberosa
BUTTERFLY WEED

How it works: This vibrant combination of orange butterfly weed (*Asclepias tuberosa*) and the mauve, dark-centered flowers of narrow-leaved *Echinacea tennesseensis* provides a contrast of floral form on plants of similar height. Both are wild flowers of the North American prairies. Butterfly weed also looks very effective with other hot-colored perennials.

Recommended partners: *Arctotis* × *hybrida* 'Flame', *Canna indica* 'Purpurea', *Hedychium coccineum* 'Tara', *Kniphofia* 'Sunningdale Yellow', *Tagetes patula* 'Striped Marvel'

H: 18–36in (45–90cm) S: 12in (30cm)
❀ Mid-summer to early autumn
◊◊ ☐-▧ Z4 pH5.5–7.5

Astilbe × arendsii hybrids

How it works: These astilbes need bog or waterside planting, or a damp border. They produce dazzling displays in colors from crimson and scarlet to mauve-pink, rose-pink, and salmon, and in white. Here, soft pink *Astilbe × arendsii* 'Ceres', a late-flowering cultivar, harmonizes with the purplish, pink-splashed leaves of *Berberis thunbergii* 'Rose Glow'.

Recommended partners: *Aruncus dioicus*, *Cornus alba* 'Elegantissima', *Hosta sieboldiana* var. *elegans*, *Iris pseudacorus* 'Variegata', *I.* 'Cambridge', *Ligularia dentata* 'Othello', *Lobelia cardinalis* 'Queen Victoria', *Sorbaria sorbifolia*

H: 20–48in (50–120cm) **S: 18in** (45cm)
Late spring to mid-summer Z5 pH5.5–7

Astilbe chinensis var. *taquetii* 'Superba'

How it works: *Astilbe chinensis* var. *taquetii* 'Superba', which flowers unusually late, has a stiffly upright habit useful for semi-formal accents in a formal border or at the water's edge. Here, its erect, carmine-pink spires, contrasted with orange *Crocosmia* 'Vulcan' and yellow kniphofias and daylilies, help to emphasize the straight geometric lines of this formal garden area.

Recommended partners: *Carex grayi*, *Euphorbia schillingii*, *Filipendula camtschatica*, *Hosta* 'Shade Fanfare', *Lysimachia clethroides*, *Mimulus aurantiacus*, *Phyllostachys nigra*

H: 4ft (1.2m) **S: 24in** (60cm) **Z4 pH5.5–7**
Late summer to mid-autumn

Astilbe 'Red Sentinel'

How it works: In this brightly colored waterside planting, *Astilbe* 'Red Sentinel' stands out against the yellow-green foliage of the dogwood *Cornus alba* 'Aurea'. In between, the lofty flowers of *Hosta* 'Tall Boy' are starting to unfurl. All three plants benefit from the pond's moisture.

Recommended partners: *Acer palmatum* f. *atropurpureum*, *Euphorbia amygdaloides* var. *robbiae*, *Iris ensata*, *Primula* Inshriach hybrids, *Sasa veitchii*

H: 36in (90cm) S: 20in (50cm)
❊ Early summer Z4 pH5.5–7

Astrantia major 'Hadspen Blood'

How it works: The intricate flowers of *Astrantia major* 'Hadspen Blood', their dusky pink umbels enclosed in a ruff of crimson bracts, harmonize perfectly with the dark foliage of *Berberis thunbergii* 'Atropurpurea Nana'.

Recommended partners: *Cotinus* 'Flame', *Foeniculum vulgare* 'Purpureum', *Heuchera villosa* 'Palace Purple', *Phormium* 'Bronze Baby', *Rosa* 'Charles de Mills'

H: 24in (60cm) S: 18in (45cm)
❊ Early to late summer Z4 pH5–7.5

Astrantia major 'Sunningdale Variegated'

How it works: In this complex tapestry of varied leaf forms, the boldly margined foliage of *Astrantia major* 'Sunningdale Variegated' is the focal point. It is joined by pale-spotted lungwort, glaucous-leaved roseroot (*Rhodiola rosea*), and golden marjoram (*Origanum vulgare* 'Aureum'). Quietly attractive dusky pink flowers appear in early summer.

Recommended partners: *Acer palmatum* var. *dissectum, Aconitum napellus, Diascia barberae* 'Blackthorn Apricot', *Hebe ochracea, Spiraea japonica*

H: 24in (60cm) **S: 18in** (45cm)
❀ **Early to late summer**
◊◊ ☐-■ ■ Z4 pH5–7.5

Astrantia 'Roma'

How it works: In early summer, the warm rose pink flowers of *Astrantia* 'Roma' and mauve *Allium cristophii* are joined by the silvery young flower stems of *Eryngium bourgatii*. By midsummer, the eryngium, by then steely blue if it is a good clone, and the astrantia will have dwarfed the spherical seedheads of the onion.

Recommended partners: *Heuchera* 'Molly Bush', *Ranunculus aconitifolius* 'Flore Pleno', *Sambucus nigra* f. *porphyrophylla* 'Gerda', *Viola cornuta*

Baptisia australis

How it works: The airy, indigo-blue spikes of *Baptisia australis* are recessive in color and less visually insistent than the lupins it resembles. This elegant herbaceous perennial forms a pleasing background for the sumptuous cupped pink blooms of *Rosa* 'Aloha'.

Recommended partners: *Artemisia ludoviciana*, *Dahlia* 'Requiem', *Delphinium* 'Sabrina', *Geranium* × *oxonianum* 'Wargrave Pink', *Rosa glauca*, *Spiraea nipponica* 'Snowmound'

H: 24in (60cm) **S: 18in** (45cm)
❀ **Early summer to late autumn**
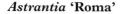 ◊◊ □-■ ■ **Z4 pH5–7.5**

H: 4ft (1.2m) **S: 24in** (60cm)
❀ **Early summer Z3 pH5.5–7.5**
◊-◊◊ □-■

Campanula 'Burghaltii'

How it works: The dusky lilac-gray bells emerging from maroon buds of *Campanula* 'Burghaltii' are the only colored flowers in this tranquil scheme of white blooms and silvery foliage, including feathery *Artemisia pontica*, spiky *Eryngium giganteum*, *Papaver orientale*, and *Lychnis coronaria* 'Alba'.

Recommended partners: *Artemisia ludoviciana*, *Dicentra* 'Stuart Boothman', *Geranium clarkei* 'Kashmir Purple', *G.* 'Sue Crûg', *Heuchera* 'Pewter Veil', *Nepeta* × *faassenii*

H: **24in** (60cm) S: **12in** (30cm)
❀ **Early to mid-summer**

 ◊◊ ☐-■ Z4 pH5–7.5

Campanula 'Kent Belle'

How it works: This cool combination features rich purplish blue *Campanula* 'Kent Belle' and the white double-flowered feverfew *Tanacetum parthenium* 'Rowallane'. *Perovskia* 'Blue Spire' grows through the feverfew and will take over its display in late summer.

Recommended partners: *Aconitum lycoctonum* subsp. *vulparia*, *Hosta fortunei* var. *albopicta* f. *aurea*, *Lamium maculatum* 'White Nancy', *Potentilla fruticosa* 'Primrose Beauty'

H: **36in** (90cm) S: **24in** (60cm)
❀ **Early to late summer**

◊◊ ☐-■ Z5 pH5–7.5

Campanula latifolia 'Gloaming'

How it works: In a semi-wild setting, trailing stems of the white-flowered Rambler rose *R.* 'Seagull' drape down to the ground to interact with the ghostly bells of the broad-leaved bellflower *Campanula latifolia* 'Gloaming'.

Recommended partners: *Anthriscus sylvestris* 'Ravenswing', *Delphinium* 'Alice Artindale', *Lilium* 'Enchantment', *Aruncus dioicus*, *Echinops bannaticus* 'Taplow Blue', *Geranium* × *oxonianum* 'Wargrave Pink'

H: 36in (90cm) S: 24in (60cm)
❀ **Early to mid-summer**
◊◊ ☐-■ Z4 pH4.5–7.5

Campanula persicifolia
PEACH-LEAVED BELLFLOWER

How it works: The sturdy and statuesque spikes of the pinkish buff perennial foxglove *Digitalis* × *mertonensis* give great structure to this combination, while the more diffuse stems of the peach-leaved bellflower (*Campanula persicifolia alba*) planted through it leaven the effect.

Recommended partners: *Nepeta* 'Six Hills Giant', *Rosa* 'Nozomi', *Thalictrum delavayi*, *Hosta fortunei*, *Scabiosa* 'Butterfly Blue'

H: 24–48in (60–120cm) S: 12in (30cm)
❀ **Early to mid-summer**
◊◊ ☐-■ Z4 pH5–7.5

Cautleya spicata **'Robusta'**

How it works: *Cautleya spicata* 'Robusta' is a relative of ginger and has broad handsome leaves, rather like those of a canna, which give it an almost tropical appearance. In this combination, its maroon calyces harmonize with the foliage of *Dahlia* 'David Howard' behind. The color of its small, hooded, yellow flowers is reflected in those of *Hypericum kouytchense* (top right), and *Calceolaria angustifolia* (bottom right).

Recommended partners: *Canna* 'Erebus', *Crocosmia* × *crocosmiiflora* 'Carmin Brillant', *Euphorbia schillingii*, *Hedychium coccineum* 'Tara', *Lobelia cardinalis* 'Queen Victoria'

Campanula takesimana

How it works: *Campanula takesimana* grows best in light to partial shade. At the front of a semi-shady border, the substantial, dusky gray-pink bells of this bellflower harmonize perfectly with clouds of tiny heuchera flowers, providing a contrast of floral form.

Recommended partners: *Ajuga reptans* 'Multicolor', *Astilbe* × *arendsii* 'Venus', *Helictotrichon sempervirens*, *Heuchera* 'Plum Pudding', *Lilium candidum*, *Rodgersia pinnata* 'Superba'

H: 24in (60cm) **S: 18in** (45cm)
❀ **Early to mid-summer**
◊◊ ☐-■ Z5 pH5–7.5

H: 36in (90cm) **S: 18in** (45cm)
❀ **Late summer to mid-autumn**
◊◊ ☐-■ ■ Z7 pH5–7.5

Centaurea montana 'Alba'
WHITE MOUNTAIN KNAPWEED

How it works: In a sunny border in late spring, the boldly shaped flowers of white mountain knapweed (*Centaurea montana* 'Alba'), extravagantly flared outward from their black-netted knops, bring light into this cottage garden mixture of columbines (*Aquilegia vulgaris*) in various colors.

Recommended partners: *Achillea* 'Moonshine', *Artemisia schmidtiana*, *Centranthus ruber*, *Digitalis lutea*, *Kniphofia* 'Atlanta', *Tulipa* 'Elegant Lady'

Chrysanthemum 'Honey'

How it works: The golden amber flowers of the florists' chrysanthemum *C.* 'Honey' combine with the flat, pink flowerheads of *Sedum spectabile* 'Septemberglut' to provide warm tints at the front of a border in early autumn.

H: 18in (45cm) **S: 24in** (60cm)
❀ **Early summer**
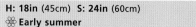 ◊◊ ☐-■ Z3 pH4.5–7.5

H: 24in (60cm) **S: 18in** (45cm)
❀ **Late summer to mid-autumn**
 ◊◊ ☐-■ Z5–9 pH5.5–7

Recommended partners: *Anemone × hybrida* 'Honorine Jobert', *Aster novi-belgii* 'Ada Ballard', *Cortaderia selloana* 'Aureolineata', *Cotinus* 'Flame', *Dahlia* 'Requiem', *Rhus × pulvinata* Autumn Lace Group, *Schizostylis coccinea* 'Major'

Coreopsis 'Sterntaler'

How it works: Although *Achillea* 'Coronation Gold' is rather taller than *Coreopsis* 'Sterntaler', it nods down to mingle with its companion, their golden yellow flowerheads producing a close color harmony. 'Sterntaler' makes fine, long-lasting cut flowers.

Recommended partners: *Aconitum napellus, Delphinium* 'Blue Nile', *Geranium* 'Johnson's Blue', *G. psilostemon, Hakonechloa macra* 'Alboaurea', *Helictotrichon sempervirens*

H & S: 16in (40cm)
❀ Late spring to late summer
 ◊-◊◊ ☐-▣ Z4 pH5.5–7.5

Cortaderia selloana 'Sunningdale Silver'

How it works: The magnificent, stiffly upright pampas grass *Cortaderia selloana* 'Sunningdale Silver' rises above *Cosmos bipinnatus* in a floriferous non-dwarf selection. Such tall cultivars have drawbacks of late flowering and early collapse, as seen here in late October, after only two weeks of full flowering: it must have a sheltered site, free of direct wind or turbulence. Alternatives for summer include: 'Icalma' (variable, to 6½ft/2m, early summer to late autumn, small, mousy plumes, bluish foliage; a clump in flower resembles a collection of rats impaled on sticks, never lovely but worse when wet); 'Patagonia' (variable, about 5ft/1.5m, early summer to late autumn, fuller plumes ageing to grayish fawn, bluish foliage); and 'Andes Silver' (rather better, 6ft/1.8m, mid-summer to mid-autumn, plumes emerging silver, attractively shaggy and very mobile but soon aging to grayish fawn). The best move freely in the breeze, adding movement to any planting, and make splendid accents.

Recommended partners: *Anemone* × *hybrida* 'Elegans', *Canna indica* 'Purpurea', *Dahlia* 'David Howard', *Ensete ventricosum* 'Maurelii'

H: 10ft (3m) S: 6ft (1.8m)

✾ **Mid-autumn to early winter**

 ◇·◇◇ ☐-■ **Z7 pH4.5–8**

Crocosmia × *crocosmiiflora* 'Lady Hamilton'

How it works: Among the many cultivars of the montbretia *Crocosmia* × *crocosmiiflora*, 'Lady Hamilton' is one of the finest and is an ideal candidate for including in planting schemes where hot, strong colors – bright yellows, golds, and rich scarlets – prevail. It is also very attractive with the softer tones of peach and apricot, as well as bronze foliage. In this scheme, its soft orange flowers combine effectively with bright yellow *Rudbeckia fulgida* var. *deamii* in a bold, long-lasting, mid-summer to early autumn scheme. The two contrast not only in the color of their flowers but in flower and foliage shape.

Recommended partners: *Aralia elata* 'Aureovariegata', *Hypericum forrestii*, *Persicaria amplexicaulis*, *Rosa glauca*, *Stipa calamagrostis*

H: 20–36in (50–90cm) **S: 9in** (23cm)
✿ **Mid-summer to early autumn**
◊◊ ☐-■ Z5–8 pH5–7.5

Crocosmia × *crocosmiiflora* 'Solfatare'

How it works: *Crocosmia* × *crocosmiiflora* 'Solfatare' has a softer flower color than many other montbretia cultivars. Here, the orange-yellow flowers and bronze-flushed leaves combine well with *Sedum telephium* 'Arthur Branch'. *S. t.* subsp. *maximum* 'Atropurpureum', its glaucous leaves and stems flushed deep purple, also makes an effective companion. Ornamental grasses, preferably with plain green leaves, can be planted among groups of montbretias.

Recommended partners: *Aralia elata* 'Aureovariegata', *Hypericum forrestii*, *Persicaria amplexicaulis*, *Rosa glauca*, *Stipa calamagrostis*

Crocosmia 'Lucifer'

How it works: The widely planted *Crocosmia* 'Lucifer' is a deserved favorite for including in exotic foliage displays. To be really effective it needs to be planted in bold groups or drifts. Here, it combines well with the pinkish purple flowers of a perennial mallow (*Malva sylvestris* subsp. *mauritanica*) and the sword-like leaves of New Zealand flax (*Phormium tenax*). Various phormiums would also make good companions, especially the bronze- or purple-leaved cultivars.

Recommended partners: *Dahlia* 'Arabian Night', *Helenium* 'Wyndley', *Hemerocallis fulva* 'Flore Pleno', *Monarda* 'Adam'

H: 20–36in (50–90cm) S: 9in (23cm)
❈ Mid-summer to early autumn
 Z5–8 pH5–7.5

H: 4ft (1.2m) S: 9in (23cm)
❈ Mid-summer
 Z5 pH5–7.5

Delphinium 'Alice Artindale'

How it works: The intricate blue pompon florets of *Delphinium* 'Alice Artindale', borne on a narrow, erect spike, are given an effective backdrop by golden hops (*Humulus lupulus* 'Aureus'), trained against a wall.

Recommended partners: *Achillea* 'Moonshine', *Galega orientalis*, *Hesperis matronalis* 'Lilacina Flore Pleno', *Lupinus* 'Polar Princess', *Onopordum nervosum*, *Rosa* 'Fantin-Latour'

H: **5ft** (1.5m) S: **24 in** (60cm)
❀ **Early to mid-summer**
◊◊ □-■ Z3 pH5–7.5

Delphinium 'Sabrina'

How it works: Although many delphiniums would be too tall to interact with the Peruvian lily *Alstroemeria* 'Vesuvius', the relatively short *Delphinium* 'Sabrina' is slightly taller and contrasts strikingly with its rich vermilion flowers.

Recommended partners: *Achillea* 'Coronation Gold', *Baptisia australis*, *Campanula persicifolia*, *Iris* 'Jane Phillips', *Philadelphus* 'Beauclerk', *Rosa* 'Maigold'

H: **4ft** (1.2m) S: **24in** (60cm)
❀ **Early to mid-summer**
◊◊ □-■ Z3 pH5–7.5

Delphinium 'Sungleam'

How it works: The vertical spikes of *Delphinium* 'Sungleam', with its soft pale butter-yellow blooms, are echoed by the upright racemes of golden-flowered, dark-stemmed *Ligularia stenocephala*. The round flowerheads of the giant scabious (*Cephalaria gigantea*) exactly match the delphinium in color, while on the wall behind, pineapple broom (*Cytisus battandieri*) also has upright, albeit shorter, yellow racemes, unifying the design.

Recommended partners: *Baptisia australis, Crambe maritima, Kniphofia* 'Goldelse', *Philadelphus coronarius* 'Aureus', *Potentilla fruticosa* 'Primrose Beauty', *Rosa* Graham Thomas ('Ausmas'), *Sambucus nigra* 'Aurea'

H: 5ft (1.5m) S: 24in (60cm)
❀ **Early to mid-summer**
Z3 pH5–7.5

Dianthus Allwoodii Alpinus Group

How it works: A bed of China roses, including *Rosa* 'Hermosa', is underplanted with mixed pinks (*Dianthus* Allwoodii Alpinus Group). The pinks have attractive glaucous foliage and include exactly the same range of colors as the roses, providing neat furnishing between and in front of them. They are distinguished by compact growth, freedom from disease, and a long flowering season.

Recommended partners: *Ajuga reptans* 'Atropurpurea', *Artemisia schmidtiana, Euphorbia seguieriana* subsp. *niciciana, Lavandula angustifolia* 'Hidcote', *Rosa* 'Cécile Brünner'

H: 6in (15cm) S: 12–18in (30–45cm)
❀ **Early to mid-summer**
 Z4 pH5.5–8

Dianthus 'Haytor White'

How it works: In this carpet of white flowers with silvery and white-variegated foliage, *Dianthus* 'Haytor White' supplies abundant bloom in front of the neatly white-edged evergreen spindle, *Euonymus fortunei* 'Emerald Gaiety'. The tall-stemmed flowers of this pink are sweetly scented.

Recommended partners: *Diascia barberae* 'Ruby Field', *Festuca glauca*, *Geum* 'Mrs J. Bradshaw', *Iris sibirica* 'White Swirl', *I.* 'Symphony', *Lavandula lanata*, *Papaver orientale* 'Cedric Morris', *Rosa* 'Frensham', *R.* Iceberg ('Korbin')

H: 18in (45cm) S: 16in (40cm)
✿ **Early summer to early autumn**
◊-◊◊ ☐-■ Z4 pH5.5–8

Diascia barberae 'Blackthorn Apricot'

How it works: *Diascia barberae* 'Blackthorn Apricot' flowers freely at the foot of a clump of *Astrantia major* 'Sunningdale Variegated', whose bright leaf edges darken to green once spring passes into summer. The apricot-pink diascia harmonizes with the astrantia's pink-flushed flowers.

Recommended partners: *Alchemilla mollis*, *Cerinthe major* var. *purpurascens*, *Eryngium giganteum*, *Helichrysum petiolare*, *Lavandula angustifolia* 'Hidcote', *Plectranthus argentatus*

H: 10in (25cm) S: 20in (50cm)
✿ **Early summer to early autumn**
◊◊ ☐-■ Z8 pH5.5–7.5

Diascia barberae 'Ruby Field'

How it works: In a steeply banked planting, coral-pink *Diascia barberae* 'Ruby Field' furnishes the base of *Penstemon* 'Schoenholzeri', whose colorful racemes of flowers fill the gap at the foot of a wall-trained *Carpenteria californica*. Like most other diascias, its slightly sprawling growth benefits from shearing after the first flush of blooms.

Recommended partners: *Euphorbia schillingii, Penstemon* 'Pennington Gem', *Phygelius aequalis* 'Yellow Trumpet', *P. × rectus* 'Salmon Leap', *Rosa* 'Yesterday'

H: 10in (25cm) S: 20in (50cm)
✽ **Early summer to early autumn**
◊◊ ☐-▪ Z8 pH5.5–7.5

Digitalis lutea
STRAW FOXGLOVE

How it works: In an appealing association for a lightly shaded position, the pale yellow flowers of *Digitalis lutea* are offset by the spidery, deep blue heads of mountain knapweed (*Centaurea montana*). Although less showy than *D. grandiflora*, straw foxglove has a compelling elegance.

Recommended partners: *Astrantia major* 'Sunningdale Variegated', *Corydalis flexuosa, Dryopteris affinis, Geranium* 'Johnson's Blue', *Meconopsis betonicifolia, Milium effusum* 'Aureum'

H: 24in (60cm) S: 12in (30cm)
✽ **Early to mid-summer**
◊◊ ▪ ■ Z4 pH5.5–7.5

Echinacea pallida
PALE PURPLE CONEFLOWER

How it works: *Echinacea pallida*, like its cousin *E. purpurea*, is well suited to the prairie or New Perennial style of planting. Here, it is mingled with *Knautia macedonica* to produce a harmony of color with flowers of contrasting form. The spidery blooms have great character and elegance but lack the substance or flower power of *E. purpurea*. Echinaceas are not blessed with good foliage and so are suited to the large-scale massing offered by the New Perennial style, allowing the effect to be produced by the repeated pattern of blooms only, massed densely or sparsely, sometimes alone, sometimes intermingled with companion plants. In such situations, the foliage is scarcely noticed. The effect produced perhaps works best when seen from a distance rather than at close range. The partners suggested for each echinacea might equally be used for one of the others.

Recommended partners: *Achillea* 'Summerwine', *A.* 'Taygetea', *Aconitum* × *cammarum* 'Bicolor', *A.* × *c.* 'Eleanora', *Agastache rugosa* f. *albiflora*, *Aster* × *frikartii* 'Mönch', *A.* 'Little Carlow', *A. pilosus* var. *pringlei* 'Monte Cassino', *Aster turbinellus* hort., *Calamagrostis* × *acutiflora* 'Stricta', *C. brachytricha*

H: 4ft (1.2m) S: 18in (45cm)
✿ **Mid-summer to early autumn**

 ◊◊ ☐-▧ Z5 pH5.5–7.5

Echinacea purpurea
PURPLE CONEFLOWER

How it works: In a border of mainly mauve-pink flowers, the slightly coarse but handsome *Echinacea purpurea* provides bold floral shape behind a froth of tiny blooms of *Heuchera villosa* 'Palace Purple', with *Lychnis coronaria* Oculata Group, large heads of *Phlox maculata*, and the narrow, dark spikes of *Persicaria amplexicaulis* 'Atrosanguinea'.

Recommended partners: *Chamerion angustifolium* 'Album', *Cirsium rivulare* 'Atropurpureum', *Cleome hassleriana* 'Helen Campbell', *Consolida* 'Frosted Skies', *Cotinus coggygria* 'Royal Purple', *Eupatorium maculatum* (Atropurpureum Group) 'Orchard Dene'

H: 24–48in (60–120cm) **S: 18in** (45cm)
✻ **Mid-summer to mid-autumn**
 ◊◊ ▪ **Z3 pH5.5–7.5**

Echinacea purpurea '*Magnus*'

How it works: The purple coneflower *Echinacea purpurea* 'Magnus', which blooms quite freely, is here joined by the smaller, harmoniously colored flowers of *Verbena bonariensis* and *Aster × frikartii*.

Recommended partners: *Gaura lindheimeri*, *Geranium* 'Blue Cloud', *Gillenia trifoliata*, *Helenium* 'Kupferzwerg', *Lychnis coronaria* 'Alba', *Lythrum salicaria* 'Feuerkerze', *Miscanthus sinensis* 'China', *Monarda* 'Prärienacht', *Sidalcea* 'Elsie Heugh'

Elymus magellanicus

How it works: In a simple but effective combination of cool colors and contrasting form, the narrow blue-green leaves of *Elymus magellanicus* arch gracefully in front of mauve-flowered musk mallow (*Malva moschata*). Unlike other elymus, this short-lived perennial grass is relatively small and lax in habit, and it prefers cool summers.

Recommended partners: *Achillea* 'Moonshine', *Eschscholzia caespitosa* 'Sundew', *Geranium* 'Mavis Simpson', *Ophiopogon planiscapus* 'Nigrescens'

H: 24–48in (60–120cm) S: 18in (45cm)
✿ Mid-summer to mid-autumn
◊◊ ▓ Z3 pH5.5–7.5

H: 6in (15cm) S: 18in (45cm)
✿ Early to late summer
◊◊ □-▓ Z4 pH5.5–7.5

Erigeron 'Gaiety'

How it works: The bright pink flowers
of the fleabane *Erigeron* 'Gaiety' and the
magenta blooms of rose campion (*Lychnis
coronaria*) are borne at the same height and
mingle together attractively if plants of
each are grown close to each other.

Recommended partners: *Artemisia alba*
'Canescens', *Ballota pseudodictamnus*,
Eryngium × *tripartitum*, *Euphorbia
seguieriana* subsp. *niciciana*, *Festuca glauca*
'Elijah Blue'

Erodium trifolium

How it works: The fairly sprawling
Erodium trifolium will scramble into
shrubby, yellow-flowered *Halimium
lasianthum* to add its flowers to those
of its support. Both like a sunny, well-
drained site.

Recommended partners: *Dianthus*
Allwoodii Alpinus Group, *Festuca glauca*
'Elijah Blue', *Geranium* × *antipodeum*
'Chocolate Candy', *Lysimachia nummularia*
'Aurea', *Molinia caerulea* 'Variegata'

H: 10–30in (25–75cm) S: 12in (30cm)
❀ **Early to mid-summer**
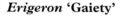 ◊◊ ☐-▓ Z5 pH5.5–7.5

H: 12in (30cm) S: 18in (45cm)
❀ **Early to late summer**
 ◊ ☐ Z8 pH6–8

Eryngium alpinum

How it works: The exquisitely shaped flowerheads of *Eryngium alpinum* are perhaps most effectively displayed against a simple, contrasting background, as provided here by *Berberis thunbergii* 'Rose Glow'.

Recommended partners: *Achillea* 'Taygetea', *Cotinus coggygria* 'Royal Purple', *Geranium pratense* 'Plenum Violaceum', *Lythrum virgatum* 'The Rocket', *Miscanthus sinensis* 'Strictus', *Phormium* 'Bronze Baby', *Phygelius* × *rectus*

Eryngium bourgatii 'Picos Blue'

How it works: The color of *Eryngium bourgatii* 'Picos Blue' is strong enough to contrast with yellow-green dogwood (*Cornus alba* 'Aurea'). The small blooms mean that the eryngium is best seen at close quarters.

Recommended partners: *Berberis thunbergii* 'Aurea', *Iris sibirica* 'Harpswell Happiness', *Phalaris arundinacea* var. *picta* 'Feesey', *Philadelphus coronarius* 'Aureus', *Phormium* 'Yellow Wave', *Potentilla fruticosa* 'Primrose Beauty', *Sisyrinchium striatum* 'Aunt May'

H: 20–30in (50–75cm) S: 18in (45cm)
✿ Mid-summer to early autumn
◊ ☐ Z5 pH5.5–7.5

H: 18in (45cm) S: 12in (30cm)
✿ Mid- to late summer
◊ ☐ Z5 pH5.5–7.5

Eryngium maritimum
SEA HOLLY

How it works: The silvery blooms of *Eryngium maritimum*, here supported by encircling *Lavandula angustifolia*, are strikingly decorative.

Recommended partners: *Achillea* Anthea ('Anblo'), *Convolvulus cneorum*, *C. sabatius*, *Dianthus* 'Doris', *Helictotrichon sempervirens*, *Miscanthus sinensis* 'Zebrinus', *Tamarix ramosissima* 'Pink Cascade'

H & S: 12in (30cm)
✿ Mid- to late summer
  ◊ ☐ Z5 pH5.5–7.5

Eryngium × *tripartitum*

How it works:

Above: Even before its stems and flowerheads flush blue, the pale, glaucous *Eryngium* × *tripartitum* makes an effective display against blue *Salvia* × *superba*.

Left: The wiry habit of *E.* × *tripartitum* allows it to support scrambling plants such as *Rehmannia elata* and the cranesbill *Geranium* × *riversleaianum* 'Russell Prichard'.

Recommended partners: *Achillea* 'Moonshine', *Allium sphaerocephalon*, *Eupatorium maculatum* 'Atropurpureum', *Geranium* 'Ann Folkard', *Hemerocallis* 'Golden Chimes', *Miscanthus sinensis* 'Morning Light'

H: 30in (75cm) S: 18in (45cm)

✿ **Mid-summer to early autumn**

 ◊ ☐ **Z5 pH5.5–7.5**

Eupatorium maculatum Atropurpureum Group

How it works: The creamy plumes of *Artemisia lactiflora* provide a contrast of form next to the rounded, dusky pink heads of *Eupatorium maculatum* Atropurpureum Group. 'Orchard Dene' (6½ft/2m) and 'Riesenschirm' (5ft/1.5m) are superior selections.

Recommended partners: *Aconitum napellus* subsp. *vulgare* 'Carneum', *Anemone* × *hybrida* 'Lady Gilmour', *Cortaderia selloana* 'Pumila', *Sedum* 'Herbstfreude'

H: 5–8ft (1.5–2.5m) S: 40in–5ft (1–1.5m) z5
❀ Mid-summer to early autumn pH5.5–7.5

Euphorbia schillingii

How it works: *Euphorbia schillingii* makes an impressive and colorful statement in mixed and herbaceous borders. Here, it contrasts strikingly with scarlet Jerusalem cross (*Lychnis chalcedonica*) in midsummer.

Recommended partners: *Asclepias tuberosa*, *Cerinthe major* var. *purpurascens*, *Helictotrichon sempervirens*, *Hosta sieboldiana* var. *elegans*, *Lobelia siphilitica*, *Ruta graveolens* 'Jackman's Blue', *Salvia nemorosa* 'Ostfriesland'

H: 36in (90cm) S: 24in (60cm)
❀ Mid-summer to mid-autumn
Z8 pH5–7.5

Euphorbia seguieriana subsp. *niciciana*

How it works: In a gravel garden, *Euphorbia seguieriana* subsp. *niciciana* provides contrasting color and variety of form with purple *Salvia nemorosa* 'Ostfriesland' and white sun rose *Helianthemum* 'The Bride'.

Recommended partners: *Allium cristophii*, *Crocosmia* 'Lucifer', *Festuca glauca* 'Elijah Blue', *Heuchera* 'Plum Pudding', *Nepeta* 'Six Hills Giant', *Leymus arenarius*, *Miscanthus sinensis* 'Zebrinus', *Monarda* 'Prärienacht'

H: 20in (50cm) S: 18in (45cm)
❀ Early summer to early autumn
◊ ☐ Z8 pH5.5–8

Filipendula 'Kahome'

How it works: This hybrid meadowsweet suits bog gardens, waterside sites, and beds or borders that do not dry out. In this mid-summer waterside planting, the feathery, rich rose-pink flowerheads of *Filipendula* 'Kahome' provide a contrast of form with the delicately colored daylily *Hemerocallis* 'Dresden Dream'.

Recommended partners: *Carex grayi*, *Hosta fortunei* 'Francee', *Iris pseudacorus* 'Variegata', *Lythrum salicaria* 'Morden Pink', *Phalaris arundinacea* var. *picta* 'Feesey'

H: 16in (40cm) S: 18in (45cm)
❀ Mid- to late summer
◊◊ ☐-☐ Z4 pH5–7.5

Foeniculum vulgare
COMMON FENNEL

How it works: In this mixture of herbs, a pleasing effect is achieved solely through the use of different kinds of foliage. The feathery leaves of fennel and bronze fennel (*Foeniculum vulgare* and 'Purpureum') are joined by the larger, bolder leaflets of angelica (*A. archangelica*) and by the narrow-leaved Spanish sage (*Salvia lavandulifolia*).

Recommended partners: *Achillea* 'Coronation Gold', *Dahlia* 'Glorie van Heemstede', *Geranium* × *oxonianum* f. *thurstonianum*, *Hedychium coccineum* 'Tara', *Rosa* 'Climbing Paul Lédé'

H: 6ft (1.8m) S: 20in (50cm)
✿ Mid- to late summer
◊-◊◊ ☐-■ Z4 pH5.5–8

Gentiana asclepiadea
WILLOW GENTIAN

How it works: *Gentiana asclepiadea* is one of the easiest gentians to grow. Here, its intense, deep pure blue flowers stand out dramatically against the yellow-green foliage of *Rubus cockburnianus* 'Goldenvale'. Grown in light shade, the rubus leaves remain bright and avoid being scorched by the sun.

Recommended partners: *Anemone* × *hybrida* 'Honorine Jobert', *Geranium* 'Johnson's Blue', *Hedera helix* 'Buttercup', *Hosta* 'Sum and Substance', *Lilium lancifolium* var. *splendens*

H: 36in (90cm) S: 24in (60cm)
✿ Mid-summer to early autumn
◊◊ ☐-■ Z6 pH5–7.5

Geraniums

Geraniums, or cranesbills, are among the most popular herbaceous plants, reflecting their versatility and prettiness, and the fact that they are generally easy to cultivate. Many grow naturally in dappled shade in woods or hedgerows. Others are meadow plants, upright in habit and suitable for a herbaceous border. Some are scramblers, able to weave through shrubs and across banks or providing good ground cover. There are hummock-forming alpine species, superb for a gravel garden, rock garden, or (the easier ones) the front of a border. A few, such as the monocarpic, tender *G. maderense* and the rather hardier, longer-lived *G. palmatum*, are not herbaceous but form bold rosettes of leaves borne on a woody stem. There are also some annuals, although these tend to be rather straggly with tiny flowers.

The flowers of geraniums are cool-colored, from soft lavender-blue to magenta and paler tints to white; they are often attractively veined – dramatic black on magenta, for example. The blooms are borne scattered across the clump, seldom in such profusion that they overwhelm their neighbors, making them ideal in a supporting role to stars of the border such as delphiniums, peonies, or old roses. One exception is *G.* × *magnificum*, which for a brief couple of weeks can produce a solid sheet of blue capable of disrupting the balance with and between its companions, unless used in a scattered drift or grown in partial shade to control its flower production. There is a handful of *G. pratense* cultivars that have double flowers; although these perhaps lack the pleasing simplicity of the single blooms, they have their own charm and are longer-lasting.

The foliage is usually tidy and respectable, without showing any strong

Deep pink *Geranium* × *oxonianum* f. *thurstonianum* and lavender-blue *G. ibericum* mingle harmoniously in this border planting, with contrasting iris leaves and the erect, deep blue spikes of *Veronica austriaca* subsp. *teucrium*.

form or texture, which must be supplied by companion plants such as irises, daylilies, or grasses. There are some silvery-leaved sorts, and chocolate- or purple-leaved cultivars are on the increase. Most are sufficiently late-leafing to be underplanted with spring bulbs or with wood anemones and celandines.

Many geraniums are excellent when used as ground cover, although the vigor and ultimate size of the chosen sort need to be carefully tailored to the neighboring plants. While smaller kinds such as *G. × cantabrigiense* are not problematic, the larger *G. macrorrhizum* and *G. × oxonianum* cultivars are so large and vigorous that they can suppress nearby roses – for example. *G. procurrens* is beautiful but irrepressible, rooting wherever it touches the ground and only practical where there is plenty of space.

Deadheading is usually desirable to keep the clumps looking tidy, prevent excess seedlings, and maintain good basal foliage. Snapping off the spent flower stems within the dome of foliage leaves no trace of interference. However, cutting the whole group to the ground with shears may be simpler. New foliage is usually produced within a couple of weeks.

An informal mix using cranesbills in a sunny glade, including pale grayish blue *Geranium pratense* 'Mrs Kendall Clark' (foreground and center), magenta *G. psilostemon*, and rich blue *G. × magnificum*, with cardoons (*Cynara cardunculus*), delphiniums, lupins, and poppies.

Geranium 'Ann Folkard'

How it works: *Geranium* 'Ann Folkard' is a plant that will sprawl through its neighbors, drawing them into a unified whole. Its flowers contrast with its foliage: combining it with the mauve blooms of *Allium cristophii* and yellow-green leaves of golden marjoram (*Origanum vulgare* 'Aureum') gives a scheme in which all the flowers contrast with all the leaves.

This cranesbill has black-veined magenta flowers and contrasting yellow-green leaves. It gives its most dazzling display when newly in bloom, especially when set against yellow-green foliage and flowers such as euphorbias or *Alchemilla mollis*, pale yellow plants such as some achilleas, or carmine or crimson flowers. Leaves are at their brightest in sun. This versatile cultivar is most suitable for ground cover or as a carpet through which other plants can be grown.

Recommended partners: *Anthemis tinctoria*, *Artemisia stelleriana* 'Boughton Silver', *Cytisus nigricans*, *Deschampsia cespitosa*, *Geranium sylvaticum* 'Mayflower', *Heuchera villosa* 'Palace Purple', *Lilium* 'Joy', *Populus alba* 'Richardii', *Rhus* × *pulvinata* Autumn Lace Group, *Rosa* 'De Rescht'

H: 24in (60cm) **S: 36in** (90cm)
✿ **Mid-summer to mid-autumn**

◊◊ ☐-■ **Z5 pH5–7.5**

Geranium × *antipodeum* 'Chocolate Candy'

How it works: The variety of flower and foliage sizes and colors adds interest to this pretty mixture of three cranesbills, in which bright pink *G.* × *antipodeum* 'Chocolate Candy', soft pink *Geranium* 'Dusky Crûg', and soft magenta *G. psilostemon* 'Bressingham Flair' all harmonize agreeably.

This cultivar is suitable for rock gardens and sunny borders with good drainage, where it associates most easily with plants from a similar climate and needing similar conditions – plants from New Zealand or the Chilean Andes, for example. Its deeply colored foliage looks best in a forward position, mixed with black mondo grass, heucheras, and other dark-leaved cranesbills such as *G. pratense* Midnight Reiter strain. Its flowers are a strong enough pink to contrast with yellow-green flowers or, even more dramatically, with silver foliage, and they also associate well with crimson and other cool colors such as mauve, lilac, or purple.

Recommended partners: *Artemisia alba* 'Canescens', *Celmisia spectabilis*, *Hebe ochracea*, *Heuchera* 'Plum Pudding', *Ophiopogon planiscapus* 'Nigrescens', *Spiraea japonica* 'Goldflame'

H: 10in (25cm) **S: 20in** (50cm)
❀ **Early summer to early autumn**
◊◊ ☐-■ **Z8 pH5.5–7.5**

Geranium 'Brookside'

How it works: *Geranium* 'Brookside' and *Ammi majus* combine together perfectly, their heights matching and the filigree of the ammi making a contrast of floral form with the cranesbill. For this combination, the ammi should be sown in spring: if allowed to self-sow or if sown in autumn, it would overtop the cranesbill and finish flowering too early. Some brushwood support, worked through the base of the cranesbill, would help it remain upright throughout its flowering season. The rich blue of the cranesbill is strong enough to allow this gently pretty scheme to be made altogether more punchy by adding boldly shaped flowers or foliage in a contrasting color such as lemon or yellow-green. The cranesbill also harmonizes effectively with glaucous, silver, or purple foliage and with cool-colored flowers. It can mingle charmingly with annuals of a similar height.

Recommended partners: *Achillea* 'Lucky Break', *Agrostemma gracile* 'Snow Queen', *Anethum graveolens* 'Mariska', *Consolida* 'Snow Cloud', *Eryngium giganteum* 'Silver Ghost', *Filipendula ulmaria* 'Aurea', *Galega* × *hartlandii* 'Candida', *Gypsophila elegans* 'White Elephant', *Hemerocallis* 'Marion Vaughn', *Leucanthemum* × *superbum* 'Aglaia'

H: 24in (60cm) **S: 5ft** (1.5m)
✿ **Early to late summer**
◇◇ ☐-☐ Z5 pH5–7.5

Geranium × *cantabrigiense* 'Cambridge'

How it works: *Geranium* × *cantabrigiense* 'Cambridge', grown through gravel to edge a bed, is infiltrated by variegated apple mint, *Mentha suaveolens* 'Variegata'. The cream edges to the mint's leaves highlight their shape, producing a pleasing pattern.

Recommended partners: *Bergenia* 'Abendglut', *Carex comans* 'Frosted Curls', *Dryopteris affinis*, *Festuca glauca* 'Elijah Blue', *Heuchera cylindrica* 'Greenfinch', × *Heucherella alba* 'Rosalie', *Lilium* 'Joy', *Molinia caerulea* 'Variegata', *Rosa glauca*

H: 12in (30cm) **S: 24in** (60cm)
✿ **Early to mid-summer**
◇◇ ☐-☐ Z5 pH5–7.5

Geranium 'Johnson's Blue'

How it works: *Geranium* 'Johnson's Blue' is a superlative and floriferous mound-forming plant for the front of beds and borders, flowering profusely over several months, especially if grown in a fairly sunny situation. In this scheme, it is used to furnish beneath Jerusalem sage (*Phlomis fruticosa*), providing a contrast of color and floral form.

Recommended partners: *Allium hollandicum, Centranthus ruber, Filipendula ulmaria* 'Aurea', *Iris chrysographes, Lamium maculatum, Lilium pyrenaicum* var. *pyrenaicum, Rosa* Iceberg ('Korbin')

H: **16in** (40cm) S: **24in** (60cm)
❀ **Early summer to mid-autumn**
◊◊ ☐-▨ **Z4 pH5–7.5**

Geranium 'Mavis Simpson'

How it works: The soft pink flowers and slightly gray foliage of *Geranium* 'Mavis Simpson' are suited to delicately colored schemes and combinations with silvery or glaucous foliage, as here with the contrasting form of the grass *Elymus magellanicus*. 'Mavis Simpson' is a sprawling plant that will also scramble effectively over its neighbors.

Recommended partners: *Achillea* 'Moonshine', *Dianthus* 'Doris', *Eryngium* × *tripartitum, Festuca glauca* 'Elijah Blue', *Heuchera villosa* 'Palace Purple', *Lilium speciosum*

H: **9in** (23cm) S: **40in** (1m)
❀ **Early summer to early autumn**
◊◊ ☐-▨ **Z6 pH5.5–7.5**

Geranium × oxonianum f. *thurstonianum*

How it works: The dusky magenta-pink flowers of the cranesbill *Geranium × oxonianum* f. *thurstonianum* harmonize with feathery bronze fennel (*Foeniculum vulgare* 'Purpureum'). The squirting cucumber (*Ecballium elaterium*) provides foliage interest in front, while the white flowers of the love-in-a-mist *Nigella damascena* 'Miss Jekyll Alba' leaven the whole.

Recommended partners: *Cotinus coggygria* 'Royal Purple', *Dicentra eximia*, *Hebe stenophylla*, *Hosta* 'Sum and Substance', *Kniphofia* 'Atlanta', *Philadelphus* 'Beauclerk'

H: 31in (80cm) S: 30in (75cm)
Late spring to mid-autumn
Z5 pH4.5–8

Geranium pratense 'Mrs Kendall Clark'

How it works: The streaked, soft blue flowers of the meadow cranesbill *Geranium pratense* 'Mrs Kendall Clark' are contrasted with the yellow-green inflorescences of cypress spurge (*Euphorbia cyparissias*). A deeper blue cranesbill would also be effective. This cultivar is choice enough for a border in sun or partial shade.

Recommended partners: *Achillea millefolium* 'Lilac Beauty', *Artemisia alba* 'Canescens', *Hosta* (Tardiana Group) 'Halcyon', *Miscanthus sinensis* 'Variegatus', *Rosa* 'Buff Beauty'

H: 40in (1m) S: 24in (60cm)
Early to mid-summer
Z4 pH4.5–8

Geranium psilostemon
ARMENIAN CRANESBILL

How it works: In a steeply banked, sunny planting of mainly cool but rich colors, *Geranium psilostemon* grows beneath blush-pink *Rosa* Heritage, with *Sedum* 'Herbstfreude' in front. *Viola* 'Mercury' and *Dianthus* 'Laced Monarch' furnish the front of the border.

Recommended partners: *Hosta sieboldiana* var. *elegans*, *Lathyrus odoratus* 'Matucana', *Miscanthus sinensis* 'Zebrinus', *Phygelius aequalis* 'Yellow Trumpet'

Geranium renardii

How it works: *Geranium renardii*, with its fascinatingly felted and netted sage-green leaves and pale blooms veined with lavender, is an excellent plant for the front of a border, here harmonizing with the coppery flowers of *Geum rivale* 'Leonard's Variety'. It is a plant that deserves to be appreciated at close range.

Recommended partners: *Anthemis tinctoria* 'E. C. Buxton', *Festuca glauca* 'Blaufuchs', *Hebe pinguifolia* 'Pagei', *Nepeta* × *faassenii*, *Salvia officinalis* 'Purpurascens'

H: 40in (1m) S: 24in (60cm)
❋ Early to late summer
◊◊ ☐-■ Z4 pH5–7.5

H & S: 12in (30cm)
❋ Early summer
◊◊ ☐-■ Z6 pH5.5–7.5

Geranium × *riversleaianum* 'Russell Prichard'

How it works: In an attractive partnership for the front of a border, *Geranium* × *riversleaianum* 'Russell Prichard' weaves among the stems of tricolor sage (*Salvia officinalis* 'Tricolor'), its magenta flowers matching the tips of the sage's young shoots.

Recommended partners: *Achillea* 'Moonshine', *Dianthus* 'Doris', *Eryngium* × *tripartitum*, *Festuca glauca* 'Elijah Blue', *Heuchera villosa* 'Palace Purple', *Lilium speciosum*

H: 9in (23cm) S: 40in (1m)
❀ **Early summer to early autumn**
◊◊ ☐-■ **Z6 pH5.5–7.5**

Geranium sanguineum var. *striatum*

How it works: The delicate pink, crimson-veined blooms of *Geranium sanguineum* var. *striatum* show among a tracery of silvery *Artemisia alba* 'Canescens', the artemisia's filigree foliage letting through the light that the cranesbill needs in order to flower.

Recommended partners: *Allium cristophii*, *Berberis thunbergii* 'Atropurpurea Nana', *Dictamnus albus* var. *purpureus*, *Euphorbia schillingii*, *Salvia nemorosa* 'Lubecca'

H: 6in (15cm) S: 8in (20cm)
❀ **Early summer to late autumn**
◊◊ ☐-■ **Z4 pH5.5–7.5**

Geum **'Lady Stratheden'**

How it works: At the peak of their flowering in early summer, *Geum* 'Lady Stratheden', with its rich, soft yellow, ruffled blooms, and scarlet *G.* 'Mrs J. Bradshaw' combine to give a dazzling display. Deep red or yellow-green foliage or blood-red flowers could enhance the effect.

Recommended partners: *Achillea* 'Fanal', *Aconitum* 'Ivorine', *Aquilegia* 'Hensol Harebell', *Geranium* 'Johnson's Blue', *Hakonechloa macra* 'Alboaurea', *Lilium* 'Enchantment', *Phormium* 'Bronze Baby', *Rosa* 'Buff Beauty'

H: 20in (50cm) **S: 24in** (60cm)
❀ **Early summer to early autumn**
▬▬▬ ◇◇ ▦ **Z5 pH5.5–7.5**

Gunnera manicata

How it works: Backed by the elegant, arching canes of the bamboo *Fargesia murielae*, *Gunnera manicata*, often called giant rhubarb, creates an exotic, almost tropical effect. Its leaves are echoed by the much smaller, umbrella-like foliage of *Darmera peltata* that furnishes the front of the planting.

This magnificent monster of a plant can make gardens of more modest size look jungle-like. Its conical flower spikes, 40in (1m) high and covered with frilled, reddish bracts, sometimes nestle beneath the leaves. It revels in moist places, especially waterside sites where reflections double its impact. It is best combined with similarly dramatic plants – bamboos and other large grasses such as arundos or the biggest miscanthus – and with plants of semi-tropical appearance, such as bananas, cannas, colocasias, palms, tetrapanax, the biggest ligularias and eupatoriums, and stooled paulownias or catalpas. Companions should be grouped on a similar scale to avoid being overwhelmed.

Recommended partners: *Canna* 'Erebus', *Catalpa bignonioides* (stooled), *Eupatorium purpureum*, *Hosta sieboldiana* var. *elegans*, *Ligularia stenocephala*, *Miscanthus sacchariflorus*, *Tetrapanax papyrifer* (stooled)

H: 8ft (2.5m) S: 13ft (4m)
❀ **Early summer**
◇◇◇   ▪ Z7 pH5.5–7.5

Gypsophila paniculata 'Compacta Plena'

How it works: The airy, delicate blush flowers of this slow-growing, spreading form of baby's breath (*Gypsophila paniculata* 'Compacta Plena') help to soften the almost too solid color of the annual Chinese pink *Dianthus chinensis* (Princess Series) 'Princess Salmon', in this pretty combination for summer display at the front of a border.

Recommended partners: *Convolvulus cneorum*, *Dahlia* 'Bednall Beauty', *Diascia rigescens*, *Geranium* 'Mavis Simpson', *Helianthemum* 'Ben Hope'

H: 10in (25cm) S: 24in (60cm)
❀ **Mid- to late summer**
◇-◇◇   □-▪ Z4 pH6–8

Hedychium coccineum 'Tara'

How it works: The orange, tropical-looking spikes of *Hedychium coccineum* 'Tara' are here set in a haze of seedheads of common fennel (*Foeniculum vulgare*), beneath the golden honey locust (*Gleditsia triacanthos* 'Sunburst').

Recommended partners: *Alonsoa warscewiczii, Canna* 'Striata', *Kniphofia caulescens, Leonotis leonurus, Phygelius* × *rectus* 'Moonraker', *Salvia coccinea* 'Lady in Red'

H: 6½ft (2m) S: 3ft (90cm)
❀ Late summer to mid-autumn
◌◌ □-■ Z8 pH5.5–7.5

Helenium 'Wyndley'

How it works: In this glowing combination for mid-summer, the flowers of the sneezeweed *Helenium* 'Wyndley', with golden petals shaded warm orange around a mahogany disc, are just overtopped by the vermilion *Crocosmia* 'Lucifer'.

Recommended partners: *Euphorbia sikkimensis, Hosta* 'August Moon', *Kniphofia* 'Wrexham Buttercup', *Miscanthus sinensis* 'Zebrinus', *Tagetes patula* 'Striped Marvel'

H: 24in (60cm) S: 18in (45cm)
❀ Early to late summer
◌◌ □-■ Z4 pH5.5–7.5

Helianthus decapetalus 'Soleil d'Or'

How it works: The rich golden yellow, outward-facing flowers of *Helianthus decapetalus* 'Soleil d'Or', seen here with *Helenium* 'Mahogany', are borne on the upper half of an erect plant, allowing it to punctuate borders with bright highlight.

Recommended partners: *Canna* 'Striata', *Coronilla valentina* subsp. *glauca*, *Hemerocallis fulva* 'Flore Pleno', *Kniphofia rooperi*, *Rosa* Graham Thomas ('Ausmas')

H: 5ft (1.5m) S: 3ft (90cm)
� **Late summer to mid-autumn**
◊◊ □-■ Z5 pH5–7.5

Helictotrichon sempervirens
BLUE OAT GRASS

How it works: The blue-green leaves of *Helictotrichon sempervirens* harmonize with the fleshy foliage of *Sedum spectabile* 'Rosenteller', while contrasting with its rose flowerheads in late summer and early autumn.

Recommended partners: *Achillea* 'Walther Funcke', *Centranthus ruber* 'Albus', *Euphorbia polychroma* 'Major', *E. rigida*, *Geranium* 'Johnson's Blue', *G.* × *oxonianum* 'Wargrave Pink'

H & S: 40in (1m)
✣ **Late spring to midsummer**
◊-◊◊ □-■ Z4 pH6–8

Hemerocallis fulva 'Flore Pleno'

How it works: Daylilies are almost indestructible plants and are invaluable assets in any garden scheme, producing superlative single or double flowers – some deliciously scented – in a wide range of colors, from late spring to late summer depending on the cultivar. In this hot-colored scheme, *Hemerocallis fulva* 'Flore Pleno' harmonizes with vermilion *Crocosmia* 'Lucifer', while the superlative lemon-yellow *Lilium* Citronella Group echoes the flower shape of the daylily. Adding a bronze foliage plant with more-rounded leaves could be effective.

'Flore Pleno' is a double cultivar with a long flowering season. The advantage of double flowers is that the individual florets last for two days, twice as long as those of most single cultivars. Its color – soft orange with deeper red markings at the base, sometimes hidden by other petals – blends well with bronze foliage and flowers in hot colors, such as red, yellow, or orange.

Recommended partners: *Cotinus coggygria* 'Notcutt's Variety', *Iris pallida*, *Kniphofia* 'Bees' Sunset', *Lilium* African Queen Group, *L.* 'Connecticut King', *Lobelia* × *speciosa* 'Cherry Ripe'

H: 30in (75cm) **S: 4ft** (1.2m)
✽ **Mid- to late summer**
○○ □-■ Z3 pH5–7.5

Hemerocallis 'Golden Chimes'

How it works: The rufous-red reverses on the outer petals of *Hemerocallis* 'Golden Chimes' unite this combination with the richly colored *Rosa* Lilli Marlene ('Korlima') and the deep bronze foliage of *Heuchera villosa* 'Palace Purple'.

Recommended partners: *Canna* 'Wyoming', *Dahlia* 'Moonfire', *Fuchsia* 'Thalia', *Phygelius aequalis* 'Yellow Trumpet', *Rosa* Westerland ('Korwest'), *Sisyrinchium striatum* 'Aunt May'

H: 36in (90cm) **S: 24in** (60cm)
✽ **Early to late summer**
○○ □-■ Z4 pH5–7.5

Hemerocallis 'Hyperion'

How it works: Held well above slim, grassy foliage, the elegant, starry flowers of *Hemerocallis* 'Hyperion' seem to leap forward when set against a contrasting background of recessive, soft lavender *Clematis* 'Perle d'Azur'.

Recommended partners: *Agapanthus* 'Lilliput', *Aralia elata* 'Aureovariegata', *Clematis* 'Prince Charles', *Helictotrichon sempervirens*, *Kniphofia* 'David', *Miscanthus sinensis* 'Zebrinus', *Phormium* 'Duet', *Rosa* Benjamin Britten ('Ausencart'), *R.* Grace ('Auskeppy'), *Yucca flaccida* 'Golden Sword'

Hemerocallis 'Sammy Russell'

How it works: *Hemerocallis* 'Sammy Russell' is here combined with *Achillea* 'Coronation Gold', showing the effective use of the achillea's grayish, feathery leaves and flat flowerheads as a contrast for the gently flared blooms of the daylily.

H: 36in (90cm) S: 30in (75cm)
❁ **Midsummer**
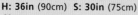 ◊◊ ☐-■ **Z5 pH5–7.5**

H: 6–48in (15–120cm) S: 12–36in (30–90cm)
❁ **Midsummer**
◊◊ ☐-■ **Z5 pH5–7.5**

Cardoons (*Cynara cardunculus*) provide bold, architectural foliage behind.

Recommended partners: *Artemisia ludoviciana, Corylus maxima* 'Purpurea', *Deschampsia cespitosa, Heuchera villosa* 'Palace Purple', *Kniphofia* 'Wrexham Buttercup', *Ligularia dentata* 'Desdemona'

Hemerocallis 'Stafford'

How it works: In a relatively steeply banked border, tall stems of *Achillea filipendulina* 'Gold Plate' provide a contrast of floral and foliage form with the rich red *Hemerocallis* 'Stafford'. They are backed by purple smoke bush (*Cotinus coggygria* 'Royal Purple'), whose foliage harmonizes perfectly with the daylily.

Recommended partners: *Artemisia ludoviciana, Corylus maxima* 'Purpurea', *Deschampsia cespitosa, Heuchera villosa* 'Palace Purple', *Kniphofia* 'Wrexham Buttercup', *Ligularia dentata* 'Desdemona'

H: 6–48in (15–120cm) **S: 12–36in** (30–90cm)
❀ **Midsummer**
◊◊ ☐-■ **Z5 pH5–7.5**

Heuchera 'Rachel'

How it works: The warm yet not too strongly colored leaves of *Heuchera* 'Rachel' work well with cool flowers such as this white musk mallow (*Malva moschata* f. *alba*). Warm "fruity" colors of high summer also make effective partners for this heuchera.

Recommended partners: *Allium cristophii*, *Festuca glauca* 'Elijah Blue', *Geranium* × *riversleaianum* 'Russell Prichard', *Rosa* Pink Bells ('Poulbells'), *Stachys byzantina*, *Tulipa* 'Burgundy'

H: **12in** (30cm) S: **18–24in** (45–60cm)
✿ **Early to late summer Z4 pH5.5–7.5**

Heuchera villosa '**Palace Purple**'

How it works: Chosen for outstanding leaf color, *Heuchera villosa* 'Palace Purple' is a handsome plant with metallic, deep coppery bronze foliage. At its best, this is glistening and sumptuously dark and, as here, makes a fine contrast with the yellow-green leaves of *Geranium* 'Ann Folkard'. Sprawling *G.* × *riversleaianum* 'Russell Prichard' furnishes in front, its flowers a touch paler than those of 'Ann Folkard' but in perfect harmony.

This popular heuchera enjoys a position in sun or partial shade and can be grown in the front of a border, in a lightly shaded woodland garden, or as ground cover. It associates well with late spring bedding, providing a foil for lighter or brighter bulbs and biennials. The tiny heuchera flowers are borne in airy sprays, but their brownish buff color is neither showy nor effective. If they detract from the impact of the foliage, the stems can be removed as they start to develop.

Recommended partners: *Achillea* 'Lachsschönheit', *Aralia elata* 'Aureovariegata', *Echinacea purpurea*, *Hemerocallis* 'Golden Chimes', *Pelargonium* 'Paul Crampel', *Rosa* Sweet Dream ('Fryminicot')

H: **20in** (50cm) S: **18in** (45cm)
✿ **Late spring to early summer**

Z4 pH5.5–7.5

Hostas

Hostas, or plantain lilies, are immensely popular plants for shade, and several thousand new varieties have been developed in the last few decades. They are useful especially for their tiny or exotically large foliage, which can be green, glaucous, or yellow-green, often variegated with white or yellow. Most also flower prolifically, the beauty of the blooms sometimes rivalling that of the leaves. Some hostas, such as *H. plantaginea* and its hybrids, have the added bonus of fragrant flowers.

All hostas grow well in partial shade and some even in full shade; some can take full sun, although variegated or yellow-green kinds can become scorched. Hostas are superlative plants for a woodland garden and are excellent for beds and borders, but they can look unnaturally exotic in a wild garden. Particularly associated with Japanese gardens, they look at home with other Japanese plants with contrasting foliage, including bamboos, smaller maples, moisture-loving irises, primulas, sedges, ferns, and hydrangeas. Hostas work well when underplanted with late winter or spring bulbs, wood anemones, or celandines – as the bulbs enter their summer dormancy, the hosta's leaves unfurl to hide their dying foliage. They are also excellent in containers, where they are perhaps most effective planted alone, with harmonies or contrasts provided by different subjects in adjacent pots.

In small gardens, the biggest sorts, such as *H. sieboldiana* and its hybrids, tend to be too large for general use or ground cover, although they are useful as strong accents, repeated if necessary at intervals along a border. Similarly, variegated or yellow-green cultivars can be rather strident if used to excess, although they too make effective accents; green- or glaucous-leaved hostas are perhaps the best for extensive plantings such as ground cover. The tiniest species and cultivars are well suited to small-scale schemes and to groupings that are to be viewed at close range.

Some, especially the largest-leaved sorts, can take up to five years to adopt their full size and characteristic habit. Conversely, if left many years without division, the leaves can become congested and reduced in size, obscuring the shape of individual leaves. Tiny species such as *H. venusta*, often dismissed for use as ground cover because so many plants are needed for a reasonably sized group, can be propagated by division up to three times a year, even in full growth, provided the offsets are kept moist. In fact, the neat, dark green leaves and entrancing flowers of this species make it exceptionally beautiful for large drifts of ground cover.

Slugs and snails can ruin the effect of hostas, particularly those with delicate, thin leaves, and should be controlled.

This planting, which consists mainly of hostas, including (clockwise from right) the cream-edged *H. fortunei* 'Spinners', bright blue-gray *H.* (Tardiana Group) 'Halcyon', yellow-green variegated *H. sieboldiana* 'Frances Williams', and the large, deeply puckered *H. s.* var. *elegans*, is saved from monotony by the addition of the contrastingly smaller leaves and flowers of cranesbills, including *Geranium* × *oxonianum*.

Hosta 'August Moon'

How it works: Although even a wispy clematis planted among hostas could obscure their handsome rosettes of leaves, the occasional trailing stem wandering from an adjacent wall or supporting shrub can create a charming incident. Here, *Clematis* 'Etoile Violette' contrasts with the bright foliage of *Hosta* 'August Moon'.

Grown for its large, yellow-green leaves and pale lavender, nearly white flowers, this is one of the most sun-tolerant yellow-green hostas, its fine color appearing less striking when plants are grown in shade. 'August Moon' is bold enough for a large garden or for use as a strong accent in a medium-sized or small site. It makes good harmonies with gold or white flowers and contrasts strikingly with blue or purple or with foliage that differs markedly in color (purple, glaucous, and bronze) or form (grasses, sedges, and ferns). Japanese maples, berberis, and other smaller shrubs are an excellent background for this hosta.

Recommended partners: *Acer palmatum* f. *atropurpureum, Berberis thunbergii* f. *atropurpurea, Carex oshimensis* 'Evergold', *Gentiana asclepiadea, Hakonechloa macra* 'Alboaurea', *Hosta sieboldiana* var. *elegans, Matteuccia struthiopteris, Primula japonica* 'Postford White'

H: 27in (70cm) S: 30in (75cm)
✿ **Midsummer Z3 pH5–7.5**
◊◊-◊◊◊ □-■

Hosta 'Buckshaw Blue'

How it works: In this dramatic grouping, handsome foliage, some of it glaucous or yellow-green, is contrasted with the salmon-pink flowers of the Hybrid Musk rose *R.* 'Cornelia' and *Rodgersia pinnata* 'Maurice Mason'. The striking blue-green *Hosta* 'Buckshaw Blue' contrasts with Bowles's golden sedge (*Carex elata* 'Aurea'), while the spurge *Euphorbia palustris* fills the space beneath the rose.

Recommended partners: *Acer palmatum* 'Bloodgood', *Astilbe chinensis* var. *taquetii* 'Superba', *Euphorbia schillingii*, *Festuca glauca* 'Elijah Blue', *Meconopsis betonicifolia*, *Milium effusum* 'Aureum', *Rodgersia pinnata* 'Superba', *Rosa* 'Reine des Centifeuilles'

H: 14in (35cm) **S: 24in** (60cm)
✿ **Midsummer Z3 pH5–7.5**

Hosta 'Hydon Sunset'

How it works: The diminutive, yellow-green, brightly gold-tipped leaves of *Hosta* 'Hydon Sunset', which scorch badly in full sun, contrast with the soft lavender, red-eyed flowers of another inhabitant of deciduous woodland, *Phlox divaricata* subsp. *laphamii* 'Chattahoochee'. Both need relative freedom from slugs and snails if they are to succeed.

Recommended partners: *Adiantum aleuticum* 'Japonicum', *Ajuga reptans* 'Atropurpurea', *Asplenium scolopendrium* 'Kaye's Lacerated', *Corydalis flexuosa* 'China Blue', *Heuchera villosa* 'Palace Purple', *Pulmonaria saccharata*, *Tiarella wherryi* 'Bronze Beauty'

H: 14in (35cm) **S: 8in** (20cm)
Mid-summer Z3 pH5–7.5

Hosta 'Sum and Substance'

How it works: Big and bold *Hosta* 'Sum and Substance' is furnished to the ground with leaves and so can be used at the very front of steeply banked borders. Here, the vigorous, tall cranesbill *Geranium* × *oxonianum* 'Claridge Druce' leavens the hosta's solidity with contrastingly small foliage and flowers. 'Sum and Substance' is perhaps the most sun-tolerant of the yellow-green kinds, and the thick leaves are relatively unpalatable to slugs and snails.

Recommended partners: *Ailanthus altissima* (stooled), *Aruncus dioicus*, *Gunnera manicata*, *Hosta sieboldiana* var. *elegans*, *Lysimachia punctata*, *Miscanthus sacchariflorus*, *Paulownia tomentosa* (stooled), *Phyllostachys nigra*

H: 30in (75cm) **S: 4ft** (1.2m)
Early to mid-summer
Z3 pH5–7.5

Irises

The diverse genus *Iris* embraces several thousand immensely useful garden plants. Herbaceous and rhizomatous sorts are considered here; *I.* 'Symphony', grown from a corm, is discussed under Bulbs (page 299). *I. ensata, I. japonica,* and their hybrids and cultivars like moist conditions and are superlative plants for waterside planting. Cultivars of *I. ensata* have large, exotically marked flowers, showy from a distance but needing close inspection for their intricacy to be appreciated. *I. chrysographes* cultivars and the related *I. delavayi* tend to be taller with grassier leaves and flowers in sumptuously dark colors; they too benefit from moist or waterside conditions and close-range viewing, their dusky blooms being scarcely visible from a distance. The hundreds of cultivars and hybrids of *I. sibirica* are also excellent marginal plants but can be grown in a border provided that the soil does not

The Tall Bearded iris *I.* 'Kent Pride' is classed as a Plicata cultivar (having a pale ground edged with a darker color). Brown varieties such as this can be combined with bronze or purple foliage and purple or warm-colored flowers.

dry out. They make a classic combination with late-flowering azaleas in situations that are neither too arid nor too shady.

Species such as the evergreen *I. unguicularis*, a precious winter-flowering iris, are suited to dry, sun-baked spots. *I. foetidissima* is invaluable in dry shade, and has attractively glossy, dark evergreen foliage and brilliant vermilion seeds, displayed for several months after its pods split open in autumn. It will grow happily at the foot of a hedge where few other plants would survive.

The Californian Hybrids, derived from species such as *I. douglasiana*, *I. innominata*, and *I. chrysophylla*, make evergreen, fairly low-growing clumps of foliage with flowers in a range of colors, often attractively veined, usually in mid- to late spring but occasionally into summer.

Spuria irises, which are derived from species such as *I. crocea*, *I. monnieri*, *I. orientalis*, and *I. sanguinea*, are the tallest and latest-flowering irises, making narrow clumps with deciduous grassy foliage. Tolerating light shade, their habit suits them to planting in borders.

Perhaps the most valuable irises are the sun-loving Bearded cultivars, ranging in size from the Miniature Dwarf Bearded sorts at about 8 in (20cm) high to Tall Bearded kinds at 27 in (70cm) or more. As a rough rule, the shortest types flower the earliest, in mid-spring, while the tallest continue into early summer.

Bearded irises are propagated by division after flowering, with young, short sections of vigorous rhizome replanted at the surface. Care should be taken not to arrange them all facing the same way, so that they move in one direction, leaving bare rhizome behind. The base of the plants can look unattractive but can be masked by interplanting with a low carpeting plant such as an acaena, or with a later-flowering bulb such as *Allium flavum*.

Tall Bearded irises such as *I.* 'Nightfall' can supply an accent among lower planting, as here with poached egg plant (*Limnanthes douglasii*) and dark-leaved heucheras.

Iris chrysographes

How it works: A waterside position is ideal for this moisture-loving iris. In this scheme, at the front of a border in early summer, the deep purple-black flowers of *Iris chrysographes*, although recessive in color and difficult to see from a distance, show distinctly against the much paler flowers of *Geranium* 'Johnson's Blue', and their upright stems provide a strong vertical accent.

Recommended partners: *Astilbe* 'Red Sentinel', *Lythrum virgatum* 'Dropmore Purple', *Monarda* 'Cambridge Scarlet', *Primula capitata*, *Tradescantia* (Andersoniana Group) 'Purple Dome'

H: 16–20in (40–50cm) S: 12in (30cm)
❀ **Early to mid-summer Z4 pH5.5–7**

Iris 'Lavinia'

How it works: In early summer, the maroon markings of *Iris* 'Lavinia' match those of *Erodium pelargoniiflorum*, while their flowers and foliage provide a contrast of size and form. The gentle coloring and pretty markings of this California hybrid are also very attractive with mauve or lilac, and with purple-flushed foliage; stronger colors may prove overwhelming, although effective contrasts can be made with deep purple.

Recommended partners: *Allium schoenoprasum*, *Dicentra peregrina*, *Erodium trifolium*, *Geranium tuberosum*, *Heuchera* 'Plum Pudding', *Rosmarinus officinalis* Prostratus Group

H & S: 16in (40cm)
❀ **Late spring to early summer Z7 pH5–7**

Iris orientalis

How it works: This combination is unified by the golden markings on the falls of *Iris orientalis*, the traces of yellow in the anthers of *Clematis* 'Sylvia Denny', and the cream variegation of *Philadelphus coronarius* 'Variegatus'.

This splendid Spuria iris is tall and elegant, with grassy foliage that makes a good foil for old roses and with white and yellow flowers that work well with rich crimson, purple, or blue. They harmonize with white and cream, soft colors such as peach and apricot, rich golden yellow, yellow-green, and glaucous foliage such as that of larger hostas. Suitable companions include peonies, lupins, and delphiniums, and medium-sized shrubs such as philadelphus and rhododendrons. Like most Spuria irises, it prefers a fairly moist site but will tolerate all but very dry soil. 'Shelford Giant' is about twice as high as *I. orientalis*, with creamier flowers.

Recommended partners: *Berberis thunbergii* 'Aurea', *Delphinium* 'Sabrina', *D.* 'Sungleam', *Hosta sieboldiana* var. *elegans*, *Lupinus* 'Polar Princess', *L.* 'Thundercloud', *Paeonia lactiflora* 'Instituteur Doriat', *Rhododendron* Blinklicht Group, *Rosa* 'Charles de Mills'

H: 40in (1m) **S: 24in** (60cm) **Z4 pH5–7.5**
❀ **Late spring to early summer**

Iris pallida 'Variegata'

How it works: The boldly striped, sword-like leaves of the Bearded iris *I. pallida* 'Variegata' supply strong form to this grouping with *Penstemon* 'Pink Endurance', whose diffuse flower spikes open after those of the iris have faded.

Recommended partners: *Anemone apennina, Cistus* × *skanbergii, Lupinus* 'Gallery White', *Phlomis fruticosa, Rosa* 'Maigold', *Rosmarinus officinalis* 'Aureus'

H: 36in (90cm) **S: 24in** (60cm)
❋ **Late spring to early summer**
◊-◊◊ □-■ Z4 pH5.5–8

Iris sibirica
SIBERIAN IRIS

How it works: In early summer, the flowers of *Iris sibirica*, borne above its leaves, combine attractively with those of white sweet rocket (*Hesperis matronalis* var. *albiflora*).

Recommended partners: *Astilbe* 'Fanal', *Cornus alba* 'Sibirica Variegata', *Rhododendron* 'Narcissiflorum', *Rosa* 'Maigold', *Salix exigua, Trollius* × *cultorum* 'Canary Bird'

H: 20–48in (50–120cm) **S: 18in** (45cm)
❋ **Early to mid-summer Z4 pH5–7.5**
◊◊-◊◊◊ □-■

Knautia macedonica

How it works: A purple smoke bush (*Cotinus coggygria* 'Royal Purple') forms a harmonious background for the crimson pincushion-like flowerheads of *Knautia macedonica*. This plant is good for the front of a border, where it will blend with other cool colors and can be used as a foil for flowers of a brighter red. Exceptionally pretty partnerships can be made with nicotianas, penstemons, eryngiums, daylilies, phlox, thalictrums, and pinks, and with flowers of contrasting form.

Recommended partners: *Achillea millefolium* 'Cerise Queen', *Allium sphaerocephalon*, *Clematis* × *durandii*, *Malva sylvestris*, *Rosa* Bonica ('Meidomonac')

Kniphofia 'Sunningdale Yellow'

How it works: Vertical accents of *Kniphofia* 'Sunningdale Yellow', backed by dusky *Rosa glauca*, echo the primrose blooms of *Anthemis tinctoria* 'Wargrave Variety', joined by golden feverfew (*Tanacetum parthenium* 'Aureum').

Recommended partners:
Early cultivars: *Baptisia australis*, *Nepeta* 'Six Hills Giant'
Later cultivars: *Agapanthus* 'Loch Hope', *Canna* 'Striata', *Salvia* × *superba*

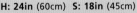

H: 24in (60cm) S: 18in (45cm)
❀ Mid- to late summer
◖◗◗ ☐-◼ Z5 pH5–7.5

H: 30–48in (75–120cm) S: 18–30in (45–75cm)
❀ Early summer to early autumn
◖◗◗ ☐-◼ Z6 pH5.5–7.5

Kniphofia uvaria 'Nobilis'

How it works: In this complex association for late summer, *Kniphofia uvaria* 'Nobilis' is the dominant plant, its bold, upright, cylindrical heads producing a definite pattern. Bright *Rudbeckia laciniata* 'Herbstsonne', creamy *Artemisia lactiflora*, and helianthus provide highlights toward the front, with duskier tones added by *Eupatorium maculatum* Atropurpureum Group and a dark-leaved *Cotinus coggygria*. *Helianthus salicifolius*, maple, and eucalyptus supply a varied background. The vermilion flowers of the poker work well in hot-colored schemes or with purple foliage and contrast effectively with yellow-green, but they are too red and not yellow enough to contrast effectively with blue. However, the duskiest violet can be used as a background to throw hot colors like this into even greater prominence. This tall cultivar is more prone to toppling than most; staking pokers inconspicuously is hard, so it is best grown where sheltered from strong wind.

Recommended partners: *Aconitum* 'Spark's Variety', *Bupleurum rotundifolium* 'Garibaldi', *Canna* 'Striata', *Catalpa bignonioides* 'Aurea' (stooled), *Crocosmia* Walberton Bright Eyes ('Walbreyes'), *Dahlia* 'David Howard', *Rosa* 'Geranium', *Rudbeckia amplexicaulis*, *R. triloba*, *Tagetes patula* 'Striped Marvel'

H: 8ft (2.5m) S: 40in (1m)
❀ **Mid-summer to mid-autumn**

 ◐-◐◐ ☐-■ Z6 pH5.5–7.5

Kniphofia 'Wrexham Buttercup'

How it works: The vertical pokers of *Kniphofia* 'Wrexham Buttercup' contrast with the horizontal layers of the variegated dogwood (*Cornus controversa* 'Variegata') and the flat plates of a creamy achillea.

Recommended partners:

Early cultivars: *Baptisia australis*, × *Halimiocistus wintonensis* 'Merrist Wood Cream', *Nepeta* 'Six Hills Giant'

Later cultivars: *Agapanthus* 'Loch Hope', *Canna* 'Striata', *Salvia* × *superba*

H: **30–48in** (75–120cm) S: **18–30in** (45–75cm)
❋ **Early summer to early autumn**
◻️◼️◻️ ◊◊ ☐-■ **Z6 pH5.5–7.5**

Leucanthemum vulgare
OXEYE DAISY

How it works: In grassland that is neither nutrient rich nor very impoverished, oxeye daisy (*Leucanthemum vulgare*) can be naturalized attractively with wild flowers liking similar regimes, such as meadow buttercup (*Ranunculus acris*).

Recommended partners: *Anthriscus sylvestris*, *Aquilegia vulgaris*, *Chaerophyllum hirsutum* 'Roseum', *Geranium phaeum*, *Heracleum mantegazzianum*, *Ranunculus repens* var. *pleniflorus*, *Trollius europaeus*

H: **12–36in** (30–90cm) S: **18–24in** (45–60cm)
❋ **Late spring to early summer**
◻️◼️◻️ ◊◊ ☐-■ **Z3 pH4.5–7.5**

Leymus arenarius
LYME GRASS

How it works: Spreading clumps of
Leymus arenarius are usually loose enough
for slender plants of contrasting form and
color, such as purple toadflax (*Linaria
purpurea*), to be grown though their
fringes, creating a pleasing mixture.

Recommended partners: *Achillea
filipendulina* 'Gold Plate', *Anthemis
tinctoria, Ballota pseudodictamnus, Glaucium
corniculatum, Nepeta* 'Six Hills Giant'

H: 4ft (1.2m) **S: 3ft** (90cm)
✿ **Mid-summer to early autumn**
�○-◇◇ □-■ **Z4 pH5.5–7.5**

Ligularia dentata '**Desdemona**'

How it works: The golden groundsel *Ligularia dentata* 'Desdemona' with its bronze-green leaves is joined by the yellow spires of *L. stenocephala*, the flat heads of *Achillea filipendulina* 'Gold Plate', and a red daylily (*Hemerocallis* 'Stafford'), against a background of purple smoke bush (*Cotinus coggygria* 'Royal Purple').

Recommended partners: *Achillea* 'Coronation Gold', *Camassia leichtlinii* 'Semiplena', *Iris pseudacorus* 'Variegata', *Rosa* Evelyn Fison ('Macev')

H: 4ft (1.2m) S: 3ft (90cm)
✿ **Mid-summer to early autumn**
◇◇◇ ■-■ Z4 pH4.5–7.5

Ligularia stenocephala

How it works: In this classic combination of moisture lovers, *Ligularia stenocephala* towers over the loosestrife *Lysimachia ciliata*, a contrast in form but a blend of colors. Other large-scale plants to combine with these two include *Gunnera manicata* and *Rodgersia podophylla*.

Recommended partners: *Astilbe* 'Red Sentinel', *Carex pendula*, *Delphinium* 'Sungleam', *Deschampsia cespitosa*, *Lobelia* × *speciosa* 'Cherry Ripe', *Rodgersia pinnata* 'Superba'

H: 5ft (1.5m) S: 3ft (90cm)
❀ Early to late summer Z5 pH4.5–7.5

Linum narbonense

How it works: In this combination for a well-drained sunny site, the blue flax *Linum narbonense* contrasts with the yellow-flowered, prostrate broom *Genista sagittalis*. An attractive, sub-shrubby spurge, *Euphorbia characias*, gives bold architectural form to the planting.

Recommended partners: *Achillea* 'Moonshine', *Cistus* × *cyprius*, *Hakonechloa macra* 'Alboaurea', *Phlomis fruticosa*, *Rosmarinus officinalis* 'Roseus', *Ruta graveolens* 'Jackman's Blue'

H: 12–24in (30–60cm) S: 18in (45cm)
❀ Early to mid-summer

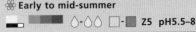

Z5 pH5.5–8

Lobelia cardinalis 'Queen Victoria'

How it works: In this extensive planting of hot-colored flowers, *Lobelia cardinalis* 'Queen Victoria', with its brilliant scarlet flowers and purple foliage, has to be grouped several plants deep for its slender spikes to give the impression of solid color. Its partners here include *Dahlia* 'Bishop of Llandaff', heleniums, and crocosmias.

Recommended partners: *Canna* 'Erebus', *Dahlia* 'Alva's Doris', *Hosta* 'Sum and Substance', *Ligularia dentata* 'Desdemona', *Molinia caerulea* 'Variegata'

H: 36in (90cm) **S: 12in** (30cm)

Mid-summer to mid-autumn

Z6 pH5–7.5

Lobelia × *speciosa* 'Cherry Ripe'

How it works: The narrow, upright habit of *Lobelia* × *speciosa* 'Cherry Ripe' and its long racemes of blooms make it especially useful for steeply banked borders such as this. In a predominantly red scheme, the lobelia is joined by *Dahlia* 'Grenadier', the scarlet hips of *Rosa* 'Geranium', and the double-flowered daylily *Hemerocallis fulva* 'Flore Pleno'.

Recommended partners: *Carex pendula*, *Corylus maxima* 'Purpurea', *Hosta sieboldiana* var. *elegans*, *Iris pseudacorus* 'Variegata', *Ligularia dentata* 'Desdemona', *Lysimachia ciliata* 'Firecracker', *Mimulus aurantiacus*, *Osmunda regalis*

H: 36in (90cm) **S: 12in** (30cm)

Mid-summer to early autumn

Z6 pH5–7.5

Lupinus 'Polar Princess'

How it works: Vigorously grown young lupins, such as the superb *Lupinus* 'Polar Princess', here making strong vertical accents against the silvery foliage of *Elaeagnus commutata*, will produce solid, columnar racemes of almost unnatural regularity in their first year of flowering, although they will bear numerous spires of varied size in subsequent years.

Recommended partners: *Allium cristophii*, *A. sphaerocephalon*, *Artemisia ludoviciana*, *Iris orientalis*, *Paeonia lactiflora* 'Duchesse de Nemours', *Papaver orientale* 'Black and White', *Rosa* Graham Thomas ('Ausmas')

H: 36–48in (90–120cm) S: 24in (60cm)
❀ **Early summer**

 ◊◊ ☐-▨ Z3 pH5.5–7.5

Lupinus 'Thundercloud'

How it works: *Euphorbia characias* subsp. *wulfenii* echoes the bold verticals of *Lupinus* 'Thundercloud', along with catmint (*Nepeta* 'Six Hills Giant') and *Erysimum* 'Bowles's Mauve'. 'Thundercloud' is one of the best purple lupins, its color being effective not only with harmonious tones such as those of blue cranesbills, but also when contrasted with yellow-green flowers or foliage.

Recommended partners: *Allium cristophii*, *A. sphaerocephalon*, *Artemisia ludoviciana*, *Iris orientalis*, *Paeonia lactiflora* 'Duchesse de Nemours', *Papaver orientale* 'Black and White', *Rosa* Graham Thomas ('Ausmas')

H: 36–48in (90–120cm) S: 24in (60cm)
❀ **Early summer**

 ◊◊ ☐-▨ Z3 pH5.5–7.5

Lychnis × *arkwrightii* 'Vesuvius'

How it works: In this dramatic grouping reminiscent of a Japanese ikebana arrangement, the vivid flowers of *Lychnis* × *arkwrightii* 'Vesuvius' contrast with the brightly variegated grass *Hakonechloa macra* 'Aureola' around the spiky foliage of a dark form of *Eucomis comosa*. The scheme could be repeated in a larger planting, replacing the grass with a less fiercely contrasting one.

Recommended partners: *Berberis thunbergii* f. *atropurpurea*, *Choisya ternata* Sundance ('Lich'), *Euphorbia schillingii*, *Hemerocallis* 'Golden Chimes', *Phormium* 'Bronze Baby', *Stipa gigantea*

H: **18in** (45cm) S: **12in** (30cm)
❀ **Early to mid-summer**
Z6 pH5.5–7.5

Lychnis coronaria
ROSE CAMPION

How it works: This lovely, easily grown silver-leaved plant is long-flowering and profuse, with flowers in a range of colors. Here, a gently contrasting salmon pelargonium scrambles into rose campions (magenta *Lychnis coronaria* and white *L. c.* 'Alba') to give a vibrant color scheme.

Recommended partners: *Campanula* 'Burghaltii', *Echinacea purpurea*, *Erigeron* 'Gaiety', *Gladiolus communis* subsp. *byzantinus*, *Malva sylvestris*, *Rosa* 'Charles de Mills', *R. gallica* 'Versicolor', *R.* 'Impératrice Joséphine', *R.* 'Tuscany Superb'

H: **31in** (80cm) S: **18in** (45cm)
❀ **Mid- to late summer**
Z4 pH5–8

Lychnis coronaria 'Alba'

How it works: In a sunny display in mid-summer, *Lychnis coronaria* 'Alba' combines with a lemon daylily (*Hemerocallis* 'Baroni'), the bold and elegant shape of the daylily blooms contrasting with those of the campion.

Recommended partners: *Campanula* 'Burghaltii', *Echinacea purpurea*, *Erigeron* 'Gaiety', *Gladiolus communis* subsp. *byzantinus*, *Malva sylvestris*, *Nepeta* 'Six Hills Giant', *Rosa* 'Charles de Mills', *R. gallica* 'Versicolor', *R.* 'Impératrice Joséphine', *R.* 'Tuscany Superb'

H: 31in (80cm) **S: 18in** (45cm)
❀ **Mid- to late summer**
◐-◐◐ ▢-▣ **Z4 pH5–8**

Lysimachia nummularia 'Aurea'
GOLDEN CREEPING JENNY

How it works: The bright yellow-green foliage and pale stems of golden creeping Jenny (*Lysimachia nummularia* 'Aurea') mingle with the glaucous, pinnate foliage of *Acaena saccaticupula* 'Blue Haze'.

Recommended partners: *Acaena microphylla* 'Kupferteppich', *Ajuga reptans* 'Atropurpurea', *Colchicum speciosum*, *C. s.* 'Album', *Hebe pinguifolia* 'Pagei', *Lobelia richardsonii*, *Matteuccia struthiopteris*, *Muscari armeniacum*, *Myosotis sylvatica*, *Scilla siberica* 'Spring Beauty', *Viola* 'Huntercombe Purple'

H: 2in (5cm) S: indefinite
Mid-summer Z4 pH4.5–7.5

Macleaya microcarpa

How it works: The tall plumes of *Macleaya microcarpa* in early summer harmonize both with the brick wall behind and with the group of mixed *Alstroemeria ligtu* hybrids in front. A soft shield fern (*Polystichum setiferum*) furnishes the base of the alstroemerias. The color of the airy spikes of this plume poppy lies somewhere among brick-red, coral, and salmon.

Recommended partners: *Alstroemeria aurea*, *Campanula latifolia* 'Gloaming', *Cotinus coggygria* 'Notcutt's Variety', *Dahlia* 'Glorie van Heemstede', *Rosa* Peach Blossom ('Ausblossom')

H: 7ft (2.2m) S: 3ft (90cm)
Early to mid-summer Z4 pH5.5–7.5

Malva moschata f. *alba*

How it works: An upright *Miscanthus sinensis* cultivar produces a fountain of foliage behind *Malva moschata* f. *alba* in a simple scheme of subdued colors. The crisp, prettily cut leaves of the musk mallow give a strong contrast of form with the ribbon-like foliage of the grass. This plant is immensely effective with other white flowers, pastel shades, and silver foliage, and with yellow-green or glaucous leaves.
Recommended partners: *Artemisia schmidtiana*, *Astrantia maxima*, *Heuchera* 'Rachel', *Hydrangea arborescens*, *Rosa* Pink Bells ('Poulbells'), *Veronicastrum virginicum* 'Album'

H: 36in (90cm) **S: 24in** (60cm)
Early summer to early autumn
Z4 pH5.5–7.5

Meconopsis betonicifolia

TIBETAN BLUE POPPY

How it works: In a partially shaded glade blessed with moist, humus-rich soil, Tibetan blue poppies (*Meconopsis betonicifolia*) and white foxgloves (*Digitalis purpurea* f. *albiflora*) create a classic combination of blue and white, the spikes of the foxgloves providing bold accents and contrast of form.
Recommended partners: *Astilbe* × *arendsii* 'Irrlicht', *Corydalis flexuosa*, *Hosta fortunei* var. *albopicta* f. *aurea*, *Matteuccia struthiopteris*, *Primula florindae*, *Rhododendron* 'Polar Bear', *Rodgersia pinnata* 'Superba'

H: 4ft (1.2m) **S: 18in** (45cm)
Early summer
Z7 pH5–6.5

Miscanthus sinensis 'Variegatus'

How it works: The cream-striped *Miscanthus sinensis* 'Variegatus' in this scheme seems almost identical in tone to silvery *Elaeagnus* 'Quicksilver', differing in form and texture but blending to give a gentle and elegant combination.

Recommended partners: *Anemone × hybrida* 'Elegans', *Chrysanthemum* Rubellum Group, *Crocosmia* 'Lucifer', *Echinacea purpurea*, *Rhus × pulvinata* Autumn Lace Group, *Rodgersia podophylla*

H: 5ft (1.5m) S: 40in (1m)
✸ Early to mid-autumn

Z6 pH5–7.5

Monarda 'Adam'

How it works: In this border of brightly colored flowers for midsummer to autumn, the relatively compact, cherry-red *Monarda* 'Adam' takes center stage. In front are golden heleniums and crimson *Phlox paniculata*, while behind, *Crocosmia* 'Lucifer', achilleas, and dark-leaved *Ricinus communis* provide both structure and bold color.

Recommended partners: *Achillea filipendulina* 'Gold Plate', *Aster divaricatus*, *Deschampsia cespitosa*, *Rudbeckia fulgida* var. *deamii*, *Salvia coccinea* 'Coral Nymph'

H: 31in (80cm) S: 18in (45cm)
✸ Mid- to late summer

Z4 pH5–7.5

Monarda 'Beauty of Cobham'

How it works: Pale pink *Monarda* 'Beauty of Cobham', used toward the front of a border of predominantly purple flowers and dark foliage, helps to lighten an otherwise leaden combination featuring the smoke bush (*Cotinus coggygria* 'Foliis Purpureis') and purple loosestrife (*Lythrum salicaria* 'Feuerkerze').

Recommended partners: *Aster* × *frikartii* 'Mönch', *Astilbe* × *arendsii* 'Ceres', *Lobelia* × *speciosa* 'Fan Scharlach', *Lythrum virgatum* 'Dropmore Purple', *Thalictrum delavayi* 'Hewitt's Double'

Nepeta govaniana

How it works: *Nepeta govaniana* is a beautiful Himalayan herbaceous perennial that expands in moist, cool conditions to form a clump of erect pointed foliage and airy racemes of subdued creamy yellow flowers. In this scheme, its flowers, which rise above a cushion of feathery *Artemisia* 'Powis Castle' and a cream achillea, contrast with the nearby lavender-blue catmint *Nepeta* 'Six Hills Giant' in mid-summer.

Recommended partners: *Agapanthus* 'Loch Hope', *Caryopteris* × *clandonensis* 'Heavenly Blue', *Hydrangea macrophylla* 'Mariesii Perfecta', *Lilium* African Queen Group, *Perovskia* 'Blue Spire', *Rosa* Crown Princess Margareta ('Auswinter')

H: 36in (90cm) **S: 18in** (45cm)
❀ **Mid- to late summer**
 ◊◊ ☐-■ Z4 pH5–7.5

H: 36in (90cm) **S: 24in** (60cm)
❀ **Mid-summer to early autumn**
◊◊ ☐-■ ■ Z5 pH5.5–7.5

Nepeta 'Six Hills Giant'

How it works: The lavender-blue flowers of the catmint *Nepeta* 'Six Hills Giant' sprawl across a gravel path next to the contrasting yellow blooms of Jerusalem sage (*Phlomis fruticosa*), harmonizing with the glaucous lyme grass (*Leymus arenarius*), confined in a verdigrised laundry copper.

Recommended partners: *Geranium* × *oxonianum* 'A.T. Johnson', *Lupinus* 'Thundercloud', *Paeonia lactiflora* 'Albert Crousse', *Rosa* 'Chinatown'

Oenothera speciosa 'Siskiyou'

How it works: *Allium senescens* has here grown through the fringes of *Oenothera speciosa* 'Siskiyou', its mauve flowerheads harmonizing with the attractively veined, satin-pink blooms of the oenothera but providing a contrast of floral form.

Recommended partners: *Cistus* × *argenteus* 'Silver Pink', *Helianthemum* 'Wisley White', *Lavandula* 'Regal Splendour', *Origanum* 'Kent Beauty', *Stipa gigantea*, *Teucrium fruticans*

H: 30in (75cm) S: 36in (90cm)
❀ **Early to late summer Z5 pH5.5–7.5**

H & S: 12in (30cm)
❀ **Early to late summer Z5 pH5.5–7.5**

Ophiopogon planiscapus 'Nigrescens'
BLACK MONDO GRASS

How it works: The glistening dark foliage of black mondo grass (*Ophiopogon planiscapus* 'Nigrescens'), closer to black than almost any other plant, contrasts with the pale green leaves of acaenas, forming a carpet beneath. The cranesbill *Geranium sessiliflorum* subsp. *novae-zelandiae* 'Nigricans' has smoky foliage intermediate in color between that of its two companions.

The insignificant flowers of this superlative ground-cover plant – small, white, and sometimes tinged with lilac – are followed by dark green berries that are shaded black with turquoise undertones.

This grass makes a good foil for contrasting foliage and flowers, especially bulbs such as colchicums, and for specimen shrubs like Japanese maples. It can also be used to make a patchwork of ground-cover foliage with leaves of contrasting form, either in harmonizing dusky colors such as those of dark-leaved heucheras, or together with contrasting pale-leaved plants like smaller yellow-green hostas or silver lamiums. It is an excellent choice for creating abstract carpet bedding designs on a large scale.

Recommended partners: *Acer palmatum* Dissectum Atropurpureum Group, *Cyclamen hederifolium* f. *albiflorum*, *Heuchera villosa* 'Palace Purple', *Iris* 'George'

H: 8in (20cm) **S: 12in** (30cm)
✿ **Mid-summer**

Z6 pH5–7

Origanum 'Rosenkuppel'

How it works: The rosy flowers and reddish-purple calyces of the marjoram *Origanum* 'Rosenkuppel' are subdued enough not to clash with sulphur-yellow *Coreopsis verticillata* 'Moonbeam' in a sunny, relatively nutrient-poor situation. The fine-textured grass *Festuca mairei* provides a pleasing contrast of form. The neighboring sedum, catmint, and *Phlomis russeliana* are ideally suited to the same conditions. Like many marjorams, 'Rosenkuppel' is tolerant of lime and has a long season of display. It is big enough and sufficiently robust to be used in New Perennial style plantings on a fairly large scale but is rather lacking in structure, so benefits from companions of more definite form. Its coloring suits it to combinations with cool colors and purple foliage, though it can also be contrasted with cream, lemon-yellow, and yellow-green.

Recommended partners: *Anthemis* Susanna Mitchell ('Blomit'), *Echinacea purpurea* 'Kim's Knee High', *Eryngium bourgatii* 'Picos Blue', *Festuca glauca* 'Blaufuchs', *Geranium* 'Mavis Simpson', *Lavatera* × *clementii* 'Barnsley Baby', *Marrubium incanum*, *Penstemon* 'Pink Endurance', *Phlomis italica* 'Pink Glory', *Phormium* 'Bronze Baby', *Salvia pratensis* Haematodes Group, *Scabiosa* 'Butterfly Blue'

H: 20in (50cm) S: 16in (40cm)
✿ **Mid-summer to mid-autumn**
◊-◊◊ ☐-▨ **Z5 pH5.5–8**

Paeonia lactiflora 'Albert Crousse'

How it works: The rose-pink blooms of *Paeonia lactiflora* 'Albert Crousse' harmonize in color and floral form with those of *Rosa* Gertrude Jekyll ('Ausbord'). Alliums in purplish mauve (*A. aflatunense* and taller *A. giganteum*) add contrast of form, their stems providing repeated vertical accents.

Recommended partners: *Alstroemeria* 'Apollo', *Aquilegia vulgaris* (mixed), *Chionodoxa forbesii*, *Iris* 'Jane Phillips', *Papaver orientale* 'Black and White', *Rosa* 'Charles de Mills'

H: 36in (90cm) **S: 24in** (60cm)
Early to mid-summer
Z6 pH5.5–7.5

Paeonia lactiflora 'Auguste Dessert'

How it works: Carmine *Paeonia lactiflora* 'Auguste Dessert' is here daringly juxtaposed against yellow loosestrife (*Lysimachia punctata*). Although the contrast of form certainly succeeds, some gardeners might prefer to achieve it with spires of a more harmonious color, perhaps using a lupin or delphinium that would also blend agreeably with pale pink *P. l.* 'Noemi Demay' behind.

Recommended partners: *Centaurea montana*, *Delphinium* 'Bruce', *Dictamnus albus* var. *purpureus*, *Lupinus* 'Thundercloud', *Potentilla fruticosa* 'Primrose Beauty', *Rosa* 'Complicata'

H & S: 30in (75cm)
✽ **Early to mid-summer**
◊◊ ☐-■ Z5 pH5.5–7.5

Phalaris arundinacea var. *picta* 'Picta'
GARDENER'S GARTERS

How it works: The bright variegation of *Phalaris arundinacea* var. *picta* 'Picta' contrasts boldly with the dark foliage of *Berberis thunbergii* 'Rose Glow'. Behind, carmine *Clematis* 'Madame Julia Correvon' harmonizes with the berberis. The stripes in the leaves carry a hint of cream, which enhances their appearance when grown among yellow, apricot, or peach-colored flowers.

Recommended partners: *Achillea* 'Lachsschönheit', *Crocosmia* × *crocosmiiflora* 'Solfatare', *Cynara cardunculus*, *Hemerocallis fulva*, *Tulipa* 'Ballerina'

H: 30–40in (75cm–1m) S: 40in (1m)
✽ **Late spring to early summer**
◊◊ ☐-■ Z4 pH5–7.5

Phlomis russeliana

How it works: This selection of *Phlomis russeliana* has flowers of clear yellow, rather than brownish buff, which make a fine contrast with lavender-blue flowers, such as those of the catmint *Nepeta sibirica*. The phlomis is sufficiently strongly colored to be seen against a background of the harmonious cream variegation of the privet *Ligustrum ovalifolium* 'Argenteum'.

Recommended partners: *Cornus alba* 'Spaethii', *Cytisus × kewensis, Digitalis purpurea* f. *albiflora, Euphorbia characias* subsp. *wulfenii, Geranium sanguineum* var. *striatum, × Halimiocistus wintonensis* 'Merrist Wood Cream'

Phlox maculata

How it works: Although strong yellow and mauve can make an uneasy alliance, the slightly paler yellow daylily *Hemerocallis* 'Marion Vaughn' and *Phlox maculata*, here with teasel (*Dipsacus fullonum*), make a more pleasant contrast.

Recommended partners: *Achillea* 'Moonshine', *Atriplex hortensis* var. *rubra, Campanula latifolia* 'Brantwood', *Cotinus coggygria* 'Royal Purple', *Echinacea purpurea, Lupinus* 'Polar Princess', *Macleaya cordata*

H: 36in (90cm) S: 30in (75cm)
✵ **Late spring to early autumn**
 ◊ ☐-■ **Z4 pH5.5–7.5**

H: 36in (90cm) S: 18in (45cm)
✵ **Early to mid-summer Z4 pH5.5–7.5**
 ◊◊-◊◊◊ ☐-■

Phlox paniculata 'Norah Leigh'

How it works: In mid-summer, the cream-variegated foliage of *Phlox paniculata* 'Norah Leigh' harmonizes with a white agapanthus, while its mauve-pink flowers with magenta eyes blend happily with the Oriental hybrid lily *Lilium* 'Black Beauty' and the Regal pelargonium *P.* 'Pompeii', a cultivar that will bloom out of doors even in climates with barely warm summers.

Recommended partners: *Campanula* 'Kent Belle', *Corylus maxima* 'Purpurea', *Geranium* × *oxonianum* 'Claridge Druce', *Heuchera* 'Plum Pudding', *Rosa* 'De Rescht'

Phormium 'Bronze Baby'

How it works: To produce a sumptuous effect at the height of the summer, in either a bed or a good-sized container, the richly colored *Phormium* 'Bronze Baby' can be planted through a carpet of flaming scarlet verbenas.

Recommended partners: *Diascia* 'Dark Eyes', *Phygelius* × *rectus* 'Pink Elf', *Potentilla fruticosa* 'Tangerine', *Skimmia japonica* 'Rubella', *Verbena* 'Lawrence Johnston'

H: 40in (1m) **S: 24in** (60cm)
✻ **Mid-summer to mid-autumn**
◊◊ ▨-▩ **Z4 pH5.5–7.5**

H & S: 24in (60cm)
✻ **Mid-summer Z8 pH5–7.5**
◊◊-◊◊◊ ▢-▨

Phormium 'Duet'

How it works: A pale blend of green and cream, *Phormium* 'Duet' and the scented pelargonium *P.* 'Lady Plymouth' make a good focal point for a container where subtle color is needed.

Recommended partners: *Ajuga reptans* 'Atropurpurea', *Hemerocallis* 'Golden Chimes', *Lysimachia nummularia* 'Aurea', *Verbena* Tapien Pink ('Sunver')

Phormium tenax 'Veitchianum'

How it works: In this striking combination relying on foliage effect alone, the creamy-yellow-striped leaves of *Phormium tenax* 'Veitchianum' make a bold statement between dark-leaved cannas and *Berberis* × *ottawensis* f. *purpurea* 'Superba'.

This variegated New Zealand flax is extremely spiky and therefore suitable for the most emphatic accents. With the broad, creamy yellow stripes on its dark green leaves, it is especially effective when used as a contrast to plants with purple foliage, and when grown with strong blue flowers or in harmonies with gold or yellow-green. As with most other plants, the price of brighter variegation is reduced hardiness. *P. t.* 'Variegatum' has narrower, creamy yellow stripes and is less striking than more brightly variegated clones, but it is hardier. Purple-flushed forms are also less hardy. Purpureum Group is recommended and has some variation in intensity of color; it harmonizes with flowers in hot colors and makes a fine contrast with yellow-green foliage.

Recommended partners: *Bergenia cordifolia* 'Purpurea', *Penstemon* 'Andenken an Friedrich Hahn', *Pittosporum tenuifolium* 'Purpureum', *Verbena* Tapien Violet ('Sunvop')

H: 40in (1m) S: 4ft (1.2m)
� Mid-summer **Z8 pH5–7.5**
 ◊◊-◊◊◊ ☐-■

H: 8ft (2.5m) S: 6ft (1.8m)
✦ Mid-summer **Z7 pH5–7.5**
 ◊◊-◊◊◊ ☐-■

Phuopsis stylosa

How it works: Vivid pink *Phuopsis stylosa* makes a sharp contrast with chartreuse *Alchemilla mollis* and bright green hart's tongue fern *Asplenium scolopendrium*, while harmonizing with *Hosta* (Tardiana Group) 'Halcyon'. The fern and the hosta provide bold structure lacking from the phuopsis, which fills the gaps between its partners to complete the ground cover. The phuopsis can produce a solid sheet of flower, so its flowerheads cannot be seen individually, and the pattern of their shape is lost. Growing in dappled shade, they are seen interspersed with glimpses of green foliage, the ensemble enlivened by shafts of light. Flower color can vary from mid-rose to shocking Schiaparelli pink *P. s.* 'Purpurea', the strength of which can be jarring among subdued woodland planting. It harmonizes with cool colors and purple or glaucous foliage and contrasts with yellow-green, white, cream, or palest yellow.

Recommended partners: *Acaena saccaticupula* 'Blue Haze', *Achillea* Anthea ('Anblo'), *Allium cristophii*, *Anthemis* Susanne Mitchell ('Blomit'), *Campanula lactiflora* 'Pouffe', *Euphorbia seguieriana* subsp. *niciciana*, *Geranium* × *antipodeum* 'Chocolate Candy', *G.* Sabani Blue ('Bremigo'), *Gladiolus tristis* var. *concolor*

H: 10in (25cm) S: 20in (50cm)
✿ **Early to late summer**
 ◊◊ ☐-■ **Z5 pH5.5–8**

Polemonium caeruleum
JACOB'S LADDER

How it works: Jacob's ladder (*Polemonium caeruleum*) contrasts with *Spiraea japonica* 'Gold Mound', accompanied by black pansies, achilleas, and wood forget-me-nots (*Myosotis sylvatica*) in a charming incident that could be equally effective used on a larger scale.

Recommended partners: *Achillea* 'Moonshine', *Allium cristophii*, *Artemisia schmidtiana*, *Euphorbia characias* subsp. *wulfenii*, *Stachys byzantina* 'Silver Carpet'

H: 24in (60cm) S: 16in (40cm)
❀ Early summer Z4 pH5–7.5

Potentilla 'Etna'

How it works: The sprawling stems of *Potentilla* 'Etna' bear blood-red flowers, a color so deep that it is scarcely visible from a distance. Here, against a background of dark foliage, 'Etna' scrambles forward across the floriferous seed-raised *Viola* 'Prince John', whose bright yellow blooms highlight those of the potentilla.

Recommended partners: *Artemisia ludoviciana* 'Silver Queen', *Berberis thunbergii* 'Aurea', *Hebe* 'Red Edge', *Hedera helix* 'Glacier', *Phygelius* × *rectus* 'Pink Elf'

H: 18in (45cm) S: 24in (60cm)
❀ Early to late summer   Z5 pH5–7.5

Potentilla nepalensis 'Miss Willmott'

How it works: In two colors that lie to either side of primary deep pink, coral *Potentilla nepalensis* 'Miss Willmott' and soft magenta *Stachys macrantha* 'Superba' contrast gently, the potentilla scrambling around, into, and over its companion. This clump-forming cinquefoil makes a looser plant than *P.* 'Etna' (left), and its flowers vary from salmon-pink to deeper cherry-pink.

Recommended partners: *Berberis thunbergii* 'Atropurpurea Nana', *Diascia barberae* 'Blackthorn Apricot', *Heuchera villosa* 'Palace Purple', *Rosa* 'Europeana'

Rehmannia elata

How it works: Standing prominently at the edge of a bed, in front of a carpet of pure blue *Ceratostigma willmottianum* and a sentinel clump of New Zealand flax (*Phormium tenax*), the exotic carmine-pink trumpets of *Rehmannia elata* mingle with racemes of the smaller, paler pink blooms of *Diascia rigescens*.

Recommended partners: *Eryngium* × *tripartitum*, *Gypsophila* 'Rosenschleier', *Nigella damascena*, *Rosa* 'Yesterday', *Salvia nemorosa* 'Ostfriesland'

H: 18in (45cm) S: 24in (60cm)
❀ Early to late summer
◊◊ ☐-■ Z5 pH5–7.5

H: 24in (60cm) S: 18in (45cm)
❀ Early to late summer
◊◊ ☐-■ Z9 pH5.5–7.5

Rodgersia podophylla

How it works: Grasses, like ferns, provide a telling contrast of form with rodgersias. Here, the bronze-flushed palmate foliage of *Rodgersia podophylla* is joined by the elegant cream-striped *Miscanthus sinensis* 'Variegatus'.

Recommended partners: *Acer palmatum* 'Ōsakazuki', *Deschampsia cespitosa*, *Dryopteris affinis*, *Euphorbia schillingii*, *Kirengeshoma palmata*, *Rhododendron luteum*

H: 3–5ft (90–1.5m) S: 24–30in (60–75cm)
✽ Early to late summer Z5 pH5–7.5

Roscoea cautleyoides

How it works: *Roscoea cautleyoides* is an exotic-looking relative of ginger, with white, yellow, or magenta-purple flowers. Here, in a semi-shaded bed of moist, humus-rich soil in early summer, the soft, creamy yellow, orchid-like blooms of the roscoea contrast in size, shape, and color with the striking blue flowers of *Corydalis flexuosa*.

Roscoea generally prefers humus-rich soil, good drainage, and some shade, and so makes an excellent plant for woodland gardens, partially shaded rockeries, and shady borders. The most common variant is 'Kew Beauty', with large, pale creamy yellow flowers that suit combinations with flowers in warm tints, stronger yellows, yellow-green, or white, and yellow-green or gold-variegated foliage. It is particularly attractive with ferns, smaller sedges, grasses, and hostas (especially purple-flowered ones), later-flowering woodland plants including patrinias, and later-flowering lilies, as long as these are not too strongly colored.

Recommended partners: *Acer palmatum* var. *dissectum*, *Carex siderosticha* 'Variegata', *Dryopteris affinis*, *Hosta* 'Ginko Craig', *Lilium regale*, *Meconopsis betonicifolia*, *Molinia caerulea* 'Variegata', *Patrinia triloba* var. *palmata*

H: 18in (45cm) S: 12in (30cm)
✽ Early to mid-summer Z6 pH5–7.5

Salvia nemorosa 'Lubecca'

How it works: At the height of summer, the violet flowers of *Salvia nemorosa* 'Lubecca', borne on a 24 in (60cm) plant, are furnished at the base by a cushion of the delicate pink cranesbill, *Geranium sanguineum* var. *striatum*. The narrow, upright habit of the species suits herbaceous and mixed borders.

Recommended partners: *Achillea* 'Coronation Gold', *Delphinium* 'Sungleam', *Deschampsia cespitosa*, *Euphorbia seguieriana* subsp. *niciciana*, *Rudbeckia fulgida* var. *deamii*

Salvia pratensis 'Indigo'

How it works: The long-flowering, airy lavender blooms of the meadow clary *Salvia pratensis* 'Indigo' provide a pleasing contrast, of both color and form, beneath the horizontal flowerheads of *Achillea filipendulina* 'Gold Plate'.

Recommended partners: *Alchemilla mollis*, *Anthriscus sylvestris* 'Ravenswing', *Artemisia* 'Powis Castle', *Delphinium* 'Butterball', *Eryngium alpinum*, *Iris* 'Nightfall', *Rosa* 'Buff Beauty', *Stipa tenuissima*, *Thalictrum flavum*

H: 24in (60cm) **S: 18in** (45cm)
✿ **Early summer to early autumn**
◐-◐◐ ☐-■ **Z5 pH5.5–7.5**

H: 36in (90cm) **S: 18in** (45cm)
✿ **Early to mid-summer Z3–4 pH5.5–7.5**
◐◐ ☐-■

Salvia × *sylvestris* 'Mainacht'

How it works: The sumptuous dark blooms of *Salvia* × *sylvestris* 'Mainacht' harmonize perfectly with *Geranium* 'Kashmir Blue'.

Recommended partners: *Aquilegia vulgaris* (mixed), *Camassia leichtlinii* 'Semiplena', *Geranium* × *oxonianum* 'A. T. Johnson', *Hemerocallis* 'Golden Chimes', *Hesperis matronalis* var. *albiflora*, *Lunaria annua* 'Variegata', *Paeonia lactiflora* 'Emperor of India', *Rosa* 'Maigold'

Salvia × *superba*

How it works: *Salvia* × *superba* has narrow spikes of lavender-blue flowers emerging from deep reddish purple calyces. In this mid-summer scheme, the richly colored flowers look striking beside the copper-red blooms of *Helenium* 'Moerheim Beauty'. Deadheading the salvia will encourage it to produce further flowers, prolonging the display.

Recommended partners: *Achillea millefolium* 'Cerise Queen', *Echinacea purpurea*, *Eryngium* × *tripartitum*, *Rudbeckia fulgida* var. *deamii*, *Thalictrum delavayi* 'Album', *Verbascum* (Cotswold Group) 'Gainsborough'

H: 24–36in (60–90cm) **S: 18–24in** (45–60cm)
❀ Mid-summer to early autumn
 ◇-◇◇ ☐-■ Z5 pH5.5–7.5

H: 24in (60cm) **S: 12in** (30cm)
❀ Early summer
 ◇◇ ☐-■ Z5 pH5.5–7.5

Sanguisorba tenuifolia 'Alba'

How it works: In this scheme of bold forms and primary colors, the white flowerheads of *Sanguisorba tenuifolia* 'Alba' are backed by the upright grass *Calamagrostis* × *acutiflora* 'Strictus', with red *Papaver commutatum* 'Ladybird' and *Crocosmia masoniorum* 'Dixter Flame', blue *Campanula lactiflora*, and yellow *Oenothera biennis*.

Recommended partners: *Artemisia ludoviciana*, *Clarkia amoena* Satin Series, *Geranium* × *oxonianum* 'Prestbury Blush', *Nigella damascena*, *Salvia* × *superba*

H: 4ft (1.2m) S: 24in (60cm)
❀ **Mid- to late summer**
◖◗ ☐-☒ Z4 pH5.5–7.5

Scabiosa 'Butterfly Blue'

How it works: *Scabiosa* 'Butterfly Blue' is furnished in front by the glaucous foliage of *Mertensia simplicissima* and the crimson heads of *Dianthus deltoides* 'Leuchtfunk', and behind by the white *Campanula persicifolia* var. *alba*. Two alliums, blue *Allium caeruleum* and mauve *A. cristophii*, push their way through the other plants.

Recommended partners: *Artemisia schmidtiana*, *Brachyscome iberidifolia*, *Eryngium bourgatii*, *Rosa* Pink Bells ('Poulbells')

H & S: 18in (45cm)
❀ **Mid-summer to early autumn**
◖◗ ☐-☒ Z5 pH5.5–8

Sisyrinchium striatum

How it works: At the front of a border adjoining a stone path, the erect stems of creamy yellow *Sisyrinchium striatum* provide a strong accent. The plant's base is furnished by a carpet of rich blue-flowered *Veronica austriaca* subsp. *teucrium*, which spills over onto the path.

Recommended partners: *Achillea* 'Moonshine', *Artemisia* 'Powis Castle', *Campanula persicifolia*, *Kniphofia* 'David', *Lavandula angustifolia* 'Hidcote', *Papaver orientale* cultivars

H: 24in (60cm) S: 12in (30cm)
❀ Early to mid-summer
▬▬ ▬▬ ◊·◊◊ ☐·▦ Z7 pH5.5–8

Solidago 'Crown of Rays'

How it works: The plumose flowerheads of *Solidago* 'Crown of Rays' contrast in color and form with the fragrant, deep purple *Heliotropium* 'Marine'. The dense flowering display of this goldenrod is seen at its best in loosely spaced or scattered groups, with other plants threaded through.

Recommended partners: *Aster amellus* 'King George', *Crocosmia* 'Lucifer', *Dahlia* 'Grenadier', *Helenium* 'Wyndley', *Sambucus nigra* 'Guincho Purple' (stooled), *Stipa capillata*

H: 24in (60cm) S: 18in (45cm)
❀ Mid- to late summer Z4 pH5.5–7.5
▬▬ ▬▬ ◊·◊◊ ☐·▦

Stachys byzantina
LAMB'S EARS

How it works: In late spring, the emerging flower stems of lamb's ears (*Stachys byzantina*) harmonize with the gray-leaved willow *Salix hastata* 'Wehrhahnii' behind. They are joined by self-seeded wood forget-me-nots (*Myosotis sylvatica*) and Miss Willmott's ghost (*Eryngium giganteum*).
Recommended partners: *Allium moly, Crocus vernus* 'Jeanne d'Arc', *Cynara cardunculus, Rosa* Peach Blossom ('Ausblossom'), *Tulipa* 'Palestrina'

Stachys macrantha 'Superba'

How it works: *Stachys macrantha* 'Superba' furnishes the front of the border neatly in front of the loosely informal Damask *Rosa* 'Celsiana'. Both bloom and fade at exactly the same time and, although the stachys might have a few later flowers, the rose is strictly once-flowering. The zingy color of the stachys perks up the combination but a third plant with more structured foliage, perhaps a Bearded iris or a relatively sun-tolerant hosta, would help compensate for the lack of form. The stachys combines well with cool colors (including rich purples, blues, and crimsons) and glaucous, silver, or purple foliage, and contrasts effectively with yellow-green. For many years, 'Superba', almost sterile in damp, cool climates, has been confused with slightly taller *S. m.* 'Robusta', the distinction between the two being further blurred by the raising of variable offspring of the latter from seed.
Recommended partners: *Acaena saccaticupula* 'Blue Haze', *Aconitum* × *cammarum* 'Eleanora', *Alchemilla mollis, Artemisia ludoviciana, Hosta* (Tardiana Group) 'Halcyon', *Crambe maritima, Gladiolus tristis* var. *concolor, Heuchera* 'Obsidian', *Iris pallida* subsp. *pallida, Viola* 'Huntercombe Purple'

H & S: 18in (45cm)
❀ **Early summer to early autumn**
Z4 pH5.5–7.5

H: 22in (55cm) **S: 16in** (40cm)
❀ **Late spring to early summer**
Z6 pH5.5–7.5

Stachys officinalis 'Hummelo'

How it works: In this prairie-like planting in the New Perennial style, the vibrant betony *Stachys officinalis* 'Hummelo' is joined by *S. o.* 'Saharan Pink', *Echinacea purpurea* 'Rubinglow', *E. p.* 'Green Eyes', and the airy grass *Molinia caerulea* subsp. *arundinacea* 'Poul Petersen'. The near-horizontal echinacea flowers contrast in form with the strikingly dark, vertical stems of 'Rubinglow' and the columnar heads of the betonies. If grown in the nutrient-poor soil they all like, this combination will remain attractive for several months without the need for staking. This betony is valuable not so much for its foliage, which is rather dull and perhaps best placed behind something more attractive, nor for its florets as for the repeated rhythm of its flowerheads. It is also suited to herbaceous borders and could be used with shrub roses.

Recommended partners: *Artemisia absinthium* 'Lambrook Silver', *Campanula persicifolia* 'Bennett's Blue', *Geranium pratense* 'Mrs Kendall Clark', *Heuchera cylindrica* 'Greenfinch', *H.* Licorice ('Tnheu044'), *Lychnis coronaria* 'Alba', *Phygelius* × *rectus* Somerford Funfair Yellow ('Yapyel'), *Prunus* × *cistena*, *Rosa* Gertrude Jekyll ('Ausbord'), *Salvia officinalis* 'Purpurascens'

H: 20in (50cm) **S: 16in** (40cm)
❁ **Early summer to early autumn**
▬▬▭ ◊·◊◊ ☐·■ **Z5 pH5.5–7.5**

Stemmacantha 'Pulchra Major'

How it works: A drift of the knapweed *Stemmacantha* 'Pulchra Major' here combines with *Delphinium* 'Rosemary Brock', *Thalictrum flavum* subsp. *glaucum*, *Allium aflatunense*, *Nectaroscordum siculum*, and *Achillea* 'Terracotta'. The allium and nectaroscordum that started the display remain as seedheads, echoing the global knops of the knapweed, which remain after the flowers fade, encased in subtly shiny, papery scales. Horizontal plates of achillea and vertical spires of delphinium add contrasting form. The subdued mauves and pinks are gently contrasted with biscuity orange achillea and sulphur thalictrum. The knapweed is best grown in sufficient quantity for its globes to establish a pattern and rhythm. The flowers provide relatively little color, though they are pleasing enough with other cool tints and silver or purple foliage. It is good for prairie-style plantings, though more tolerant of wet, heavy soils than is usually supposed.

Recommended partners: *Achillea* 'Summerwine', *Agastache* 'Blue Adder', *Agrostemma gracile* 'Snow Queen', *Allium* 'Globemaster', *Artemisia ludoviciana* 'Silver Queen', *Aster × herveyi* 'Twilight', *Echinacea purpurea* 'White Swan'

H: 30in (75cm) **S: 20in** (50cm)
❀ Early to late summer

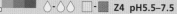 ◊·◊◊ ☐·■ Z4 pH5.5–7.5

Stipa capillata

How it works: The glistening, almost white seedheads of *Stipa capillata* shimmer against the sun, providing a contrast of form with *Eryngium planum* 'Blaukappe', its flowerheads flushed steely blue.

Recommended partners: *Achillea* 'Fanal', *Aster* × *frikartii* 'Mönch', *Echinops ritro*, *Kniphofia* 'Sunningdale Yellow', *Phormium* 'Duet', *Rudbeckia fulgida* var. *sullivantii* 'Goldsturm', *Scabiosa* 'Butterfly Blue'

H: 36in (90cm) S: 24in (60cm)
❀ **Early to late summer**
◊-◊◊ ☐-■ **Z7 pH5.5–7.5**

Veratrum nigrum

How it works: In this use of contrasting bold foliage but harmonious flowers, *Veratrum nigrum* furnishes in front of the elegant hybrid plume poppy, *Macleaya × kewensis*. The poppy's biscuit-colored flowers are borne in panicles similar in shape to those of the veratrum.

Recommended partners: *Cercidiphyllum magnificum, Cornus alba* 'Sibirica Variegata', *Lilium* 'Enchantment', *L. martagon, Meconopsis betonicifolia, Saxifraga fortunei*

H: 6ft (1.8m) S: 24in (60cm)
❀ Mid- to late summer Z4 pH5.5–7.5

Verbascum 'Helen Johnson'

How it works: In this charming mix of flowers, *Verbascum* 'Helen Johnson' stands behind young leaves of the grass *Miscanthus sinensis* and the yellow plate-like heads of *Achillea clypeolata*, with white sweet rocket (*Hesperis matronalis* var. *albiflora*) in the background.

Recommended partners: *Anthriscus sylvestris* 'Ravenswing', *Artemisia ludoviciana, Clematis* 'Pastel Blue', *Rosa* 'Climbing Paul Lédé', *Stipa calamagrostis*

H: 36in (90cm) S: 12in (30cm)
❀ Early to late summer Z4 pH6–7.5

Verbascum 'Megan's Mauve'

How it works: In this thoroughly mingled and charming scheme, *Verbascum* 'Megan's Mauve' is combined with *Heuchera* Ebony and Ivory ('E and I'), *Allium cristophii*, *Papaver orientale* 'Patty's Plum', Bearded iris, *Allium hollandicum* 'Purple Sensation', achillea, hemerocallis, salvia, and bronze fennel (*Foeniculum vulgare* 'Purpureum'). The flowers are predominantly from mauve to blue, with a touch of white and yellow to lighten the ensemble. A modicum of bronze foliage helps prevent the relatively subdued flowers being overwhelmed by bright green leaves. Varied shapes (round poppies and onions, flat achilleas, spires of verbascum, and a froth of heucheras) add interest. Like *V.* 'Helen Johnson' (page 279), 'Megan's Mauve' rarely overwinters in damp, cool climates, even in relatively nutrient-poor, dry, sharply drained conditions.

Recommended partners: *Achillea* Anthea ('Anblo'), *Anaphalis margaritacea* 'Neuschnee', *Anthemis* Susanna Mitchell ('Blomit'), *Artemisia stelleriana* 'Boughton Silver', *Cistus* × *hybridus*, *Convolvulus cneorum*, *Eschscholzia californica* 'Buttermilk', *Festuca glauca* 'Elijah Blue', *Lavandula pedunculata*, *Nigella damascena*, *Omphalodes linifolia*, *Parahebe perfoliata*

H: 4ft (1.2m) **S: 16in** (40cm)
❀ **Early summer to mid-summer**
◊-◊◊ ▢ **Z5 pH5.5–8**

Verbena 'Homestead Purple'

How it works: *Verbena* 'Homestead Purple' provides a carpet beneath upright *Miscanthus sinensis* 'Morning Light', whose silvery variegation harmonizes with the verbena's flowers. It can be used thus with summer-flowering bulbs or fountain- or rosette-forming plants like other grasses or yuccas. Alternatively, it can be used in containers or at the front of a border.

Recommended partners: *Helictotrichon sempervirens*, *Ipomoea batatas* 'Sweet Carolina Light Green', *Triteleia ixioides* 'Starlight', *Yucca filamentosa* 'Bright Edge'

H: 8in (20cm) S: 30in (75cm)
✽ **Late spring to late autumn**
◯-◯◯ ☐-▨ **Z8 pH5.5–7.5**

Veronica austriaca subsp. *teucrium* **'Crater Lake Blue'**

How it works: Low-growing *Veronica austriaca* subsp. *teucrium* 'Crater Lake Blue', with its long-lasting racemes of rich, deep blue flowers, provides a foil for the blooms of *Osteospermum* 'Pink Whirls', with their spoon-tipped petals. Other hybrids include gentian-blue 'Kapitän', 12in (30cm) tall, and vivid sky-blue 'Shirley Blue', just 2–4in (6–10cm).

Recommended partners: *Crambe maritima, Eryngium × tripartitum, Euonymus fortunei* 'Emerald 'n' Gold', *Salvia × sylvestris* 'Mainacht', *Sisyrinchium striatum*

H & S: **12in** (30cm)
❀ **Late spring to mid-summer**
◊◊ ☐-■ Z5 pH5.5–7.5

Viola **'Nellie Britton'**

How it works: *Viola* 'Nellie Britton' is one of the most successful hybrids, with small, dainty flowers in an uncommon shade of dusky mauve-pink (pink is a relatively rare color among viola cultivars). In this softly pretty planting scheme, its flowers match exactly those of the speedwell *Veronica spicata* 'Erika', whose foliage is lightly silvered, harmonizing with the white-edged leaves of *Ajania pacifica*.

Recommended partners: *Epimedium × versicolor* 'Sulphureum', *Hebe pinguifolia* 'Pagei', *Helichrysum petiolatum, Heuchera* 'Plum Pudding', *Myosotis sylvatica, Nemophila menziesii*

H: **6in** (15cm) S: **12in** (30cm)
❀ **Late spring to mid-summer**
◊◊ ■-■ Z4 pH5.5–7.5

Bulbs

Easy and rewarding plants, summer bulbs can be grown through a carpet of lower plants and incorporated into beds and borders. Many, including lilies, crinums, and gladioli, have bold, elegantly shaped blooms that can bring bright color and a touch of class to summer planting that, without them, might be mundane.

Introducing bulbs

In gardening, the word "bulb" is used very loosely to refer to any plant with a more-or-less swollen, underground storage organ that can be dried and sold as a conveniently packaged object: bulb catalogs offer true bulbs (daffodils, lilies, muscari, tulips), corms (crocosmias, crocuses, gladioli), and assorted tubers, tuberous roots, and rhizomes (aconites, anemones, dahlias). The vast majority of these "bulbous" plants share a common lifestyle as perennials, returning annually to their underground resting state. They come from a range of natural habitats, including desert margins, alpine pastures, and deciduous woodlands, most requiring them to grow, flower, and die down in the short space of time that the conditions are favorable. Bulbs also usually have short-lived, brightly colored blooms, a quality that is needed to attract pollinating insects, and many have fairly uninteresting, often strap-shaped foliage. In other respects, such as height and flower presentation and form, they are extremely varied.

Gardening with bulbs

In reasonably sheltered gardens, there can be bulbs in flower year-round: imposing lilies and gladioli, irises and zantedeschias, for example, look stunning in summer.

Bulbs are inexpensive when they are bought in bulk, and some suppliers are willing to sell even quite small quantities fairly cheaply. Summer starts with later camassias and Dutch and English irises. Spring alliums are followed by yet more summer onions, including many new hybrids. Lilies constitute the most important genus of summer bulbs, like the onions more expensive than most spring bulbs but still an excellent value.

In a crowded summer border, it might be harder for bulbs to compete; they might dwindle, so some "topping-up" might be necessary from year to year. However, bulb species in more-open sites such as rock gardens will often spread themselves by seeding.

Beds and borders

Summer-flowering bulbs can be integrated into borders and used in much the same way as herbaceous

A gravel mulch retains moisture for arum lily *Zantedeschia aethiopica* and the sedge *Cyperus involucratus*. The many new hybrid arum lilies include some hardy enough to grow outdoors in cooler climates.

Lilies like *Lilium speciosum* are invaluable for pots, where bare ankles and any necessary supporting canes can easily be hidden behind shorter plants.

rounded forms, or punctuation among those with soft foliage, such as fennel and artemisias.

Bulbs in pots

Most bulbs are ideal for pot culture, and many will enjoy the special conditions that can be created; for example, lime-hating lilies can be grown in containers of acidic growing mediums in chalk or limestone areas. Some lilies are stem-rooting and need to be planted deep, making it difficult to fit them into conventional pots. Larger containers or tubs are a solution, but chimneypots have also been used. Because their flowering season varies over a long period, it can help to have enough lilies to provide a succession, putting them in place as they start to bloom and removing them when they fade. Those cultivars that tend to lean to the sun will need their pots turned often. Ornamental onions and lilies, perhaps underplanted with annuals, make ideal subjects for large pots in summer.

Window boxes bring the flowers closer to eye level, where their delicate markings and, with some, wonderful scent can be more fully appreciated.

plants. Lilies are perfect for pairing with tall delphiniums or placing in front of Shrub or Climbing roses, both combinations being popular in cottage gardens, while gladioli and irises will provide strong focal points among cranesbills and other plants with lax or

Naturalizing bulbs

A few bulbs, such as later camassias, can be naturalized in grass to flower in early summer. These are vigorous enough to compete with grasses if nutrient levels are fairly low. The first of the meadow saffrons, such as *Colchicum byzantinum*, usually appear in the closing days of August and again are able to compete in moderately impoverished sward. The grass needs to be cut after seed of the early summer bulbs has been shed but before the colchicums emerge, removing the clippings so that the soil remains fairly impoverished and grasses do not prevail over bulbs and wildflowers.

Provided nutrients have been diminished sufficiently by removing mowings over several years, wild orchids will usually establish themselves from seed blown in on the wind. Native species bloom over a long period from April to September, giving gardeners who want to encourage them a headache over when to mow without disturbing their growth cycle. (Clearly, it helps to let them shed seed.) Perhaps the solution is to tailor the mowing regime to the predominant species.

Flowering from late spring into summer, the fragrant *Gladiolus tristis* var. *concolor* combines charmingly with the wallflower *Erysimum* 'Bowles's Mauve'.

Allium carinatum subsp. *pulchellum*

How it works: The slightly diffuse flowerheads of *Allium carinatum* subsp. *pulchellum* are made up of dainty amethyst florets that droop until pollinated, after which they turn upward. In this planting scheme, they are intimately mixed with the taller, starry flowerheads of *Eryngium* × *oliverianum*, to striking effect.

A. c. subsp. *pulchellum* is ideal for interweaving with shorter ground-cover plants and for combining with cranesbills, catmints, or eryngiums. Their coloring works well with silver, glaucous, or purple foliage, and cool flower colors such as crimson, lavender, pale pink, pale mauve, and white. A white-flowered variant is *A. c.* subsp. *pulchellum* f. *album*.

This planting combination would perhaps work even better with an eryngium that grows to the same height as the allium – for example, *E. bourgatii* 'Picos Blue'.

Recommended partners: *Artemisia stelleriana* 'Boughton Silver', *Heuchera* 'Amethyst Myst', *Populus alba* 'Richardii'

H: 18in (45cm) S: 2in (5cm)
✿ **Mid- to late summer**
 ◊-◊◊ ☐-■ Z6 pH5–7.5

Allium cristophii

How it works: *Allium cristophii* produces stout stems topped with bold globes of mauve, starry flowers that mature to parchment-colored seedheads that are almost as eye-catching as the flowers themselves. Its broad leaves start to die back at flowering time and are best hidden by foliage from neighboring plants. In this planting scheme, the ornamental onion is flowering at exactly the same height as love-in-a-mist *Nigella damascena* 'Miss Jekyll', the leaves of the nigella hiding the allium's untidy dying foliage. *A. cristophii* can be interplanted with bush roses and old Shrub roses, although these need to be pruned fairly hard to allow sunlight to reach the allium leaves early in the year and to match the height of its flowerheads.

Recommended partners: *Allium sphaerocephalon, Anemone × hybrida* 'Honorine Jobert', *Geranium* 'Ann Folkard', *Lavandula pedunculata* subsp. *pedunculata, Rosa* 'Prince Charles', *Spiraea japonica* (yellow-green leaved)

H: 18in (45cm) S: 12in (30cm)
✾ **Early to mid-summer**
◯-◯◯ ☐-▨ Z4 pH5–8

Allium giganteum

How it works: The round flowerheads of *Allium giganteum* and smaller round-headed leek *A. sphaerocephalon* echo each other in shape and harmonize with silver *Artemisia ludoviciana*. Warm *Helenium* 'Moerheim Beauty' is just subdued enough not to overwhelm it, while yellow-green euphorbia adds piquancy. The many florets in each head of *A. giganteum*, flowering in succession, give it an exceptionally long flowering season. It is perhaps best used in generous quantities in a drift or extended group, as here, drawing the eye from one association to the next, rather than as a small and static huddle produced by a handful of bulbs. It is the parent of many excellent hybrids, such as 'Globemaster', with heads 8in (20cm) across. The hybrids are usually sterile so do not self-sow, while *A. giganteum* can produce many seedlings that will replenish the planting if there is room and light for them to develop. Its color suits it to harmonies with cool colors, glaucous, purple, and silver foliage, and to contrasts with yellow-green.

Recommended partners: *Achillea* 'Summerwine', *Atriplex hortensis* var. *rubra*, *Campanula lactiflora* 'Alba', *Eryngium giganteum*, *Euphorbia sikkimensis*, *Salvia pratensis* Haematodes Group

H: 4ft (1.2m) S: 12in (30cm)
❀ **Early to late summer**
 ◇-◇◇ ▫-▪ **Z6 pH5–7.5**

Allium sphaerocephalon
ROUND-HEADED LEEK

How it works: *Allium sphaerocephalon* is an easy bulb for a gravel garden or sunny border, where it is useful as a unifying theme if repeated at intervals in informal drifts. Its slender growth allows it to weave prettily through groups of other plants.

Save for a collar of narrow bracts, the egg-shaped flowerheads of *Eryngium × tripartitum* in the scheme below left match the larger ones of *Allium sphaerocephalon* and harmonize in color. In the equally harmonious scheme below right, *Knautia macedonica* matches *A. sphaerocephalon* perfectly in color,

H: **24in** (60cm) S: **3½in** (8cm)
✻ **Early to late summer**
 ○-○○ ☐-■ **Z6 pH5–7.5**

along with lilac *Viola cornuta*, blue cornflowers (*Centaurea cyanus*), and bold seedheads of *Allium cristophii*.
Recommended partners: *Bupleurum rotundifolium*, *Eryngium planum* 'Blaukappe', *Euphorbia palustris*, *Gaura lindheimeri* 'Whirling Butterflies', *Gypsophila paniculata* 'Flamingo'

Camassia leichtlinii 'Semiplena'

How it works: The creamy white, star-shaped flowers of *Camassia leichtlinii* 'Semiplena' are borne on stiffly upright stems above an underplanting of magenta and yellow columbines. The very dark background, which is provided by *Berberis thunbergii* f. *atropurpurea* above and *Ligularia dentata* 'Desdemona' below, sets off the creamy camassia flowers to dramatic effect.
Recommended partners: *Ceanothus* 'Concha', *Eupatorium rugosum* 'Chocolate', *Geranium* × *oxonianum*, *Lunaria annua* 'Variegata', *Rosa* 'Helen Knight'

H: 31in (80cm) S: 9in (23cm)
❀ **Late spring to early summer**
 ◊◊ **Z4 pH5–8**

Galtonia candicans

How it works: The white bells of *Galtonia candicans* rise above the old Dwarf Bedding Group dahlia *D.* 'Hatton Castle' in a striking late summer display. The dahlia disguises the galtonia's foliage, which tends to become untidy as flowering time nears. Other dahlias that would also make good companions for the galtonia are 'Gallery Art Deco' and 'Orange Nugget'.

Recommended partners: *Agapanthus* 'Loch Hope', *Agastache* 'Firebird', *Artemisia lactiflora* Guizhou Group, *Dahlia* 'Bednall Beauty', *Filipendula rubra* 'Venusta', *Lilium* 'Black Beauty', *Nicotiana langsdorffii*, *Papaver orientale* 'Sultana'

H: 4ft (1.2m) **S: 12in** (30cm)
✤ **Late summer**

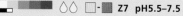 ◊◊ ▢-▩ **Z7 pH5.5–7.5**

Gladiolus communis subsp. *byzantinus*

How it works: Magenta-flowered *Gladiolus communis* subsp. *byzantinus* and *Geranium psilostemon* have contrasting flower shapes that combine well. Their rich color is leavened by the silver leaves of rose campion (*Lychnis coronaria*), which will add its own magenta blooms before the gladiolus fades. *G. c.* subsp. *byzantinus* is vigorous and very easy to grow from cormlets.

Recommended partners: *Cistus* × *purpureus*, *Cytisus* × *praecox* 'Warminster', *Iris pallida*, *Lavandula pedunculata* subsp. *pedunculata*, *Phormium* 'Bronze Baby', *Rosmarinus officinalis*

H: 36in (90cm) **S: 12in** (30cm)
✤ **Early summer**

◊-◊◊ ▢-▩ **Z7 pH5.5–7**

Gladiolus **Grandiflorus Group**

How it works: A drift of showy *Gladiolus* 'Dancing Doll' (there is also a Butterfly Group cultivar of this name) is combined with other plants with vertical habits, including pure blue *Salvia patens* and *Penstemon* 'Mother of Pearl'. These form an effective contrast with the rounded flowerheads of *Phlox paniculata* cultivars. *Gladiolus* 'Windsong' would look equally good in such a planting.

Hybrid gladioli of the Grandiflorus Group are available in every color except pure blue, black, and blue-green. The giant-, large-, and medium-flowered hybrids have great impact and an almost tropical exuberance that suits large-scale planting schemes. Their spiky habit makes bold accents, and any stiffness can be masked by planting shorter, mound-forming plants in front.

Recommended partners: *Cleome hassleriana*, *Dahlia* 'Arabian Night', *Lavatera* × *clementii* 'Barnsley', *Miscanthus sinensis* 'Kleine Silberspinne', *Penstemon* 'King George V', *Phygelius* × *rectus*

H: 5–6ft (1.5–1.8m) **S: 8in** (20cm)
✿ **Early to late summer**
△-△△ ☐-■ Z9 pH5.5–7

Gladiolus small-flowered hybrids

How it works: The sumptuous red blooms of *Gladiolus* 'Georgette', one of several of this name, harmonize in color but contrast in form with the dainty hanging bells of *Fuchsia magellanica* 'Versicolor', working well against the fuchsia's pale leaves.

Recommended partners: *Erysimum* 'Bowles's Mauve', *Euphorbia palustris*, *Philadelphus* 'Manteau d'Hermine', *Phlomis purpurea*, *Rosa* Sweet Dream ('Fryminicot'), *Spiraea japonica* 'Bullata'

H: 40in–4ft (1–1.2m) **S: 6in** (15cm)
❀ **Early to late summer**

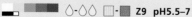 ◊-◊◊ ☐-■ **Z9 pH5.5–7**

Iris 'Symphony'

How it works: The bright colors of Dutch Group *Iris* 'Symphony' shine among the orange flowers of *Geum* 'Prinses Juliana' and an Oriental poppy (*Papaver orientale*). Adding more of the iris and poppy, perhaps with some bronze foliage, would also be effective.

The flowering season of Dutch irises extends beyond that of spring bulbs such as tulips and narcissi, bridging the gap between these and many summer flowers. 'Symphony' is an excellent cultivar, as is 'Apollo', both of them white and yellow bicolors. Other yellowish Dutch irises include 'Royal Yellow' and 'Golden Harvest', with golden yellow falls and paler standards; and 'Yellow Queen', in golden yellow, with an orange blotch on the falls. With their upright, narrow habit, they are all useful for planting among slightly shorter herbaceous or biennial plants with simpler shapes or significantly different colors or with small to medium-sized shrubs, such as smaller ceanothus and Shrub roses.

Recommended partners: *Aquilegia chrysantha* 'Yellow Queen', *Ceanothus* 'Puget Blue', *Erysimum* × *marshallii*, *Papaver nudicaule*, *Potentilla fruticosa* 'Hopleys Orange', *Rosa xanthina* 'Canary Bird', *Spiraea japonica* Golden Princess ('Lisp')

H: 26in (65cm) S: 4in (10cm)
✿ **Late spring to early summer**
 ◊◊ Z7 pH5.5–7.5

Lilium African Queen Group

How it works: This is a dramatic combination of warm colors consisting of *Lilium* African Queen Group, *Crocosmia* 'Lucifer', and the double daylily *Hemerocallis fulva* 'Flore Pleno'.

The lilies in the African Queen Group typically have large, trumpet-shaped flowers in shades of rich yellow and apricot-orange. 'African Queen' was selected as the best seedling of the Group and has flowers in more intense colors: the petals are warm deep tangerine-apricot inside and warm mahogany brown suffused with yellow outside. Its bold shape and beautiful lines, also characteristic of other lilies in this Group, make a strong architectural impact and add a striking note of superlative quality wherever it is used. The dark stems contribute to the effect, making this an excellent plant to associate with bronze foliage and warm colors such as apricot, peach, and soft orange. It is also strongly fragrant.

Recommended partners: *Canna* 'Phasion', *Foeniculum vulgare* 'Purpureum', *Hosta* 'Sum and Substance', *Physocarpus opulifolius* 'Diabolo', *Rosa* Graham Thomas ('Ausmas'), *Weigela* Briant Rubidor ('Olympiade')

H: 6ft (1.8m) S: 8in (20cm)
❀ **Mid- to late summer**
◼◼◼◼ ◊◊ ▢-◼ Z5 pH5.5–7.5

Lilium Bellingham Group

How it works: The warm orange *Lilium* Bellingham Group forms a striking contrast with sumptuous indigo *Delphinium* King Arthur Group, its blooms enlivened by their white eyes. The flowers of L. Bellingham Group are unscented.

Recommended partners: *Anchusa azurea*, *Euphorbia palustris*, *Meconopsis* × *sheldonii*, *Osmanthus heterophyllus* 'Purpureus', *Rhododendron* 'Delicatissimum'

H: 6½ft (2m) S: 8in (20cm)
❀ **Early to mid-summer**
◼◼◼◼ ◊◊ ▢-◼ Z5 pH5–7.5

Lilium 'Black Beauty'

How it works: This summer combination of flowers in similar shades of rose-pink and crimson includes the large, scented blooms of the Oriental Hybrid lily *Lilium* 'Black Beauty', upward-facing Texensis Group *Clematis* 'Duchess of Albany', and *Anisodontea capensis*. They form a close harmony that is charming and intricate at close range – although from a distance it would be hard to distinguish the individual blooms.

    L. 'Black Beauty' is robust and aristocratic in form. With good cultivation in a humus-rich soil, it should produce a prodigious candelabra of blooms, each stem bearing dozens of flowers – as many as 150 have been reported on one stem. The complex architecture and geometry of a well-grown flower spike, with its secondary and tertiary branching, has a pleasing symmetry that can be destroyed if any limbs of the candelabra are lost through damage from slugs.

Recommended partners: *Anemone × hybrida* 'September Charm', *Atriplex hortensis* var. *rubra*, *Buddleja davidii* 'Nanho Petite Indigo', *Fuchsia magellanica*, *Phlox paniculata* 'Harlequin', *Phygelius aequalis* 'Sani Pass', *Weigela florida* 'Foliis Purpureis'

H: 6ft (1.8m) S: 8in (20cm)
✿ **Mid-summer**
◌◌ ☐-■ **Z6 pH5–6.5**

Lilium candidum
MADONNA LILY

How it works: Careful planting of the hybrid lavender *Lavandula × intermedia*, both in front of and behind *Lilium candidum*, has hidden the Madonna lily's untidy basal foliage.

Recommended partners: *Artemisia* 'Powis Castle', *Dianthus* 'Mrs Sinkins', *Lavandula × chaytoriae* 'Sawyers', *Nepeta* 'Six Hills Giant', *Nigella damascena* 'Oxford Blue', *Rosa* 'De Rescht', *R. glauca*

H: 5ft (1.5m) S: 12in (30cm)
✿ **Early to mid-summer**
◌◌ ☐-■ **Z6 pH5.5–8**

Lilium 'Connecticut King'

How it works: *Lilium* 'Connecticut King', with its strong yellow, star-shaped, and upward facing flowers, provides the focal point in this hot mixture of orange daylilies (*Hemerocallis fulva* 'Flore Pleno') and red *Crocosmia* 'Lucifer'. The upright stems of this very vigorous and easy-to-grow lily bear dark green, glossy foliage.

Recommended partners: *Achillea* 'Inca Gold', *Coreopsis* 'Sunray', *Delphinium grandiflorum*, *Lychnis chalcedonica*, *Miscanthus sinensis* 'Zebrinus', *Tagetes patula* Favorite Series (mixed)

H: **40in** (1m) S: **8in** (20cm)
✿ **Early to mid-summer**
◻︎ ◻︎ ◻︎-◼︎ Z5 pH5.5–7.5

Lilium 'Enchantment'

How it works: *Lilium* 'Enchantment' contrasts boldly with *Lavandula* × *intermedia* Old English Group. Yearly mid-spring pruning of the lavender will be needed in order to let in enough light for the lily.

Recommended partners: *Acanthus mollis* 'Hollard's Gold', *Achillea* 'Moonshine', *Alchemilla mollis*, *Campanula glomerata* 'Superba', *Canna indica* 'Purpurea', *Centaurea cyanus*, *Corokia* × *virgata* 'Bronze King', *Hemerocallis* 'Corky', *Lysimachia ciliata* 'Firecracker', *Phygelius* × *rectus* 'Sunshine', *Rosa* Amber Queen ('Harroony')

H: **36in** (90cm) S: **8in** (20cm)
✿ **Early summer**
◻︎ ◻︎ ◻︎-◼︎ Z5 pH5.5–7.5

Lilium 'Joy'

How it works: *Lilium* 'Joy' (syn. 'Le Rêve') harmonizes with the blooms of *Geranium* 'Ann Folkard', joined by gently contrasting bluish bracts of *Cerinthe major* var. *purpurascens*, *Salvia patens* 'Cambridge Blue', and the sharp yellow-green leaves of the cranesbill.

Recommended partners: *Achillea millefolium* 'Lilac Beauty', *Astrantia major* 'Roma', *Berberis thunbergii* 'Pink Queen', *Campanula* 'Burghaltii', *Geranium pratense* Midnight Reiter strain, *Gypsophila paniculata* 'Flamingo', *Heuchera* 'Raspberry Regal', *Hosta* 'Krossa Regal', *Rosa glauca*, *Salvia officinalis* 'Purpurascens', *Stachys byzantina*

H: 30in (75cm) **S: 8in** (20cm)
✸ **Mid-summer**
◊◊ ☐-■ Z6 pH5–6.5

Lilium 'Pretender'

How it works: Here, the starry blooms of *Lilium* 'Pretender' are set in a cloud of tiny flowers of the rather lax herbaceous *Clematis recta*. The lily, like 'Enchantment', is classed as an Asiatic hybrid and usually has about 10 well-spaced blooms borne almost on the same level, suiting them to a treatment where, as here, they appear set above a sheet of other flowers. As for all lilies, it pays to buy the biggest bulbs, both to minimize the risk of virus disease and to get the most blooms flowering over the longest period. The clematis needs some support to keep its flowers just below those of the lily and can sprawl untidily if left to its own devices. 'Pretender' is suited to combinations with hot colors – glaucous, red, yellow-green, or purple foliage and hot-colored flowers – and is sufficiently light orange to be contrasted with rich blue. It can clash exquisitely with magenta and is good with yellow-green flowers.

Recommended partners: *Camassia leichtlinii* 'Semiplena', *Campanula lactiflora* 'Prichard's Variety', *Delphinium* (Belladonna Group) 'Volkerfrieden', *Dianthus barbatus* 'Messenger Red', *D. b.* 'Messenger Scarlet', *Geranium* 'Brookside', *G. psilostemon*, *Hosta sieboldiana* var. *elegans*

H: 24in (60cm) **S: 8in** (20cm)

❀ **Early summer**

 ◊◊ ▢-◾ ◼ Z5 pH5–7.5

Lilium regale

How it works: In this white-flowered scheme, which would be equally effective with larger groups of each plant, *Lilium regale* is joined by *Hydrangea arborescens* 'Grandiflora', feverfew (*Tanacetum parthenium*), Miss Willmott's ghost (*Eryngium giganteum*), and the seedheads of *Allium aflatunense*. Vigorous and easy to grow, *L. regale* has superbly shaped and very sweetly scented white trumpets.

Recommended partners: *Astilbe × arendsii* 'Cattleya', *Cryptotaenia japonica* f. *atropurpurea*, *Nicotiana langsdorffii*, *Oenothera fruticosa* 'Fyrverkeri', *Ruta graveolens*, *Weigela* 'Victoria'

H: 6ft (1.8m) S: 8in (20cm)
✣ **Mid-summer**

 Z5 pH5–7.5

Ornithogalum pyramidale

How it works: This combination uses the feathery silver leaves of tender shrubby *Artemisia arborescens* to hide the untidy dying foliage of *Ornithogalum pyramidale* and to infill between the bulb's spindly flower stems. The artemisia can be grown from cuttings taken in late summer or early autumn, overwintered under glass, and planted out as soon as the danger of frost has passed.

Recommended partners: *Ageratina altissima* 'Chocolate', *Cerinthe major* var. *purpurascens*, *Echinops ritro* 'Veitch's Blue', *Eucalyptus gunnii*, *Nigella damascena* 'Miss Jekyll', *Osmanthus heterophyllus* 'Purpureus', *Phormium* 'Bronze Baby'

H: 40in (1m) S: 8in (20cm)
❀ **Early summer**
�○-�○�○ ☐-■ Z7 pH5.5–7.5

Tigridia pavonia
PEACOCK FLOWER

How it works: This carmine selection of *Tigridia pavonia*, flopping obligingly to place itself among the matching, sprawling *Verbena* 'Sissinghurst', creates a fascinating picture to be viewed at close range at the front of a border.

Recommended partners: *Argyranthemum* 'Jamaica Primrose', *Canna* 'Champigny', *Dahlia* 'Roxy', *Phormium* 'Yellow Wave', *Salvia greggii* 'Peach', *Solenostemon* 'Walter Turner'

Watsonia fourcadei

How it works: A clump of coral-red *Watsonia fourcadei* is here given ample room to display its imposing habit to the full. Its blooms contrast with large *Agapanthus praecox* subsp. *orientalis* and a smaller agapanthus. White Japanese anemones (*Anemone* × *hybrida*) leaven the rich colors.

H: 18in (45cm) **S: 9in** (23cm)
❀ **Mid-summer to early autumn**
 ◊◊ ☐ **Z9 pH5–7**

H: 18–60in (45–150cm) **S: 16in** (40cm)
❀ **Early spring to early autumn**
 ◊◊ ☐ **Z9 pH5–7**

Watsonia 'Stanford Scarlet'

How it works: The rich coral-red flowers and sword-like foliage of *Watsonia* 'Stanford Scarlet' and spiky *Cordyline australis* 'Torbay Dazzler' create a bold, almost tropical effect. It combines well with hot-colored flowers and purple or yellow-green foliage, but its hue is soft enough to be used with peach, salmon, or apricot.

Recommended partners: *Agastache* Acapulco Orange ('Kiegador'), *Eschscholzia californica*, *Heuchera* 'Obsidian', *Kniphofia* 'Bees' Sunset', *Nicotiana langsdorffii*

Recommended partners: *Agapanthus* 'Loch Hope', *Agastache* 'Firebird', *Beschorneria yuccoides*, *Canna* 'Cleopatra', *Dahlia* 'Bednall Beauty', *Hedychium gardnerianum*, *Hemerocallis* 'Frans Hals', *Kniphofia* 'Timothy', *Leonotis leonurus*, *Lobelia tupa*, *Nandina domestica*, *Phormium* 'Yellow Wave', *Phygelius × rectus* 'Sunshine', *Yucca gloriosa*

H: 18–60in (45–150cm) **S: 16in** (40cm)
❀ **Early spring to early autumn**
◊◊ □ **Z9 pH5–7**

Zantedeschia aethiopica

ARUM LILY

How it works: In hot climates, the arum lily (*Zantedeschia aethiopica*) will flower happily in partial shade, where it can be combined with other shade-loving plants, such as the dainty *Begonia* 'Ricinifolia', with its elegant sprays of pink flowers.

Recommended partners: *Astilbe* 'Deutschland', *Canna* 'Erebus', *Dryopteris filix-mas*, *Filipendula rubra* 'Venusta', *Iris* 'Butter and Sugar', *Rodgersia aesculifolia*

H: 36in (90cm) **S: 24in** (60cm)

Late spring to mid-summer Z8 pH5–7.5

Zigadenus elegans

How it works: An airy veil of green and cream flowers of *Zigadenus elegans* is enlivened by the brilliant magenta, dark-veined blooms of the sprawling, long-flowering cranesbill *Geranium wallichianum* 'Syabru' in front of a carpet of *G. macrorrhizum*.

A very hardy bulb, *Zigadenus elegans* is a sun-lover for the front of a warm border, although it will tolerate some shade in areas with hotter summers. It needs very good drainage, so it is good in a gravel garden. The quiet color of its flowers suits it to close-range inspection, and it looks attractive growing through low ground-cover plants, particularly against a background of dark foliage. It combines well with glaucous foliage and with other flowers in white, soft yellow, pure blue, very deep blue, or purple, as well as yellow-green, such as summer-flowering euphorbias.

Recommended partners: *Agapanthus* 'Bressingham Blue', *Agastache rugosa*, *Crambe maritima*, *Eryngium alpinum* 'Blue Star', *Eschscholzia californica* 'Alba' (spring sown), *Euphorbia seguieriana* subsp. *niciciana*, *Phygelius aequalis* 'Yellow Trumpet', *Verbena rigida*, *Veronica spicata*

H: 27in (70cm) S: 3½in (8cm)
❀ **Mid- to late summer Z5 pH5.5–7.5**
 ◊-◊◊ ☐-■

Annuals

Invaluable for summer
display, annuals, biennials,
and frost-tender perennials
have abundant flowers, while
many, including vegetables
such as black kale and
lettuces, also have striking
foliage. They are extremely
versatile, working well
among more-permanent
plants in bedding as well
as playing an important role
when grouped in pots and
hanging baskets.

Introducing annuals

Often the brightest flowers and most spectacular foliage in gardens are provided by the shortest-lived plants – the annuals, biennials, and tender perennials, are used for late spring and summer display. (Those not reliably hardy in Zone 8 are included here.) True annuals and biennials are plants that invest all their energy into one season of flower and seed production before dying. Tender perennials are from climates without cold winters; this means many evolved to flower freely over a very long period. The result is maximum flower power, a feature that plant breeders have often intensified by producing astonishing color ranges on compact and uniform plants.

Seed-raised plants

Hardy annuals are easy to sow where they are to flower, then thinned out to final spacings when they are established. One particularly delightful way of using them is in a mixture: many seed companies offer packets of mixed tall or short annuals, while more adventurous gardeners may like to concoct their own mixes for a particular height, flowering time, or range of colors. Sown sparsely in straight rows and thinned to small clumps of seedlings, 6–8in (15–20cm) apart, they will soon go on to produce a colorful display.

Dahlias provide bold colors and strong shapes in borders from mid-summer until the autumn frosts.

Biennials need to be sown the year before they are required to flower and then put in their flowering positions in autumn or spring. Some hardy annuals can be treated in the same way. Being sown the previous late summer or autumn means that flowers appear earlier on larger plants, thus widening the possible flowering combinations. Sweet peas are ideal for this treatment.

Half-hardy annuals and many tender perennials are also easy to raise from seed. In cold areas, they should be sown in pots or trays somewhere bright and warm, such as on a windowsill or in a greenhouse, and the seedlings must not be planted in the garden until no further frosts are expected.

Formal and informal bedding

Annuals and tender perennials are very popular for bedding, and a huge range of effects can be achieved. Plants may be arranged in patterns or mixed loosely together to create a tapestry of mingled colors and varied forms. Careful selection of colors, forms, and textures can produce gentle, romantic moods or bright, vibrant ones. For example, the vivid red salvia, once so popular for formal beds in public parks, is now available in a variety of softer colors, which produce a much more delicate display. Where there is more space, taller-growing

In this imaginative composition, scarlet *Salvia coccinea* and pelargoniums have been mixed with clashing carmine impatiens and nicotiana.

tender perennials with bold foliage can be used to produce exciting subtropical or junglelike areas in the garden – bananas, cannas, and ricinus are all excellent choices.

Drifts of quiet color – cosmos, lavateras, and nigellas – will enrich a subtle bed, while cannas, dahlias, ricinus, and many salvia will bring a border of hot-colored roses, kniphofias, and purple-leaved shrubs to a fiery climax.

Aeonium 'Zwartkop'

How it works: A well-branched plant of *Aeonium* 'Zwartkop' contrasts dramatically against the near-white stems of *Leucophyta brownii*. Aeoniums are tender perennial succulents with rosettes of leaves that are fascinating for their geometrical perfection. The leaves of 'Zwartkop' age from bronze through deep chocolate to lustrous black. Both plants in this scheme benefit from a sunny site with good drainage and relatively low nitrogen availability.

Recommended partners: *Cordyline australis* Purpurea Group, *Dahlia* 'Bishop of Llandaff', *Fuchsia* 'Thalia', *Lotus berthelotii*, *Plectranthus argentatus*, *Ricinus communis* 'Carmencita', *Senecio cineraria* 'Silver Dust'

H: 18in (45cm) S: 14in (35cm)
❀ Late spring

 Z10 pH5.5–7

Ageratum houstonianum 'Old Grey'

How it works: At the front of a border, the small flowerheads of *Ageratum houstonianum* 'Old Grey' and bicolored florets of *Nemesia* 'KLM' contrast in size with the larger, more solid flowers of *Petunia* (Pearl Series) 'Pearl Azure Blue' and *Salpiglossis* 'Kew Blue', all of them in harmonious shades. The name 'Old Grey' is misleading because the flower color is really a soft lavender-blue.

Recommended partners: *Argyranthemum gracile* 'Chelsea Girl', *Brachyscome iberidifolia* 'Summer Skies', *Helichrysum petiolare*, *Heliotropium arborescens* 'Princess Marina', *Osteospermum* 'White Pim', *Senecio cineraria* 'Cirrus'

H: 18in (45cm) S: 12in (30cm)
❀ Early summer to early autumn

 Z10 pH5.5–7.5

Alonsoa warscewiczii

How it works: A veil of shining scarlet florets of *Alonsoa warscewiczii* on harmonizing red stems shows up brightly against the dusky reddish purple foliage of a smoke bush (*Cotinus coggygria*) cultivar in a steeply banked detail at the front of a border.

Recommended partners: *Calceolaria* 'Camden Hero', *Canna indica* 'Purpurea', *Cordyline australis* Purpurea Group, *Dahlia* 'Bednall Beauty', *D.* 'Yelno Harmony', *Fuchsia* 'Thalia', *Lobelia* × *speciosa* 'Fan Orchidrosa', *Lysimachia nummularia* 'Aurea', *Nicotiana* 'Domino Red', *N.* 'Lime Green', *Pelargonium* 'Paul Crampel', *Salvia splendens*

H: 18in (45cm) **S: 12in** (30cm)
✤ **Early summer to mid-autumn**
◌◌ ▢-▢ **Z10 pH5–7.5**

Ammi majus

How it works: The flattish, lacy heads of *Ammi majus* contrast in form and color with the blue columns of the larkspur *Consolida ajacis* 'Blue Spire', they are exactly the same height here. Both plants can be grown from either an autumn or a spring sowing. When sown in autumn, the ammi will reach about 4ft (1.2m), with the larkspur ultimately growing slightly taller. Sown in spring, the ammi would be 30in (75cm), with the larkspur eventually a little taller.

Recommended partners: *Briza maxima*, *Lunaria annua* 'Variegata', *Paeonia lactiflora* 'Albert Crousse', *Rosa* 'Impératrice Joséphine', *Weigela* Lucifer ('Courtared')

H: 30–48in (75–120cm) **S: 18–24in** (45–60cm)
✤ **Early summer to mid-autumn**
◌◌ ▢-▢ **Z6 pH5.5–7.5**

Antirrhinum majus 'Black Prince'

How it works: Spikes of the snapdragon *Antirrhinum majus* 'Black Prince' and the rounded flowerheads of sweet William (*Dianthus barbatus* Nigrescens Group) contrast in form while matching perfectly in color. Snapdragons are available in a wide range of sizes and colors.

Recommended partners: *Atriplex hortensis* var. *rubra*, *Cosmos bipinnatus* 'Sonata White', *Cotinus coggygria* 'Royal Purple', *Ricinus communis* 'Carmencita', *Verbena rigida*

H: 18in (45cm) S: 8in (20cm)
❈ **Early summer to early autumn**
▰▰▱▱ ◊◊ ▢-▰ Z9 pH5.5–7.5

Argyranthemum foeniculaceum hort.

How it works: The white petals and golden discs of *Argyranthemum foeniculaceum* hort. lift the recessive tints of lavender, lilac, and indigo supplied by sea lavender (*Limonium latifolium*), *Geranium himalayense*, horned violets (*Viola cornuta*), and the annual clary, *Salvia viridis* 'Claryssa Blue'.

Recommended partners: *Heliotropium arborescens* 'Princess Marina', *Pelargonium* 'Paul Crampel', *Petunia* 'Frenzy Buttercup', *Salvia farinacea* 'Victoria', *Senecio cineraria* 'Silver Dust', *Verbena* 'Silver Anne'

H: 30in (75cm) S: 24in (60cm)
❈ **All year**
▰▰▱▱ ◊◊ ▢-▰ Z9 pH5–7.5

Argyranthemum 'Jamaica Primrose'

How it works: In late summer and early autumn, *Argyranthemum* 'Jamaica Primrose' remains in full bloom, combining beautifully with warm, bronze-orange *Rudbeckia hirta* Rustic Dwarf Group and the sprawling yellow *Bidens ferulifolia*, which fills in the space in front of both, spilling onto the adjoining path.

Recommended partners: *Agapanthus* 'Loch Hope', *Arundo donax* var. *versicolor*, *Dahlia* 'David Howard', *Helichrysum petiolare* 'Variegatum', *Nicotiana* 'Lime Green', *Nigella damascena* 'Miss Jekyll', *Perovskia* 'Blue Spire', *Salvia farinacea* 'Strata'

H & S: **40in (1m)**
❁ **Late spring to mid-autumn**
 ◊◊ ☐-■ Z9 pH5–7.5

Arundo donax var. *versicolor*

How it works: With their eye-catching variegation, the upright stems of the grass *Arundo donax* var. *versicolor* provide a striking accent among the harmonious flowers of yellow corn marigolds (*Glebionis segeta*), white Japanese anemones (*Anemone* × *hybrida* 'Honorine Jobert'), and behind, the shrubby *Bupleurum fruticosum*.

Recommended partners: *Canna indica*, *Cleome hassleriana* Color Fountain Series, *Dahlia coccinea*, *Melianthus major*, *Musa basjoo*, *Ricinus communis* 'Carmencita', *Verbena bonariensis*

H: **6ft (1.8m)** S: **24in (60cm)**
❁ **Mid- to late autumn** Z9 pH4.5–7.5
■ ◊◊-◊◊◊ ☐-■

Atriplex hortensis var. *rubra*
RED ORACH

How it works: The large, dusky purple-red leaves of *Atriplex hortensis* var. *rubra* fill in the gaps between and unify the cool colors of various perennials – *Allium giganteum*, with spherical flowerheads, pale blue *Campanula lactiflora*, and *Salvia verticillata* 'Purple Rain'.

Recommended partners: *Cotinus coggygria* 'Royal Purple', *Dahlia* 'Bishop of Llandaff', *Echinops bannaticus* 'Taplow Blue', *Eryngium giganteum*, *Hemerocallis* 'Stafford', *Nicotiana* 'Lime Green', *Plectranthus argentatus*

H: 4ft (1.2m) S: 12in (30cm)
✿ **Early to mid-summer**
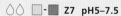 ◊◊ ▢-◼ **Z7 pH5–7.5**

Brachyscome iberidifolia
SWAN RIVER DAISY

How it works: This charming incident with dark-eyed, vivid lavender *Brachyscome iberidifolia* set in a carpet of sweet alyssum (*Lobularia maritima*) could be repeated on a larger scale, perhaps with contrasting soft yellow or yellow-green foliage and flowers for greater impact.

Recommended partners: *Crambe maritima*, *Eschscholzia caespitosa* 'Sundew', *Heliotropium arborescens* 'Princess Marina', *Petunia* 'Frenzy Buttercup', *Verbena peruviana* 'Alba'

H: 12–18in (30–45cm) S: 12in (30cm)
✿ **Early to late summer**
◊◊ ▢-◼ **Z10 pH5.5–7.5**

Brassica oleracea (Acephala Group) 'Red Peacock'

How it works: The radiating purple-flushed leaves and magenta midribs of the ornamental kale *Brassica oleracea* (Acephala Group) 'Red Peacock' make a focal point in this container planting, harmonizing with *Osteospermum* 'Pink Whirls', *Verbena* 'Hidcote Purple' (top), and sprawling *V. tenuisecta* (bottom). From a mid-spring sowing, this will become even more brilliantly variegated with purple-pink through autumn and winter.

Recommended partners: *Argyranthemum foeniculaceum* hort., *Petunia* Surfinia Blue ('Sunblu'), *Solenostemon* 'Lord Falmouth'

H & S: 16in (40cm)
Late spring to mid-summer
Z5–6 pH6–8

Canna 'Erebus'

How it works: This exotic combination, mainly of tender plants, includes salmon-pink *Canna* 'Erebus', scarlet *Lobelia cardinalis* 'Queen Victoria', the ray-like umbels of papyrus (*Cyperus papyrus*), a dark-leaved canna, and the cider gum (*Eucalyptus gunnii*). The canna's flowers act as the focal point of the group, harmonizing with the red blooms and contrasting gently with the glaucous foliage of the gum.

Recommended partners: *Cordyline australis* Purpurea Group, *Dahlia* 'Alva's Doris', *Diascia rigescens*, *Fuchsia* 'Thalia', *Ricinus communis* 'Carmencita', *Verbena bonariensis*

H: 4ft (1.2m) **S: 20in** (50cm) **Z9 pH5.5–7.5**
Mid-summer to early autumn

Cerinthe major var. *purpurascens*

How it works: This cool-colored planting combination consists of *Cerinthe major* var. *purpurascens* and lavender (*Lavandula angustifolia*) – both of them favorite food plants of bees – behind a clipped edging of dwarf boxwood (*Buxus sempervirens* 'Suffruticosa').

Recommended partners: *Eschscholzia caespitosa* 'Sundew', *Euphorbia characias* 'Blue Hills', *Iris* 'Jane Phillips', *Lilium* 'Joy', *Miscanthus sinensis* 'Kleine Fontäne'

H: **18in** (45cm) S: **12in** (30cm)
❀ **Early to late summer**
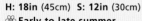   Z9 pH5.5–7.5

Cleome hassleriana
SPIDER FLOWER

How it works: White and purplish crimson spider flowers (*Cleome hassleriana*) are ideally matched in height to *Verbena bonariensis*, whose small purple flowerheads produce a soft haze of contrasting blooms. In front, *Cosmos bipinnatus* closely corresponds with the colors of the spider flowers but provides a contrast of floral form.

The relatively tall height of *C. hassleriana* makes it useful for growing at the back of an annual border or in drifts through a herbaceous or mixed border. Good cultivars include 'Violet Queen', 'Cherry Queen', 'Pink Queen', pure white 'Helen Campbell', and Color Fountain Series. These cultivars mix well with cool pink, crimson, lilac, purple, or white flowers, and with glaucous, purple, and white-variegated foliage, such as some larger miscanthus cultivars. They are excellent with dahlias and larger China asters (*Callistephus* cultivars), while for a tropical effect they can be mixed with cannas, melianthus, and larger-flowering tender solanums. Spider flowers require warm summers to thrive.

Recommended partners: *Aster × frikartii* 'Wunder von Stäfa', *Crambe maritima*, *Dahlia* 'Gerrie Hoek', *Lathyrus rotundifolius*, *Populus alba* 'Richardii' (stooled)

H: 4ft (1.2m) S: 18in (45cm)
❀ **Mid- to late summer**
◊◊ ▢-▧ Z10 pH5.5–7

Consolida ajacis
LARKSPUR

How it works: The columnar racemes of this attractive rich blue cultivar of *Consolida ajacis* are tall enough to appear among and just above the contrasting white flowers of an annual mallow (*Lavatera trimestris* 'Mont Blanc').

Recommended partners: *Ammi majus*, *Antirrhinum majus* 'White Wonder', *Clarkia unguiculata* Royal Bouquet Series, *Lychnis coronaria* 'Alba', *Plecostachys serpyllifolia*

H: 12–48in (30–120cm) S: 9–12in (23–30cm)
❀ **Early to late summer**
◊◊ ▢-▧ Z7 pH5.5–7.5

Cordyline australis Purpurea Group

How it works: In its third year, *Cordyline australis* Purpurea Group will just outgrow the matching dark foliage and scarlet flowers of *Dahlia* 'Bednall Beauty', making a strong focal point in a border.

Recommended partners: *Canna* 'Wyoming', *Chamaerops humilis* 'Vulcano', *Dahlia* 'Alva's Doris', *Nicotiana* 'Lime Green', *Pelargonium* 'Orangesonne', *Ricinus communis* 'Impala'

Dahlia 'Arabian Night'

How it works: The rounded, blood-red blooms and dark foliage of *Dahlia* 'Arabian Night' contrast strikingly in form with those of the sword-leaved, vermilion-flowered *Crocosmia* 'Lucifer'. Note that only about three blooms here (bottom center) are 'Arabian Knight' – the others are a paler type that it usually produces.

Recommended partners: *Amaranthus caudatus* 'Viridis', *Atriplex hortensis* var. *rubra*, *Berberis* × *ottawensis* f. *purpurea* 'Superba', *Canna* 'Roi Humbert'

H: 20ft (6m) **S: 10ft** (3m)
❀ **Early to late summer**
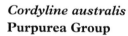 ◊◊ ▢-■ Z9 pH5.5–7.5

H: 40in (1m) **S: 18in** (45cm)
❀ **Mid-summer to mid-autumn**
■■■ ◊◊ ▢-■ Z9 pH5–7.5

Dahlia 'Glorie van Heemstede'

How it works: The luminous blooms of *Dahlia* 'Glorie van Heemstede' shine beneath a cloud of biscuit-colored florets of a plume poppy (*Macleaya microcarpa*), beside the lacy yellow-green flowers of common fennel (*Foeniculum vulgare*).

Recommended partners: *Agapanthus* 'Blue Moon', *Elaeagnus pungens* 'Maculata', *Melianthus major*, *Miscanthus sinensis* 'Zebrinus', *Nicotiana langsdorffii*, *Rosa* 'Buff Beauty'

H: 4½ft (1.4m) S: 24in (60cm)
❀ **Mid-summer to mid-autumn**
◐◐ ☐-■ Z9 pH5–7.5

Dianthus barbatus
SWEET WILLIAM

How it works: A restful effect is achieved by combining harmonious, cool-colored flowers with glaucous and gray-green foliage in this grouping consisting of mixed *Dianthus barbatus*, opium poppies (*Papaver somniferum*), and shrubby *Artemisia* 'Powis Castle'.

Recommended partners: *Antirrhinum majus* 'Black Prince', *Aquilegia vulgaris* (mixed), *Digitalis purpurea* Foxy Group, *Lupinus* 'Polar Princess', *Rosa* 'Fantin-Latour'

H: 4–27in (10–70cm) S: 8–12in (20–30cm)
❀ **Late spring to early summer**
◐◐ ☐-■ Z4 pH5.5–8

Diascia 'Dark Eyes'

How it works: In this piquant color combination of contrasting plants in a container, coral-pink *Diascia* 'Dark Eyes', *Verbena* Tapien Violet ('Sunvop'), and *Helichrysum petiolare* 'Limelight' intermingle and trail gracefully over the edge.

Recommended partners: *Alonsoa warscewiczii*, *Calibrachoa* Million Bells Trailing Blue ('Sunbelkubu'), *Isotoma axillaris*, *Lobelia erinus* 'Sapphire', *Petunia* 'Frenzy Buttercup', *Scaevola* Blauer Fächer ('Saphira')

H: 9in (23cm) S: 20in (50cm)
❀ **Early summer to mid-autumn**
██ ◊◊ □-█ **Z9 pH5.5–7.5**

Diascia rigescens

How it works: The rich pink blooms of *Diascia rigescens*, borne on dense, clearly defined spikes, harmonize with the red centers of their companion pinks and provide contrast of floral form. Both are ideal for the front of a sunny border, backed by mound-forming plants such as catmints.

Recommended partners: *Convolvulus cneorum* (foliage), *Helianthemum* 'Wisley White', *Petunia* 'Scarlet Ice', *Rehmannia elata*, *Verbena* Temari Blue ('Sunmariribu'), *V.* Temari Scarlet ('Sunmarisu')

H: 12in (30cm) S: 20in (50cm)
❀ **Early summer to early autumn**
██ ◊◊ □-█ **Z9 pH5.5–7.5**

Digitalis purpurea f. *albiflora*
WHITE FOXGLOVE

How it works: The narrow, one-sided spikes of *Digitalis purpurea* f. *albiflora* provide bold vertical accents in this relatively informal scheme with old roses, *Thalictrum aquilegiifolium*, and white sweet rocket (*Hesperis matronalis* var. *albiflora*).

Recommended partners: *Abutilon vitifolium* var. *album*, *Euphorbia polychroma* 'Major', *Heuchera villosa* 'Palace Purple', *Meconopsis betonicifolia*, *Rosa* 'Complicata', *R.* 'Fantin-Latour', *R.* 'Gruss an Aachen', *R. multiflora*, *R.* 'Penelope'

H: 4–6½ft (1.2–2m) S: 20in (50cm)
✿ **Early summer**

 ◊◊ ☐-■ Z5 pH4.5–8

Digitalis purpurea 'Sutton's Apricot'

How it works: The spikes of *Digitalis purpurea* 'Sutton's Apricot' match the flat flowerheads of an elderberry (*Sambucus nigra* 'Guincho Purple'), while offering an intriguing contrast in form; the white foxgloves (*D. p.* f. *albiflora*) lighten the effect.

Recommended partners: *Abutilon vitifolium* var. *album*, *Euphorbia polychroma* 'Major', *Heuchera villosa* 'Palace Purple', *Meconopsis betonicifolia*, *Rosa* 'Complicata', *R.* 'Fantin-Latour', *R.* 'Gruss an Aachen', *R. multiflora*, *R.* 'Penelope'

H: 4–6½ft (1.2–2m) S: 20in (50cm)
✿ **Early summer**

 ◊◊ ☐-■ Z5 pH4.5–8

Eryngium giganteum
MISS WILLMOTT'S GHOST

How it works: The handsome flowerheads of Miss Willmott's ghost (*Eryngium giganteum*), their striking silvery bracts with a hint of blue, benefit from the plain background of contrasting foliage provided by *Berberis thunbergii* 'Aurea'.

Recommended partners: *Campanula* 'Burghaltii', *Eschscholzia californica* Thai Silk Series, *Glaucium corniculatum*, *Helianthemum* cultivars, *Helictotrichon sempervirens*, *Lilium regale*, *Salvia sclarea* 'Vatican White', *Stachys byzantina*

H: 36in (90cm) **S: 12in** (30cm)
❀ **Early to mid-summer**

�-△-◇◇ ☐-■ **Z6 pH5–8**

Fuchsia 'Thalia'

How it works: The upright *Fuchsia* 'Thalia' adds height to this bold container planting, in which silver-leaved *Senecio viravira* is used to contrast with the fuchsia's dark foliage and bright flowers, as well as filling in around its stalky base. The Ivy-leaved, red-flowered *Pelargonium* 'Yale' scrambles through the senecio and tumbles over the side of the pot.

Recommended partners: *Beta vulgaris* 'Bull's Blood', *B. v.* 'Mr McGregor's Favourite', *Canna* 'Erebus', *Dahlia* 'Bishop of Llandaff', *Diascia rigescens*, *Nicotiana* 'Lime Green'

H: 31in (80cm) **S: 18in** (45cm)
❀ **Early summer to late autumn**

◇◇ ☐-■ **Z10 pH5–7**

Gaillardia pulchella 'Red Plume'

How it works: The warm, rich color of *Gaillardia pulchella* 'Red Plume' is here contrasted with the cool delicacy of blue lace flower (*Trachymene caerulea*), which was started under glass from a spring sowing. The domed flowerheads of both match perfectly in shape and size.

Recommended partners: *Dimorphotheca pluvialis, Eschscholzia californica* 'Orange King', *Nicotiana langsdorffii, Osteospermum* 'White Pim', *Scabiosa atropurpurea* 'Blue Cockade'

H: 14in (35cm) S: 6in (15cm)
❀ Mid- to late summer
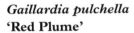 ◊◊ ☐-■ Z10 pH5.5–7.5

Glaucium corniculatum
RED HORNED POPPY

How it works: The red-horned poppy (*Glaucium corniculatum*) provides contrasting glaucous foliage and harmonious red flowers in front of *Helenium* 'Moerheim Beauty', whose rusty red blooms are borne just above the poppy.

Recommended partners: *Atriplex hortensis* var. *rubra, Crambe maritima, Eryngium giganteum, Eschscholzia californica* Thai Silk Series, *Limnanthes douglasii, Papaver somniferum*

H: 12in (30cm) S: 16in (40cm)
❀ Early summer to early autumn
◊-◊◊ ☐-■ Z7 pH5.5–7.5

Helianthus 'Moonwalker'

How it works: The annual sunflower *Helianthus* 'Moonwalker', a hybrid derived from *H. annuus* and *H. debilis* subsp. *cucumerifolius*, branches to provide a succession of flowers, contrasting here with *Verbena hastata* and the spring-sown, short-growing sweet pea *Lathyrus odoratus* 'Chatsworth'.

Tall annual sunflowers scarcely interact with other plants, but the less ungainly, branching hybrids produce bold effects in sunny borders. Other hybrids, with pale, creamy yellow flowers and a dark disc, include 'Valentine' and 'Vanilla Ice', both 5ft (1.5m). 'Velvet Queen', 6ft (1.8m), is a sumptuous mahogany-red and a good foil for warm and hot colors, while 'Prado Red' (syn. 'Ruby Sunset') is more uniform. (The recommended partners given below are for every sort of annual *Helianthus*.)

Recommended partners:
Yellow/light orange: *Arundo donax*, *Echinops bannaticus* 'Taplow Blue', *Macleaya cordata*
Bright colors: *Berberis* × *ottawensis* f. *purpurea* 'Superba', *Canna* 'Roi Humbert', *Dahlia* 'Alva's Doris'
Subdued colors: *Achillea filipendulina* 'Gold Plate', *Tithonia rotundifolia* 'Goldfinger'

H: 6ft (1.8m) S: 36in (90cm)
※ Mid-summer to early autumn
◌◌ □-■ Z7–9 pH5–7

Helichrysum petiolare 'Roundabout'

How it works: The small-leaved *Helichrysum petiolare* 'Roundabout', its white-felted foliage edged with cream, intermingles with the sprawling *Verbena* 'Kemerton', contrasting well with its magenta-purple blooms. This planting combination could be used equally successfully in a container or at the front of a border.

Recommended partners: *Agapanthus* 'Loch Hope', *Colchicum speciosum* 'Album', *Diascia* 'Dark Eyes', *Lysimachia nummularia* 'Aurea', *Pelargonium* 'Hederinum', *Petunia* 'Buttercream', *Rosa* 'American Pillar', *Scaevola aemula*

H: 8in (20cm) S: 16in (40cm)
※ Late summer to mid-autumn
◌◌ □-■ Z9 pH5–7.5

Heliotropium arborescens 'Princess Marina'

How it works: The rich purple blooms and dark leaves of *Heliotropium arborescens* 'Princess Marina' tend to be recessive, not showing up well from a distance unless lifted by paler flowers or foliage, such as the brightly edged *Plectranthus madagascariensis* 'Variegated Mintleaf'.

Recommended partners: *Ageratum houstonianum* 'Old Grey', *Argyranthemum foeniculaceum* hort., *Centaurea cineraria* subsp. *cineraria*, *Dahlia* 'Yelno Harmony', *Verbena* Temari Scarlet ('Sunmarisu')

H & S: 12in (30cm)
✤ **Early summer to mid-autumn**
◻◻ ◻-◼ **Z10 pH5.5–8**

Impatiens New Guinea hybrids

How it works: New Guinea hybrid *Impatiens*, like bicolored 'Sunglow' and rich salmon 'Meteor', are immune to the mildew that kills busy Lizzies and can be used outdoors in warm climates, with artillery plant, *Pilea microphylla*, and *Asparagus densiflorus* 'Sprengeri', both usually houseplants.

Recommended partners: *Antirrhinum majus* Coronet Series, *Begonia* (Semperflorens Cultorum Group) Cocktail Series, *Lobelia* × *speciosa* 'Fan Orchidrosa', *Scaevola aemula*

H: 4–24in (10–60cm) S: 8–24in (20–60cm)
✤ **Early summer to mid-autumn**
◻◻ ◻-◼ **Z10 pH5–7**

Ipomoea tricolor 'Mini Sky-blue'

How it works: *Ipomoea tricolor* 'Mini Sky-blue' here weaves over and through two tender sub-shrubby perennials used as summer bedding plants: harmonious rich lavender *Salvia farinacea* 'Blue Victory' and gently contrasting creamy yellow-variegated, white-flowered *Osteospermum* 'Silver Sparkler'.

This restrained morning glory is excellent in the second rank of a sunny border or in containers in a sunlit spot. Here it will scramble over neighboring plants, introducing a natural grace that other annuals and bedding plants often lack. Its flowers, which tend to close at about midday, are sky-blue, in some cases with a hint of mauve, and very effective with yellow-green or glaucous foliage, or with blue, white, or cream flowers, and in contrasts with yellow flowers. Companion plants need to be sturdy enough to support its meandering stems, so small to medium-size shrubs or sub-shrubs make the best hosts.

Recommended partners: *Argyranthemum* 'Jamaica Primrose', *Berberis thunbergii* 'Aurea', *Ceanothus* × *delileanus* 'Gloire de Versailles', *Coronilla valentina* subsp. *glauca*, *Fuchsia magellanica* var. *gracilis*, *Salvia guaranitica*

H: 4ft (1.2m) S: 10–18in (25–45cm)
❀ **Mid-summer to early autumn**
  ◊◊ ▮ **Z10 pH6–8**

Lantana camara 'Orange Beauty'

How it works: A carpet of *Lantana camara* 'Orange Beauty' provides a foil for the spectacular and extravagant purple-flushed, variegated foliage of *Canna* 'Phasion'.

Recommended partners: *Agapanthus* 'Lilliput', *Carex comans* (bronze), *Cordyline australis* Purpurea Group, *Miscanthus sinensis* 'Strictus', *Ricinus communis* 'Impala'

H: **12in** (30cm) S: **5ft** (1.5m)
❀ **Late spring to late autumn**
◊◊ ☐-■ **Z10 pH5.5–7**

Lavatera trimestris 'Rose Beauty'

How it works: Pairing *Lavatera trimestris* 'Rose Beauty' with scarlet *Salvia coccinea* 'Lady in Red' gives the thrill of a near clash and contrast of form.

Recommended partners: *Alcea rosea* Chater's Double Group, *Consolida ajacis* (blue), *Gypsophila paniculata* 'Bristol Fairy', *Nicotiana* 'Lime Green', *Veronica spicata*

H: **30in** (75cm) S: **18in** (45cm)
❀ **Early summer to early autumn**
◊◊ ■ **Z7 pH5.5–7.5**

Layia platyglossa
COASTAL TIDYTIPS

How it works: Coastal tidytips *Layia platyglossa* can be grown from a spring sowing as an annual or, in Z9 or warmer zones and sheltered, sunny situations in Z8, as a biennial from an autumn sowing. Here, it is combined with compact selections of other Californians that can be treated in the same way, California poppy *Eschscholzia californica* and *Phacelia campanularia* 'Blue Wonder', to create a charming carpet.

Recommended partners: *Anthemis punctata* subsp. *cupaniana*, *Calendula officinalis* 'Orange Daisy', *Crambe maritima*, *Nemophila menziesii* var. *menziesii*

H: 12–18in (30–45cm) S: 18in (45cm)
✿ Mid- to late summer
◯-◯◯ ▢-▩ Z9 pH5–7.5

Lobelia richardsonii

How it works: In a partially shaded bed beneath trees, there is sufficient light for *Lobelia richardsonii* to flower freely and for Bowles's golden sedge (*Carex elata* 'Aurea') to color well. This site also suits the handsomely goffered hart's tongue fern (*Asplenium scolopendrium* 'Crispum Bolton's Nobile'), which thrives in shade and becomes scorched by the sun.

Usually raised as an annual from cuttings, *L. richardsonii* is a tender evergreen perennial. It is a good pot and hanging basket plant that can also be used in bedding and at the front of a border. Its pale sky-blue flowers blend with cool colors and silver and glaucous foliage and contrast well with yellow-green foliage or flowers and soft yellow blooms. It looks very effective with *Helichrysum petiolare* cultivars; petunias, especially smaller-flowered cultivars; and achimenes. When grown on its own, it has a prostrate habit, but next to a plant of modest height, such as *Hebe* 'Quicksilver', it will scramble through its companion.

Recommended partners: *Argyranthemum foeniculaceum* hort., *Bidens ferulifolia* 'Shining Star', *Calibrachoa* Million Bells Lemon ('Sunbelkic'), *Festuca glauca* 'Blaufuchs', *Tagetes tenuifolia* 'Lemon Gem'

H: 4in (10cm) S: 12in (30cm)
❀ Early summer to mid-autumn
 ◌◌ ▨ Z10 pH5.5–7.5

Lobelia × *speciosa* (Fan Series) 'Fan Orchidrosa'

How it works: Magenta *Lobelia* × *speciosa* 'Fan Orchidrosa' is planted close to the edge of the bed, its bold vertical spikes emphasizing the bed's curve. Gently clashing busy Lizzies (*Impatiens walleriana* 'Accent Salmon') furnish below and between.

Recommended partners: *Atriplex hortensis* var. *rubra*, *Euphorbia schillingii*, *Hakonechloa macra* 'Aureola', *Nicotiana* 'Lime Green', *Tithonia rotundifolia* 'Sundance', *Verbena rigida*

H: 27in (70cm) S: 12in (30cm) Z6 pH5.5–7.5
❀ Mid-summer to mid-autumn
◌◌-◌◌◌ ▨

Lobularia maritima 'Snow Crystals'

How it works: A carpet of sweet alyssum *Lobularia maritima* (syn. *Alyssum maritimum*) 'Snow Crystals' is interspersed with *Senecio cineraria*. This ghostly scheme could be used as a foil for brighter color or for black. Alyssum has long been a staple of Victorian-style bedding, as in the patriotic combination with red *Pelargonium* 'Paul Crampel' and blue *Lobelia erinus*, which though hackneyed is still effective. A neat and compact cultivar like this, producing such a solid sheet of white bloom, is ideal for use in formal schemes as an edging, serving to underscore the edge of the bed, thus emphasizing its shape and, if it is set in turf, the separation of lawn from planting. Its fine, almost structureless texture makes it a good foil for plants with bold architectural form, such as some larger succulents. It is also richly honey-scented.

Recommended partners: *Aeonium* 'Zwartkop', *Agapanthus* 'Navy Blue', *Agave americana* 'Mediopicta Alba', *Colocasia esculenta* 'Black Magic', *Diascia* Coral Belle ('Hecbel'), *Echeveria secunda* var. *glauca* 'Gigantea', *Lobelia erinus* 'Crystal Palace', *Pelargonium* (Black Velvet Series) 'Black Velvet Scarlet'

H: 4in (10cm) **S: 8in** (20cm)
✽ **Mid- to late summer**

 ◊-◊◊ ☐-■ **Z6 pH5.5–8**

Malva sylvestris **'Brave Heart'**

How it works: In this harmony of crimson flowers of similar outline, the common mallow *Malva sylvestris* 'Brave Heart' mingles with *Knautia macedonica* and *Lychnis coronaria* Atrosanguinea Group, whose gray-green stems and foliage leaven the scheme.

Recommended partners: *Achillea* 'Moonshine', *Briza maxima*, *Calendula officinalis* 'Orange King', *Crocosmia* 'Lucifer', *Euphorbia cyparissias*, *Nicotiana* 'Lime Green'

H: 4ft (1.2m) **S: 24in** (60cm)
�֍ **Late spring to mid-autumn**

▬▬ ◊◊ ☐-■ **Z5–9 pH5.5–8**

Nemophila menziesii
BABY BLUE EYES

How it works: The blue flowers of *Nemophila menziesii* are joined by the white flowers of *Osteospermum* 'Gold Sparkler', contrasting yellow *Viola aetolica* and the five-spot (*Nemophila maculata*), to produce a charming *millefleurs* tapestry of flowers.

Recommended partners: *Argyranthemum* 'Jamaica Primrose', *Euphorbia rigida* (foliage), *Hakonechloa macra* 'Alboaurea'

H: 8in (20cm) **S: 12in** (30cm)
�֍ **Early to late summer**

▬▬ ◊◊ ☐-■ **Z7 pH5.5–7.5**

Nicotiana (Domino Series) 'Domino Red'

How it works: In this richly colored scheme, *Nicotiana* 'Domino Red' is joined by the flat yellow flowerheads of *Achillea filipendulina* 'Gold Plate', the yellow daisy flowers of *Rudbeckia laciniata* 'Herbstsonne', bright red *Dahlia* 'Bishop of Llandaff', the orange spikes of *Kniphofia uvaria* 'Nobilis', orange *Crocosmia paniculata* and *C.* 'Vulcan', the puckered leaves of the beets *Beta vulgaris* 'Mr McGregor's Favourite' and *B. v.* 'Rhubarb Chard', pelargoniums, and verbenas. Since 2001, tobacco blue mold has caused damage to common flowering tobaccos in moist climates.

Recommended partners: *Canna indica* 'Purpurea', *Cosmos bipinnatus, Helichrysum petiolare, Heuchera* 'Plum Pudding', *Perilla frutescens* var. *crispa, Plectranthus argentatus, Rosa* 'Frensham', *R.* Iceberg ('Korbin')

H: 16in (40cm) **S: 8in** (20cm)
✤ **Early summer to mid-autumn**
◊◊ ☐-■ Z9 pH5–7.5

Nicotiana langsdorffii

How it works: In this blend of flowers and foliage in subdued colorings, two species of tobacco are used for their elegant form. In the foreground, *Nicotiana langsdorffii* casts a veil of nodding apple-green bells in front of the handsome foliage of *N. sylvestris*, whose extraordinary, long-tubed flowers cascade in front of the feathery cut-leaved elder, *Sambucus racemosa* 'Plumosa Aurea'.

Recommended partners: *Consolida* 'Frosted Skies', *Cotinus coggygria* 'Royal Purple', *Delphinium* 'Sungleam', *Hydrangea paniculata* 'Greenspire', *Onopordum nervosum*

H: 4ft (1.2m) S: 16in (40cm)
❀ **Early summer to mid-autumn**
◊◊ ☐-■ **Z10 pH5–7.5**

Nigella damascena
LOVE-IN-A-MIST

How it works: This charmingly simple, single variant of love-in-a mist (*Nigella damascena*) exactly matches exotic-looking *Rehmannia elata* in height, mingling attractively with it. Love-in-a-mist bears distinctive, inflated seedpods and feathery foliage that is a useful filigree infill between more-solid plants such as Bearded irises.

Recommended partners: *Achillea* 'Moonshine', *Allium cristophii*, *Geranium* × *oxonianum* f. *thurstonianum*, *Rosa gallica* 'Versicolor', *R.* 'Raubritter', *R.* 'Tuscany Superb'

H: 8–30in (20–75cm) S: 6–9in (15–23cm)
❀ **Early to late summer**
◊◊ ☐-■ **Z6 pH5–7.5**

Onopordum nervosum

How it works: The dramatic pale leaves of *Onopordum nervosum* transform this subtly colored scheme, which blends pink blooms of *Pimpinella major* 'Rosea' and *Rosa glauca* with glaucous foliage from the rose and *Thalictrum flavum* subsp. *glaucum*, which also contributes yellow-green buds.

Recommended partners: *Acanthus spinosus, Artemisia ludoviciana* 'Silver Queen', *Cotinus coggygria* 'Royal Purple', *Crambe cordifolia, Lavatera × clementii* 'Barnsley', *Miscanthus sacchariflorus, M. sinensis* 'Variegatus', *Rosa* 'Highdownensis', *R.* 'Pink Perpétué', *Salix exigua, Sambucus nigra* 'Guincho Purple'

H: 10ft (3m) **S: 40in** (1m)
❀ Mid- to late summer
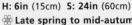 ◊◊ ▢-■ Z6 pH5.5–7.5

Osteospermum 'White Pim'

How it works: The carpeting habit of *Osteospermum* 'White Pim' allows it to be used at the front of a shallowly banked border, in a bed of fairly flat planting, or in a large rock garden, with other plants of similar low and spreading habit, such as *Veronica austriaca* subsp. *teucrium* 'Kapitän', seen here. It works well with cool colors and glaucous, silver, or purple foliage.

Recommended partners: *Aeonium* 'Zwartkop', *Argyranthemum* 'Jamaica Primrose', *Brachyscome iberidifolia, Felicia petiolata, Nemophila menziesii, Plectranthus argentatus*

H: 6in (15cm) **S: 24in** (60cm)
❀ Late spring to mid-autumn
◊◊ ▢-■ Z8 pH5.5–7.5

Papaver commutatum 'Ladybird'

How it works: When allowed to self-sow or if sown in autumn in Z9 or warmer climates (or sheltered sites in Z8), *Papaver commutatum* 'Ladybird' will bloom with *Gladiolus communis* subsp. *byzantinus* in early summer. This method tends to give bigger, longer-flowering plants of the poppy, whose boldly blotched scarlet blooms clash vibrantly with the dark-stemmed, magenta gladiolus. The poppy can also be grown from seed sown *in situ* in mid- to late spring, with plants flowering from mid-summer on.

It combines attractively with hot colors and dark foliage, contrasts effectively with yellow-green, and like the softer-red, less-emphatically blotched common poppy *Papaver rhoeas*, can be used to make a cheerful, cornfield mix in primary colors with cornflower (*Centaurea cyanus*) and corn marigold (*Glebionis segetum*). It will glow even more ardently if combined with intense green foliage.

Recommended partners: *Ammi majus*, *Anethum graveolens* 'Hedger', *Atriplex hortensis* var. *rubra*, *Crambe maritima*, *Euphorbia donii*, *E. dulcis* 'Chameleon', *Omphalodes linifolia*, *Orlaya grandiflora*, *Petroselinum crispum* 'Bravour'

H: 18in (45cm) **S: 12in** (30cm)
❀ **Early to late summer Z9 pH5.5–7.5**

Papaver rhoeas, Shirley poppy

How it works: Although once containing only pastel colors, double Shirley poppies now often comprise mostly richer tints. If given space to make large, vigorous plants, they will bloom into late summer, their warm tints harmonizing here with *Calendula officinalis* Fiesta Gitana Series. Groups derived from Shirley poppies include Cedric Morris, Fairy Wings, Mother of Pearl, and double Angels' Choir.

Recommended partners: *Agrostemma githago, Briza maxima, Centaurea cyanus, Leucanthemum vulgare, Malva sylvestris, Papaver somniferum, Rosa* 'De Rescht'

H: 24in (60cm) **S: 18in** (45cm)
✽ **Early to late summer Z5 pH5.5–7.5**

Papaver somniferum
OPIUM POPPY

How it works: After flowering, the glaucous pods of opium poppy (*Papaver somniferum*) remain attractive, combined here with *Salvia sclarea* var. *turkestanica, Phlox paniculata*, and alliums. The color range of this annual poppy is extensive.

Recommended partners: *Allium sphaerocephalon, Aquilegia vulgaris* (mixed), *Artemisia ludoviciana* 'Silver Queen', *Briza maxima, Dianthus barbatus, Helictotrichon sempervirens, Iris* 'Kent Pride', *Lavatera trimestris, Nigella damascena* 'Miss Jekyll', *Rosa glauca*

H: 24–48in (60–120cm) **S: 12in** (30cm)
✽ **Early to late summer**
◊◊ ☐-■ **Z7 pH5–7.5**

Pelargonium 'Hederinum'

How it works: The long-jointed stems of pink-flowered *Pelargonium* 'Hederinum' and red *P.* 'Roi des Balcons Impérial' look spectacular cascading from balconies and window boxes, lacking the congestion of more compact sorts. This is the oldest Ivy-leaved pelargonium cultivar, dating back to 1786. *P.* 'Hederinum Variegatum', one of its variations, has white variegation.

Recommended partners: *Helichrysum petiolare, Ipomoea tricolor* 'Mini Sky-blue', *Lobelia erinus* 'Sapphire', *Lophospermum erubescens, Plectranthus argentatus, Thunbergia alata*

H: 12in (30cm) **S: 5ft** (1.5m)
✿ **Late spring to mid-autumn**
�▬ ◊-◊◊ ☐-■ Z9 pH5–7.5

Pelargonium (Multibloom Series) 'Multibloom Salmon'

How it works: *Pelargonium* 'Multibloom Salmon' and *Zinnia* 'Dreamland Coral' make good companions, with flowers of harmonious colors but contrasting form on plants of the same height.

Recommended partners: *Abutilon pictum* 'Thompsonii', *Canna* 'Lucifer', *Cordyline australis* Purpurea Group, *Lobularia maritima* 'Snow Crystals', *Nicotiana langsdorffii, Petunia* Surfinia Blue ('Sunblu'), *Phormium* 'Bronze Baby', *Senecio cineraria* 'Silver Dust', *Verbena* Tapien Violet ('Sunvop')

H & S: 12in (30cm)
✿ **Late spring to mid-autumn**
▬▬▬ ◊-◊◊ ☐-■ Z9 pH5–7.5

Penstemon 'Andenken an Friedrich Hahn'

How it works: *Penstemon* 'Andenken an Friedrich Hahn', one of the hardiest hybrid penstemons, furnishes the base of the gold-variegated *Phormium tenax* 'Veitchianum', supplying rich color to complement the phormium's long, dramatic leaves.

Recommended partners: *Alstroemeria ligtu* hybrids, *Dianthus* 'Doris', *Lavandula angustifolia* 'Hidcote', *Miscanthus sinensis* 'Variegatus', *Nicotiana* 'Lime Green', *Rosa* 'Geranium', *Verbena* 'Silver Anne'

H: 24in (60cm) **S: 18in** (45cm)
✿ Mid-summer to mid-autumn
 ◊◊ ▊ Z6 pH5–7.5

Penstemon 'Chester Scarlet'

How it works: The relatively upright stems of *Penstemon* 'Chester Scarlet', furnished along most of their length with flowers, are ideal for a steeply banked border behind mound-forming plants, as here with lady's mantle (*Alchemilla mollis*) and contrasting silver-leaved *Artemisia ludoviciana*.

Recommended partners: *Pelargonium* 'Paul Crampel', *Perilla frutescens* var. *crispa*, *Phygelius* × *rectus* 'Pink Elf', *Verbena* Tapien Violet ('Sunvop'), *Zinnia elegans* 'Envy'

H: 26in (65cm) **S: 16in** (40cm)
✿ Mid-summer to mid-autumn
▊ ◊◊ ▊ Z8 pH5–7.5

Penstemon 'King George V'

How it works: The sheer gorgeousness of the blooms of *Penstemon* 'King George V' lends it to richly colored planting schemes, as seen here with orange kniphofias and the dark-leaved *Actaea simplex* Atropurpurea Group.

Recommended partners: *Canna indica* 'Purpurea', *Cordyline australis* Purpurea Group, *Dahlia* 'Bishop of Llandaff', *Diascia rigescens*, *Phormium tenax* Purpureum Group

H: 26in (65cm) **S: 18in** (45cm)
❀ Mid-summer to mid-autumn
 ◊◊ ▪ Z9 pH5–7.5

Pericallis 'Royalty Sky Blue'

How it works: From a sowing under glass in late winter to early spring, cinerarias can be used for mid-summer to autumn display outdoors. Here, *Pericallis* 'Royalty Sky Blue' forms a striking contrast with the striped grass *Hakonechloa macra* 'Aureola'.

Recommended partners: *Helichrysum petiolare*, *Heuchera villosa* 'Palace Purple', *Salvia farinacea* 'Victoria', *Senecio cineraria* 'Silver Dust'

H & S: 16in (40cm)
❀ Mid-summer to late autumn
 ◊◊ ▪ Z9 pH5.5–7.5

Perilla frutescens var. *crispa*

How it works: This is a sumptuous combination with *Perilla frutescens* var. *crispa* and *Salvia coccinea* 'Lady in Red' in mid-summer. The perilla will grow taller as the season advances and will overtop the salvia, allowing it to be used as a formal accent or dot plant.

Recommended partners: *Begonia semperflorens* Cocktail Series, *Dahlia* 'Bednall Beauty', *Pelargonium* Multibloom Series, *Salvia splendens* 'Vanguard', *Verbena* 'Kemerton'

H: 40in (1m) S: 12in (30cm)
✵ Mid-summer to mid-autumn
■□ ◊◊ ■ Z9 pH5.5–7.5

Petunia (Frenzy Series) 'Frenzy Light Blue'

How it works: The soft lavender-blue *Petunia* (Frenzy Series) 'Frenzy Light Blue' is contrasted with sulphur-yellow *P.* 'Buttercream'. *Helichrysum petiolare* 'Limelight' adds a contrast of form.

Recommended partners:

Mixed: *Helichrysum petiolare* 'Roundabout', *Perilla frutescens* var. *crispa*, *Senecio cineraria* 'Silver Dust'

Yellow: *Agapanthus* 'Lilliput', *Ageratum houstonianum* 'Old Grey', *Brachyscome iberidifolia*

H: 4–16in (10–40cm) S: 4in–4ft (10cm–1.2m)
✵ Early summer to mid-autumn
■□ ◊◊ □-■ Z9–10 pH5–7.5

Petunia (Ice Series) 'Scarlet Ice'

How it works: Petunias, lobelias, and pelargoniums can be combined to provide cheerful color with a variety of floral form. In this window box, the shape of *Petunia* (Ice Series) 'Scarlet Ice' is emphasized by its white edging; it is joined by other petunias in white, pink, and purple, *Pelargonium* 'Decora Rouge', and *Lobelia erinus* 'Sapphire'.

Recommended partners:

Mixed: *Helichrysum petiolare* 'Roundabout', *Perilla frutescens* var. *crispa*, *Senecio cineraria* 'Silver Dust'

Yellow: *Agapanthus* 'Lilliput', *Ageratum houstonianum* 'Old Grey', *Brachyscome iberidifolia*

H: 4–16in (10–40cm) **S: 4in–4ft** (10cm–1.2m)

✿ **Early summer to mid-autumn**

◊◊ ▢-■ **Z9–10 pH5–7.5**

Salvia sclarea 'Vatican White'

How it works: The white candelabras of *Salvia sclarea* 'Vatican White' form a backdrop for the bright blooms of an early yellow kniphofia and the contrasting blue flowers of viper's bugloss (*Echium vulgare*) in early summer. Its green calyces and flower stems give an overall impression of pale greenish white rather than pure white.

Recommended partners: *Achillea* 'Coronation Gold', *Campanula persicifolia* 'Telham Beauty', *Delphinium* 'Alice Artindale', *Hemerocallis* 'Corky', *Iris* 'Curlew', *Papaver orientale* 'Black and White', *Rosa* 'Tuscany Superb'

H: 36in (90cm) **S: 18in** (45cm)
❀ Early to mid-summer
◊◊ ☐-■ Z6 pH5–7.5

Scaevola aemula

How it works: In this cool-colored carpet of plants, a compact, rich lavender cultivar of the fanflower *Scaevola aemula* is combined with magenta busy Lizzies (*Impatiens walleriana* 'Accent Violet') and a short *Ageratum houstonianum* cultivar, leavened by the silvery trails of *Helichrysum petiolare*.

Recommended partners: *Calibrachoa* Million Bells Lemon ('Sunbelkic'), *Diascia* 'Lilac Belle', *Leucophyta brownii*, *Lysimachia congestiflora* 'Outback Sunset', *Osteospermum* 'White Pim', *Pelargonium* Rose Evka ('Penevro'), *Plectranthus forsteri* 'Marginatus', *Torenia* Rose Moon ('Dantoromoon')

H: 8–12in (20–30cm) **S: 12–24in** (30–60cm)
❀ Early summer to mid-autumn
◊◊ ☐-■ Z10 pH5.5–7.5

Tithonia rotundifolia '**Goldfinger**'

How it works: The Mexican sunflower *Tithonia rotundifolia* 'Goldfinger' is an imposing plant for the second or third rank of a bed or border. Here, it associates easily with the taller reddish brown sunflower *Helianthus* 'Velvet Queen', gently clashing mauve *Lavatera thuringiaca*, and osteospermums. Mexican sunflowers vary in height from 1 to 6ft (30cm to 1.8m).

Recommended partners: *Crocosmia* 'Late Lucifer', *Haloragis erecta* 'Wellington Bronze', *Kniphofia uvaria* 'Nobilis', *Lobelia* × *speciosa* 'Fan Scharlach', *Nicotiana* 'Lime Green'

H: 3ft (90cm) S: 18in (45cm)
❀ Late summer to mid-autumn
◊◊ ☐-■ Z10 pH5.5–7.5

Tolpis barbata

How it works: *Tolpis barbata*, here flopping gracefully across the gravel in which it has seeded itself, might seem thin-textured and insubstantial if grown alone, but it can mingle well with the foliage or flowers of another plant – as here with the golden hop (*Humulus lupulus* 'Aureus').

Recommended partners: *Cerinthe major* var. *purpurascens*, *Felicia amelloides* (variegated), *Molinia caerulea* 'Variegata', *Perilla frutescens* var. *crispa*, *Pilosella aurantiaca*, *Solenostemon scutellarioides* Wizard Series

H: 20in (50cm) S: 12in (30cm)
❀ Early to late summer
◊◊ ☐-■ Z7 pH5.5–7.5

Verbena 'Silver Anne'

How it works: Harmonious colors and contrasting floral form are seen in this striking combination of *Verbena* 'Silver Anne' and *Penstemon* 'Andenken an Friedrich Hahn'. The strongly fragrant flowers of *V.* 'Silver Anne' open carmine-pink and become paler with age.

Recommended partners: *Helichrysum petiolare*, *Salvia farinacea* 'Strata', *Sedum telephium* 'Arthur Branch', *Senecio cineraria* 'Silver Dust', *Silene coeli-rosa* Angel Series

H: **12in** (30cm) S: **24in** (60cm)
❀ **Mid-summer to mid-autumn**
◊◊ ▢-▨ **Z9 pH5.5–7.5**

Verbena 'Sissinghurst'

How it works: Deep carmine *Verbena* 'Sissinghurst' and clear pink *Diascia vigilis*, seen here with the tubular-flowered *Penstemon* 'Evelyn', are both sprawling plants that can interweave and mix with each other and their neighbors to make delightful harmonies in beds, borders, or containers.

Recommended partners: *Antirrhinum majus* 'Black Prince', *Leucophyta brownii*, *Osteospermum* 'Pink Whirls', *Salvia officinalis* 'Purpurascens', *Tigridia pavonia*

H: **6–8in** (15–20cm) S: **36in** (90cm)
❀ **Early summer to early autumn**
◊◊ ▢-▨ **Z9 pH5.5–7.5**

Viola tricolor 'Helen Mount'

How it works: In a charming cottage garden mix that has no pretensions to color scheming, compact *Viola tricolor* 'Helen Mount' (syn. *V. t.* 'Johnny-jump-up'), the pink *Dianthus deltoides* 'Leuchtfunk', and the low-growing cransbill *Geranium* (Cinereum Group) 'Ballerina' fill a narrow border at the foot of a garden wall.

Best grown as a biennial for late spring and early summer display, *V. tricolor*, with the common name of heartsease or Johnny-jump-up, is a charming perennial with very variable flowers, usually in a combination of lavender-blue, yellow, and white. From this, several more distinct cultivars have been developed. They include 'Helen Mount', in lavender and yellow; 'Bowles's Black', nearly black with a tiny yellow eye; 'Prince Henry', in rich purple; and 'Prince John', in golden yellow. Although *V. tricolor* is more heat-tolerant than many hybrid violas, hot, dry summers curtail flowering, but where summers are cool and moist, plants will flower until mid-summer and, if then cut back, again in autumn.

Recommended partners: *Aquilegia vulgaris* (mixed), *Erysimum* 'Bowles's Mauve', *Muscari armeniacum*, *Rosa elegantula* 'Persetosa', *Tulipa* 'Queen of Night', *T.* 'Spring Green'

H: 3–5in (8–13cm) S: 4–6in (10–15cm)
❀ **Mid-spring to mid-autumn**
◊◊ ■-■ Z4 pH5.5–7.5

Hardiness zones

The hardiness zone for each plant according to the system devised by the United States Department of Agriculture (USDA) is given towards the end of each entry. The letter 'Z' is followed by a number relating to the minimum winter temperature that a plant will tolerate according to the chart opposite. Comparing this with a zoned map of average winter minimum temperatures gives a helpful indication of where the plant should survive the winter without protection. However, zones can be only a rough guide. The hardiness of a plant depends on a great many factors, including the depth of its roots, its water content at the onset of frost, the duration of cold weather, and, especially for evergreens, the force of the wind.

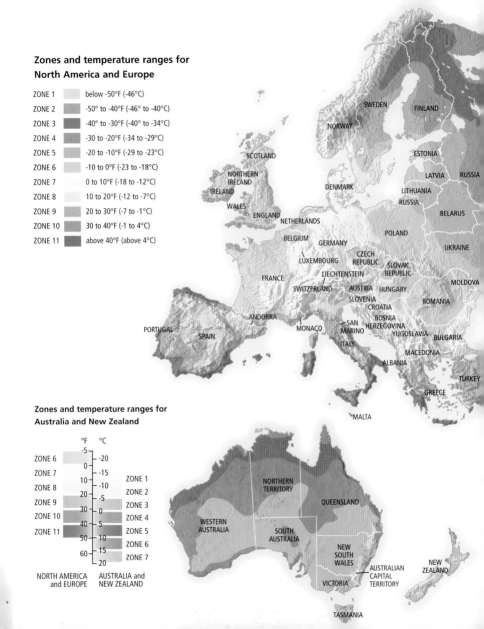

Zones and temperature ranges for North America and Europe

ZONE 1	below -50°F (-46°C)
ZONE 2	-50° to -40°F (-46 to -40°C)
ZONE 3	-40° to -30°F (-40 to -34°C)
ZONE 4	-30 to -20°F (-34 to -29°C)
ZONE 5	-20 to -10°F (-29 to -23°C)
ZONE 6	-10 to 0°F (-23 to -18°C)
ZONE 7	0 to 10°F (-18 to -12°C)
ZONE 8	10 to 20°F (-12 to -7°C)
ZONE 9	20 to 30°F (-7 to -1°C)
ZONE 10	30 to 40°F (-1 to 4°C)
ZONE 11	above 40°F (above 4°C)

Zones and temperature ranges for Australia and New Zealand

	°F	°C	
ZONE 6	-5	-20	
ZONE 7	0	-15	ZONE 1
ZONE 8	10	-10	ZONE 2
ZONE 9	20	-5	ZONE 3
ZONE 10	30	0	ZONE 4
ZONE 11	40	5	ZONE 5
	50	10	ZONE 6
	60	15	ZONE 7
		20	

NORTH AMERICA and EUROPE   AUSTRALIA and NEW ZEALAND

Index

Picture credits

Key a above, b below, l left, r right

Alamy Rob Whitworth 180al, Rob Whitworth/RHS Wisley 274–5; **Adrian Bloom** 219al; **Jonathan Buckley** 7, 36ar, 42ar, 47al, 175, 204ar, 229a; **Eric Crichton** 106; **John Fielding** 38, 43ar, 48ar, 51al, 54ar, 59ar, 60ar, 61al, 69ar, 78, 99ar, 100al, 108–9, 114al, 132ar, 141ar, 148, 156al, 167–8c, 170al, 172bl, 182ar, 184al, RHS Wisley 185br, 189al, 213al, 222bl, 225, 228–9, 233ar, 246al, 252br, 256, 257ar, 259al, 260, 267l and r, 296br, 298al, 302, 310ar, 318ar, 322ar, 328al, 330ar, 334l and r, 335, 351l and r, 352br, 355l and r; **GAP Photos** Andrea Jones 12–13, Elke Borkowski 25, 273, 314–5; Graham Strong 17, J S Sira/Chelsea Flower Show 73, Jerry Harpur 289, Jo Whitworth/design Nana Habet 30, John Glover 166r, 186–7, John Glover/design Penelope Hobhouse 22–3, John Glover/design Paul Dyer 288, Jonathan Buckley/design Christopher Lloyd 238–9, Jonathan Buckley/design Christopher Lloyd 346–7, Jonathan Buckley/design Sue and Wol Staines/Glen Chantry 288, Jonathan Buckley/design Tom Stuart Smith 287, Marcus Harpur/Beth Chatto garden, Essex 31, Matt Anker 26–7; Richard Bloom 159, 284–5, Richard Bloom/Dennis Schrader's Garden, USA 160–1, Richard Bloom/design Piet Oudolf/Scampston Hall Garden 254–5, Richard Bloom/design Tom Stuart Smith/RHS Wisley Bicentenary Glasshouse Garden 164, Suzie Gibbons 210; **The Garden Collection** Andrew Lawson/Coughton Court 19, Derek Harris 280–1, Derek Harris/design Jane Hudson and Erik de Maeijer 172–3c, Derek Harris/design Kate Frey 337, Jonathan Buckley/design Carol and Malcom Skinner 29, Jonathan Buckley/design Sarah Raven 292–3; **John Glover** 3bc, Knot Garden, Little Hill 10l, 117ar, 138al, 271ar; **Harpur Garden Library** Jerry Harpur 154; **Andrew Lawson** 2, 3br, 9, 10r, 14, 19, The Priory Kemerton 23ar, 32ar, 33al, 36al, 37br, 39bl, 40, 42al, 44br, 45, 46ar, 48al, 49al, 52al and ar, 53al, 54al, 55ar, 57, 58bl, 61ar, 62al, 63, 65al and ar, 70–1, 73ar, 74, 75, 77, 79al and ar, 81bl, 84al, 85ar, 86al and ar, 88l and r, 89, 90, 90–1, 91, 93, 94, 95, 96ar, 97l and r, 98, 99al, 101al, 110, 112l and r, 113al, 115, 116al, 118al, 119, 120l and r, 121l and r, 122al and ar, 123ar, 125, 126al and ar, 127al, 129, 130, 133al, 134, 136–7, 138al, 139l and r, 140l and r, 141al, 144, 145ar, 146, 147, 149, 157l and r, 158ar, 162bl, 166l, 167ar, 168l and r, 170ar, 17l and r, 173br, 174, 177al, 178bl, 180ar, 184–5c, 188, 189ar, 191br, 193ar, 196, 197l and r, 198al, 200, 201bl, 202ar, 203ar, 204al, 207, 208–9, 212al, 214al, 215al, 216l and r, 218ar, 220, 221, 222–3c, 223r, 224, 230l and r, 233ar, 234–5, 236ar, 240bl, 241, 242, 243al, 244ar, 245al, 246al, 247, 248al, 249l and r, 250al, 251ar, 252bl, 253, 259ar, 261, 264l and r, 265l and r, 269al, 270ar, 271al, 278, 279ar, 283l and r, 294al and c, 297, 300, 301, 303, 304l and r, 305, 308, 310al, 312al, 316, 318al, 319al, 320l and r, 323al, 324l, 325, 326l and r, 327l and r, 329al, 332, 336al, 342l and r, 343, 344l and r, 348ar, 350al, 352bl, 356ar, 35; **Marianne Majerus** Andrew Lawson 132, Saltmarshe Hall, Yorkshire 262–3, design Piet Oudolf/Scampston Hall, Yorkshire 194–5; **S & O Mathews** 312–3c; **Clive Nichols Garden Pictures** 114, Wollerton Old Hall, Shropshire 124, 145al, 155, 191bl, 231, Pettifers, Oxfordshire 276–7; **Jerry Pavia Photography Inc** 67br, 142–3, 176ar, 282, 306–7, 311, 340–1; **Brigitte & Philippe Perdereau** 34–5; **Photolibrary Group** David Askam 135, Lynne Brotchie 257bl, Brian Carter 50al, Christi Carter 127ar, 336ar, Ron Evans 298–9, John Glover 192ar, Sunniva Harte 158al, 279bl, Clive Nichols 105, Howard Rice 113ar, J S Sira 33br, 111ar, 333, Juliette Wade 350ar, Mel Watson 328ar, Didier Willery 41; **Photoshot Photos Horticultural** 56, 111al, 116–7c, 118ar, 192al, 217; **Howard Rice** 44bl, 46al, 58–59c, 60al, 62ar, 66bl, 68al, 133ar, Bressingham Gardens 150–1, 219ar, 268br; **W Anthony Lord** 3bl, 32al, 37bl, 38br, 43al, 47ar, 49ar, 50ar, 51al, 53al, 55al, 64al and ar, 66–7c, 69al, 80, 81r, 82c, 83ar, 84–5c, 87, 92, 96al, 100ar, 101ar, 102–3, 107, 123al, 128, 131, 153, 156ar, 167al, 169, 176al, 177ar, 178bl, 179, 181l and r, 182ar, 183l and r, 190l and r, 193al, 198ar, 199l and r, 201a, 202al, 203al, 205, 206, 211, 212ar, 213ar, 214ar, 215ar, 218al, 227, 232, 236al, 237ar, 240br, 243ar, 244al, 245ar, 248ar, 250ar, 251bl, 158l and r, 268bl, 269br, 270al, 272, 295ar, 296bl, 309, 317, 319ar, 321l and r, 322al, 323ar, 324r, 329ar, 330al, 331 and r, 338, 339, 345l and r, 348al, 34l and r, 353, 35l and r, 356bl.